CONFLICT AND DECISION-MAKING IN CLOSE RELATIONSHIPS

European Monographs in Social Psychology
Sponsored by the European Association of Experimental Psychology

Series Editor:
Professor Rupert Brown, Institute of Applied and Social Psychology, University of Kent, Canterbury, Kent CT2 7LZ

The aim of this series is to publish and promote the highest quality of writing in European social psychology. The editor and the editorial board encourage publications which approach social psychology from a wide range of theoretical perspectives and whose content may be applied, theoretical or empirical. The authors of books in this series should be affiliated to institutions that are located in countries which would qualify for membership of the Association. All books will be published in English, and translations from other European languages are welcomed. Please submit ideas and proposals for books in the series to Rupert Brown at the above address.

Published
The Quantitative Analysis of Social Representations
Willem Doise, Alain Clemence, and Fabio Lorenzi-Cioldi

A Radical Dissonance Theory
Jean-Léon Beauvois and Robert-Vincent Joule

The Social Psychology of Collective Action
Caroline Kelly and Sara Breinlinger

Social Context and Cognitive Performance
Jean-Marc Monteil and Pascal Huguet

Conflict and Decision-Making in Close Relationships
Erich Kirchler, Christa Rodler, Erik Hölzl, and Katja Meier

Forthcoming Titles
Social Development and Adult Identity
John Bynner, Nick Emler, and David Romney

Attitudes of Mind: The Pragmatic Theory of Rational Cognition
Maria Lewicka and Karl Halvor Teigen

Stereotyping as Inductive Hypothesis Testing
Klaus Fiedler and Eva Walthier

Conflict and decision-making in close relationships

Love, money and daily routines

Erich Kirchler,
Christa Rodler, Erik Hölzl, and Katja Meier

University of Vienna, Austria

First published 2001 by Psychology Press Ltd
27 Church Road, Hove, East Sussex, BN3 2FA

www.psypress.co.uk

Simultaneously published in the USA and Canada
by Taylor & Francis Inc.
325 Chestnut Street, Suite 800, Philadelphia, PA 19106

Psychology Press is part of the Taylor & Francis Group

British Library Cataloguing in Publication Data
A catalogue record for this book is available from the British Library

Library of Congress Cataloging-in-Publication Data
Conflict and decision-making in close relationships : love, money, and
    daily routines /
Erich Kirchler . . . [et al.].
        p. cm.—(European monographs in social psychology ISSN 0892-7286)
    Includes bibliographical references and index.
    ISBN 0-86377-811-9
    1. Marriage—Decision making. 2. Couples—Decision making.
    3. Households—Decision making. I. Kirchler, Erich. II. Series.

HQ728 .C617 2000
306.81—dc21

                                                            00-042546

ISBN 0-86377-811-9

Cover design by Amanda Barragry
Typeset in Times by Mayhew Typesetting, Rhayader, Powys
Printed and bound in the UK by TJ International Ltd, Padstow, Cornwall

Contents

Preface

Love, money, and everyday matters in the shared home are the topics of this work. The routines of everyday life in close relationships are described, analysed and interpreted using psychological concepts.

Romantic relationships on the one hand, and the processes and results of decision-making on the other, have long attracted the interest of social research scientists. Decisions in close relationships have, however, been neglected, particularly everyday decision-making involving couples and children. Close relationships have been studied for clinical-psychological reasons, in order to understand dysfunctional processes and to develop targeted intervention programmes. Meanwhile research into decision-making has offered wide scope to economists and social scientists. It has helped them to understand the relationship between economic processes and human behaviour patterns in general. The study of decision-making in close relationships is expected to make a contribution to the wider understanding of such relationships, since the relationship is reflected in joint decisions, even about financial matters, and the manner in which the joint decision is taken indicates the quality of the relationship. In addition, analysis of joint decision-making explains how partners operate in situations where resources are scarce, and how they jointly seek to realise economic and relationship goals.

The studies of decision-making, and particularly of purchasing decisions, in private households summarised here are drawn from the period going back to the start of the 1980s. For almost 20 years research on household decision-making has been conducted at the Universities of Linz and Vienna, Austria. After several years of research, some of the focuses of research and the underlying processes now seem clear and comprehensible. However, scientific studies set up to explore and test hypotheses repeatedly throw up new questions, requiring deeper and more comprehensive analysis. Further studies and more precise questioning have brought us ever closer to a focus on the actual pattern of decision-making in close relationships, and we hoped ultimately to reach the point where we could present an empirically based overview that would do justice to the complexities of everyday life in the home and which would offer a "manageable model" for decision-making in relationships. However, the latest research work, the Vienna Diary Study, which was intended to provide answers to the many unsolved questions we had gathered, showed that the reality cannot be represented in a model, not even a complex one, without a worrying amount of simplification.

Moreover, increasing dissection of joint decisions drew our attention deeper into the focus of research, with the result that ultimately the sense of overview was in danger of being lost, thereby raising the question of appropriate distance between the researcher and the focus of the research. When a landscape is surveyed from an aeroplane, or viewed from the highest mountain-top, or analysed on a walk through it, it remains the same focus of research, but the perspective changes according to the visible elements and details, and their relationship to one another. In some research areas we may be too close to the couples' decisions, but what is the optimal distance? When does proximity obscure what we are looking at rather than revealing further details?

This book is divided into five main chapters which follow a chapter on a phenomenological study of decision-making as reported by three couples in the Vienna Diary Study, together with a chapter on definitions and outlines covering love, money, and everyday matters. The five main chapters look at romantic relationships, decision-making, methods of researching decision-making in private everyday life, influence in decision-making in close relationships, and decision dynamics. Where we talk of romantic relationships, we look at goals, structures, and the dynamics of the relationship. In the chapter about decision-making we discuss the processes and topics involved. A lengthy chapter is devoted to methods of researching decision-making, because partners in close relationships may react to outside observers in such a way that intrusion into the private sphere negates the purpose of the research. Finally decision-making, particularly financial decision-making, by couples is discussed: We look at the relative influence of the partners, the interconnectedness of activities within the home, the tactics used to gain influence and the results of disagreements and decision-making. Earlier studies are quoted, but the main focus is the results of the Vienna Diary Study of 1996–1999, which are reported extensively.

We end this preface with words of thanks to the numerous friends, colleagues and institutions that have supported our work. Our thanks go to all those who have spurred us on to further work by their pertinent questioning, and to those whose critical questions have pressed us to provide more precise answers. Many people, mainly couples and their children, made themselves available to us as participants or "interested researchers" in numerous studies, and they deserve our special thanks. In particular, we wish to thank Rupert Brown at the University of Kent at Canterbury, whose commissioning of this work as part of his series of books on social psychology began the whole process.

This work, and in particular the Vienna Diary Study, was given financial assistance by the Austrian research funding agency *Fonds zur Förderung wissenschaftlicher Forschung* under the project title "P11242-OEK". We thank all those working at the agency for their unstinting support.

The diary project was carried out at the Institute for Psychology at the University of Vienna, with the assistance of Tanja Auenhammer, Ernestine Georgeacopol, Regina Rettig, Astrid Tietz, and Judith Ulm. We owe them much thanks for their tireless work during a lengthy period of research. In particular, we thank Boris Maciejovsky, who cast a critical eye over the text and made many suggestions for improvements.

Finally we give our thanks to Vivien Ward at Routledge, Taylor & Francis for her friendly encouragement.

All scientists, especially those engaged in the study of social phenomena and particularly of close relationships, are called upon to use language that is gender-neutral. To improve the readability of the text we have chosen not to use repetitions (female/male partner, she and he, etc.), and have usually used the male singular form throughout. It should be understood that statements apply equally to women and men, unless there is explicit reference to specific gender differences.

Erich Kirchler,
Christa Rodler, Erik Hölzl and Katja Meier
Vienna, April 2000

CHAPTER ONE

Decisions in the Shared Home

The aim of this work is to describe the decisions taken by partners in the course of everyday life in close relationships. Analysis is undertaken mainly of economic decisions taken jointly by men and women. Thus the focus is on romantic relationships, on money, and on other demands in everyday life. In order to understand economic decision-making, account must be taken not only of the relationship between the decision-makers, but also of other background elements to the decision. It is becoming increasingly clear that it is necessary to understand everyday life in the home in its totality before any composite part of it will make sense.

Anyone seeking to study joint decision-making in private households will surely ask themselves key questions, which they then seek to answer, such as: Which of the partners is mainly responsible for making which decisions? What affects the relative balance of influence between the partners? How do the partners try to influence or convince each other?

Over the course of 10 years of reflection and empirical research about decision-making, countless data have been collected which offer answers. Admittedly, it is rare to find clear answers, for often the results of one study contradict those of a similar study, and questions that originally appear similar may actually be addressing different things.

Many research attempts to find answers to questions on joint decision-making implicitly make assumptions about decision-making. These assumptions can often not be justified once the dynamics of disagreements and decision-making between partners in everyday life settings have been thoroughly observed. Numerous studies are devised as if the process involved pinpointing a phenomenon that is clearly distinct from other phenomena, or as if partners were aware that they were in the process of reaching a joint decision, expressing their wishes, gathering information, evaluating or choosing. In fact partners spend relatively little time at home interacting with one another and even less time talking to each other. If there is a disagreement over a particular issue, they often try to avoid conflict and postpone decision-making, instead of considering the objective arguments relating to the issue in order to reach decisions that maximise their own or joint benefit. Actual decision-making is rarely observed, but it is important and can have lasting influence on the relationship.

Decisions have neither a clearly definable start nor a clear end. In the flow of joint activities it often only becomes clear with hindsight that a decision has been reached. Where partners reflect on their decision-making behaviour, they quite often try to understand and interpret their conversations and actions retrospectively as a meaningful sequence of interactions that led to a particular goal.

Decisions within private households, including financial decisions, do not follow the normative–rational model, which acts as a basis for decision-making in economics as a whole. It is only in exceptional instances that both partners take time out from the endless routine activities around the house and consciously reach a joint decision, having weighed up their own wishes, the alternative options and the advantages and disadvantages of each choice. Anyone seeking to offer an adequate description of joint decision-making in close relationships needs to unravel the maze of everyday life patiently and, as far as possible, without pre-judging the issues. This will enable them to identify segments of interactions that could represent fragments of decision-making, slowly putting the pieces together to build up a picture of decision-making.

After years of studying economic decision-making in shared homes, no simple theoretical model can be put forward that could be tested in further studies and assist in creating a prescriptive model to offer insights as to how to reach sensible decisions that nurture relationships. Currently a gap still exists between normative decision-making models and the experience of everyday life in the home, and it is therefore more necessary than ever to involve the participants in decision-making themselves as researchers in their everyday lives, identifying and recording their actions. In this way an evidence base can be built up for economic decision-making and many other activities around the home, which can then be subjected to detailed analysis. The analysis of many such records, built up over a long period of time, and not conducted using a narrowly focused instrument according to some preconceived and rigid concept, may finally throw some light on the dynamics of decision-making in close relationships.

THE VIENNA DIARY STUDY

Answers to various questions about joint economic decision-making were sought in a series of studies starting in the mid-1980s (Kirchler, 1988a, 1988b, 1988c, 1989). Above all, the diary study conceived at the University of Vienna in 1995 and begun in winter 1995–6, to which this work repeatedly refers, sought to investigate conversations, disagreements, and decision-making of various kinds over a long period of time, in order to answer some important, still open questions (Kirchler, Rodler, Hölzl, & Meier, 1999). An analysis was made of decisions that occurred sequentially over a period of time, in order to identify which factors determined the influence of the partners over purchasing decisions and over other financial and non-financial decisions. Alongside the partners' relative resource contributions, relative competence, and relative interest in a particular decision, the study sought to evaluate the extent to which an individual partner's relative influence over past decisions and relative benefit from past decisions determined his or her relative influence over a current decision. The Vienna Diary Study, which brought together conversations, disagreements, and decisions made by 40 couples over the course of a year, examined the significance of influence determinants in satisfactory and less satisfactory relationships and in relationships where one or other partner dominated, or where both partners had roughly the same say. The regulation of influence over a period of time, like the regulation of exchangeable resources in general, appears to depend on the quality of the relationship between the partners. With regard to relative influence and benefit to the partners in the past, we examined whether different "reserves of influence" and "benefit debts" were operating in satisfactory and unsatisfactory relationships, and whether the disadvantaged partner sought to equalise the uneven distribution of influence and benefit.

In the Vienna Diary Study disagreements and financial and non-financial decisions between partners were studied. At the time of the decision being made, the relative interest of the partners in the decision was recorded, together with their relative subject knowledge, but above all their relative influence and the possible resultant debt of influence or benefit. Detailed recording of these variables allows us to identify the weight of past influence and benefit debt on the current distribution of influence, alongside the relative interest and the subject knowledge of the partners.

In order to analyse the significance of influence determinants in differently structured relationships, it was necessary to carry out the study with satisfied and less satisfied couples in egalitarian, patriarchal, or matriarchal relationships. The study was conducted over a long time-frame, recording all the different decision-making situations that were experienced, so that we could investigate the links in controlling influence across different types of decision, e.g. financial and non-financial decisions, decisions involving value, probability or distributional issues, etc.

The study also looked at the tactics used by one partner to influence the other. It was assumed that alongside the objective–logical arguments, partners in close relationships would also seek to use flattery, the offer of special attention, threats etc., to defend their viewpoint and to gain compliance. To understand the dynamic of such interactions, a study was made of which tactics were used in response to "deployment" of a particular tactic by the other partner.

The following issues, which form the essential basis of the Vienna Diary Study, are also central to this book:

(a)   The identification of influence determinants in disagreements and in joint decision-making.
(b)   An analysis of the history of decision-making as a particular determinant of influence.
(c)   The study of tactics used to exert influence.

Other aspects remain open to further study, including the outcomes of decision-making, fairness, satisfaction, and the rationality of decisions. The series of issues addressed requires a detailed description of everyday life in close relationships and consideration of the way in which spouses reconstruct jointly experienced everyday events.

Participation in the Diary Study was open solely to couples who had lived together in a shared home for several years and who had at least one child of school age. The decision to select couples with one or more dependent children was made firstly to ensure a relatively homogeneous sample with comparable family situations. Couples with children were chosen because they represent prototypes of the family, and because the frequency of conflicts appears to be higher in phases of family life where there are dependent children. In total, 40 men and 40 women took part in the study and kept a diary for a year.

The conception and the implementation of the Vienna Diary Study are described later (see Chapter 5) in greater detail. At this stage we confine our description to the detail that the diary was based on a collection of identical sets of questions, which were filled out every evening. Every evening both partners were asked to reflect on the day just ended and to record separately how long they had spent together, what they had talked about, whether there had been disagreements, and how they would assess the current warmth of the relationship between them. After this they were asked to answer further questions about any disagreements that they had indicated. After describing various aspects of the situation during the discussion, participants recorded their knowledge of the topic under discussion and their level of interest in a decision. They described the context of the conversation and indicated their relative influence and relative benefit from the outcome. They also recorded the tactics they had used in order to move towards agreement over the issue, as well as the type of disagreement.

Finally, they were asked about the fairness of the decision-making and their level of satisfaction with the outcome of the conversation.

The diary includes a vast amount of data, offering insights into everyday life as it is lived over a long time period. The structured set of questions enables quantitative analysis of specific questions. However, it is also valuable to interpret the records as a whole, drawing up a comprehensive picture of events using qualitative analyses. Disagreements can be "fished out" from the daily "stream of events" recorded by the partners, briefly analysed and finally returned to the flow as other topics attract the attention, perhaps to reappear later further downstream. Qualitative analysis of disagreements that were repeatedly raised over time and rarely resolved, but were concluded at some point, led to the realisation that decisions in close relationships are not isolated events with a defined beginning and a definable end. Often the partners cannot see that they are "grappling" with a decision, and as the disagreement is repeatedly brought up there is often a change in the goal of the decision-making process. If couples are asked in retrospect about their behaviour during such a decision-making process, they are often not able to describe the dynamics of the decision-making accurately; rather, they "straighten out" the process and rationalise their behaviour so that not only does the decision reached appear desirable, but also the process itself seems focused on the goal and sensibly conducted to the observer. The case studies that follow, taken from the Vienna Diary Study, exemplify this.

CASE STUDIES FROM THE VIENNA DIARY STUDY: STORIES OF THREE DECISIONS

The following decision-making accounts were found in the diaries of three couples. The cases are powerful examples of how everyday decision-making takes place in patterns far removed from normative, rational models.

Michael and Gina Buy a Car

Michael and Gina have lived together for 18 years and have three children, the youngest of whom is 10 years old. Gina is 38, attended a vocational school and works in a sales capacity for a technical department. Michael is 3 years younger than Gina, followed a course of further education and at the time of the events was working as a homemaker and looking for work. The monthly net household income was between 1400 and 1700 Euro. There was disagreement over how the money was managed: Gina stated that the money was pooled and both partners had access to a joint account, whereas Michael said that they kept separate accounts. Both described their relationship as dominated by Gina, and moderately satisfying.

In the partner diaries, the first mention of the need to buy a car appeared in mid-summer 1996. There were a number of separate conversations where the subject was discussed, and several disagreements. It repeatedly arose in discussions and disagreements over other matters, particularly with regard to Michael finding paid employment, during a period of over a month before a car was finally bought at the end of the summer.

On Sunday 28 July 1996, Gina recorded a disagreement about a new car. Michael's diary makes no mention of this. A few days later the partners again discussed buying a car. Both felt happy and described the disagreement, which they indicated to be slight. There were greater disagreements regarding untidiness in the kitchen and troubles one of their children was having at school. Following a short conversation about the car, the subject was not raised again for over a week. Other problems seemed more pressing: buying a bicycle for their son, Michael's return to work, job applications, and overall career plans.

On 8 August 1996, both partners recorded a conflict over buying a car in their diaries. Gina again raised the matter, and both considered whether they should buy a minibus or a second-hand car, or whether they could do without a car. The total sum involved would be around 7000 Euro. Whereas Gina felt that they had rarely discussed buying a car up till that point, Michael reported that they had often discussed the topic. Michael said he was more knowledgeable about cars than Gina was. Both said that the topic was important to them. The mood of the half-hour conversation was described as relatively objective. Both partners indicated that they had attempted to use rational arguments and clear expression of their wishes to influence the other. Both had roughly equal influence and described the course of the discussion as fair and the outcome of the conversation as satisfactory. A decision was not reached, however, and the topic was shelved after half an hour.

Two days later the conversation was resumed. Alongside other topics of conversation, such as their son's stay in England, a visit to a jazz concert, and work in the workshop (as a hobby), the cost of a new car was discussed. None of these topics led to serious conflicts, and the partners recorded their mood as good. The car was again discussed the next day, because the old car had broken down with the whole family on board and the car battery had had to be replaced. Gina recorded that she and Michael agreed on the need to buy a new car.

On 13 August 1996 Gina wrote that she and Michael had had a discussion about money matters, while Michael reported under "other details" that he had had a discussion with Gina because a planned visit to view a car had not taken place.

Three days later, Michael wrote that he had discussed buying a new car with his wife. Both agreed about the course of the conversation, which lasted five minutes. Gina recorded that she had already often spoken about a new car and said that she was more knowledgeable than Michael about the matter. Both said the topic was important to them. Gina judged the mood of the conversation to be unpleasant. Both of them, but most of all she herself, had been non-objective and relatively emotional. She had had more influence over him than he over her. Whereas he expressed his wishes openly, she responded with negative emotions and pointed out the useful-ness for the children of the car that she wanted to buy. Michael responded not with objective argument, but by distorting facts and by threatening withdrawal of resources. Gina ended the conversation with negative emo-tions and was annoyed.

They had another conversation, about ten minutes long, about the planned car purchase five days later. Only Gina provided a detailed record of it. The discussion again centred on whether to buy a new car or keep the old one. Michael began the conversation. The mood of the conversation was described as pleasant, with both partners discussing objectively and relatively unemotionally. Both had roughly equal say. Michael began by stating his wishes clearly. Gina reacted, as in the previous discussion, by pointing out the usefulness of the car for the children. He tried to influence her using objective arguments. She emphasised her own wishes and needs. At this Michael withdrew from the conversation. A final decision was again deferred.

Four days later the diaries again recorded the car purchase as a source of conflict. The following day, price comparisons in connection with a car purchase were discussed alongside other topics, such as the expense of 250 Euro for their daughter's holiday, or housework. There were no recorded disagreements.

On 25 August 1996 their son had to be collected from the airport, plants needed watering and other tasks needed to be done. They again discussed buying a car. Gina's diary made it clear that the couple had been to see cars that day. There were no further detailed descriptions relating to the planned car purchase. There was a brief discussion on the following day, with Michael noting that the fixed costs for a new car were too high.

The high fixed costs were again discussed the next day. The partners again disagreed. Gina recorded that Michael did not want to buy a new car. Michael questioned the sense of buying a new car, or owning a car at all, and compared the cost of around 2000 Euro annually for a new car with the cost of fares for trains, buses, and taxis. He reported being exceptionally objective and unemotional during the discussion, whereas Gina assessed her discussion style as more emotional and felt that she had exerted more influence over Michael than he on her. The tactics as recorded enable us to reconstruct the course of the discussion, which was assessed to be relatively fair and the outcome of which was ultimately satisfactory to both parties. Michael reported that he presented the facts as they appeared to him, whilst he felt Gina built indirect coalitions by indicating the usefulness of the car for the children and by distorting the facts. Gina recorded the course of the conversation differently: After initially insisting on her position, she indicated seeking integrative solutions, whereas Michael withdrew from confrontation with her after expressing his wishes. The decision was reached to purchase a car during this conversation. Gina had won the argument.

On 28 August 1996, the cost of buying a car was again discussed. Both partners agreed, and felt happy during the conversation. Another conversation about the car was recorded the following day, and the mood of the conversation was described as pleasant. On 30 August 1996, Michael and Gina bought their new car, at a cost of 6300 Euro.

A few days later the couple again recorded discussions on buying the car, on selling the old car and on waiting impatiently for the documentation for the new car. A day later, the partners discussed the cost of registering their new car, and on 6 September 1996 they were able to register it officially. For the next three weeks there are further references to the sale of the old car, its price and the costs of officially de-registering it. After this the desires and concerns about the car disappear from the diaries.

In this instance, the questionnaire about relative influence, which couples completed alongside the diaries, is also revealing. At the start of the diary-keeping, and again after six months and at the end of the year, the partners were each asked, in the context of a hypothetical car purchase, who would express their wishes, who would collect the information, and who would make the final decision. Here, both Michael and Gina recorded that they would reach the decision together; conforming to stereotypes, Michael would gather information autonomously and then both partners would make a decision together, in accordance with a relationship-nurturing ideal. This evidence conflicts with that of the diaries, which shows that decisions about major purchases extend over long periods of time and are quite unsystematic, with chance disagreements frequently being thrown up and discussions being brief affairs interrupted by other topics or by one partner withdrawing from the confrontation. Gina had much more influence than is stereotypically the case, or than is indicated in either of their questionnaires, which tend to conform to a socially constructed view of what represents a relationship-nurturing ideal.

Peter and Mary Look for a Birthday Present for Their Son

Peter and Mary have been married for 17 years. Peter is 43, and Mary is 7 years younger. They live together with their 15-year-old son and 11-year-old daughter in a flat in a suburb of Vienna. Peter works for the Austrian Railways and Mary works part-time in a legal office. Both rate their relationship as very satisfactory. Both think that in general Peter takes the lead, and both describe themselves as a fairly traditional couple. The income of both partners is jointly managed.

Peter and Mary were looking for a birthday present for their son. They had to make a fairly straightforward decision, but in the course of discussions it led to disagreements and ultimately to an end that was not intended. The initial goal, of buying a birthday present, was not achieved.

On 27 October 1996 Peter and Mary spent about four hours with one another, during which time they spoke for about an hour about housework and Peter's visit to a model railway exhibition with their son. They also spoke angrily about their relationship and about their daughter, who felt that she was being treated unfairly. Mary, whom Peter describes as egoistic, was particularly annoyed because he had not listened to her opinion and had unilaterally spent around 170 Euro on a model train set for his collection, and had not bought a planned birthday present for their son costing around 80 Euro. Peter described Mary as narrow-minded. He admitted having taken an autonomous decision, but stated that the train he had bought was for himself and his son together. The discussion about the purchase of the model train was also brought up at lunch-time. One of the children raised the subject of model trains. The mood during the conversation was negative. Opinions differed as to whether the purchase was appropriate. In the joint discussion between Peter and Mary she felt that she had had no influence at all on the decision; Peter had decided on his own. He indicated that his influence over the decision had been around 60%, compared to Mary's 40%. Unlike Peter, Mary described the decision as unfair, concluding that he had acted against her expressed wishes and without seeking to get her agreement, and in addition he had all the benefit of this decision—a fact Peter agreed with in his diary.

Regarding the decision-making dynamic of 27 October 1996, Mary noted that she had threatened the withdrawal of resources, had repeatedly insisted on her opinion and had finally left the room. Peter recorded that Mary had expressed negative emotions, threatened, lied and tried to build coalitions with the children. After he had taken action, making no concession towards her point of view, she broke off the argument over the purchase. Peter recorded in his diary that he for his part had remained objective, had explained his decision to buy the train as a present for his son as well as for himself, and had openly presented the reasons for his actions. He too insisted on his point of view. Mary described Peter as dishonest, saying that he had reminded her of earlier favours she had received and made her feel guilty by doing so, and that he was ultimately also seeking to find coalition partners to justify his actions.

The model train was bought on 27 October 1996, for Peter's collection, it would appear. In fact, there are earlier references in the diary to discussions about a model train, admittedly as a present for the son. On 15 August 1996, a bank holiday, the discussion about a suitable birthday present began. The couple spent ten hours together and spoke a lot with each other, discussing amongst other things a birthday party and a visit to friends. With regard to a birthday present, Peter and Mary were of quite different opinions. There were plans to buy some parts of a model railway. The cost was not to be more than 100 Euro. The conversation about the model railway lasted around five minutes and was not particularly pleasant. Peter accused Mary of using non-objective arguments and felt that she had dominated the discussion. Mary attributed 80% of the influence to herself, and 20% to Peter. Both partners believed that they had equal benefit from a present for their son. Both recorded that the discussion was ultimately not unfair, but the outcome pleased only Mary.

On 1 September 1996, Peter and Mary discussed housework and their relationship. They did not discuss the birthday present, but at lunch with the children they discussed buying a part of a model railway for Peter's collection. The cost of the part (11 Euro) was small. Peter and Mary spoke objectively about the purchase, even if Mary was somewhat more emotional than Peter. Whereas Peter attributed 70% of the influence and 90% of the benefit from the decision to himself, Mary felt that he had not only had more of the influence, but that he also had all the benefit.

Next day, Peter and Mary spent about 30 minutes together. They talked for a few minutes about pressures of work and complained about not having enough time for each other. The start of the school term was briefly mentioned, and the birthday present was again discussed. Mary felt that Peter wanted to spend too much money and this led to a disagreement. The mood of the conversation worsened in comparison to the day before. Mary recorded that she had argued non-objectively, had hardly had any influence on the discussion and, compared to Peter, had hardly had any benefit from it. She felt the course of the discussion and the outcome were unfair, and she was unhappy for that reason. Peter's diary for the day has no entry about this conflict.

Up until 27 October 1996 neither Peter nor Mary record further discussions about the present for their son. The matter of the model railway—which at one time had been considered as an appropriate and not too expensive present—was settled by an autonomous decision on Peter's part. He bought himself a present and the birthday present for his son had to be accommodated around that.

Tony, Helen, and the Purchase of a Guitar

Tony and Helen have been married for 16 years and live with their two children, the younger of whom is 6 years old, in Vienna. Helen (32) attended a vocational school and is a housewife. Tony (38) is an academic and works in a state school. The net household income, which is jointly managed, is between 2500 and 3000 Euro per month. Tony and Helen describe their relationship as very satisfactory, more dominated by Helen, and modern with respect to gender roles.

In the diaries of this couple there was a series of disagreements surrounding the purchase of a guitar for Tony. After a discussion, where the couple could not agree, Tony decided autonomously to buy the guitar, although at first he did not carry out his decision. He sought to gain Helen's agreement. The following day there was again a disagreement. Almost two months later Tony bought the guitar, without Helen's agreement. Following that there was a renewed argument.

On Sunday 4 August 1996, the couple recorded spending about an hour together and talking for about 20 minutes. Helen did not feel particularly good about their relationship. By contrast, Tony felt relatively happy about the relationship, but somewhat constrained. Alongside a discussion about leisure time, they talked about the cost of buying a guitar. During this discussion Tony was resting and Helen was doing the housework. Tony wanted to buy a guitar costing around 1000 Euro for himself, and had already gathered information about various guitars. Helen was not particularly interested in the topic, and had little information or knowledge of the subject. The mood of the conversation was described by both as moderately pleasant. Whereas Helen was relatively emotionless, Tony was very emotional during the discussion. Tony had more influence in this discussion than Helen (she rated it at 100%, he rated it at 90%). The decision to buy a guitar was postponed.

In the conversation, which both partners described as completely unfair, Tony began by presenting the objective basis for the purchase and expressing his wishes. Helen remained insistent that she did not agree with the cost involved in buying the guitar. After this, Tony sought to use objective arguments to change Helen's point of view. She reacted by withdrawing, and ending the conversation. Both partners' diaries agree about the tactics used by each person during the conversation. Helen was not at all satisfied with the outcome of the conversation; Tony was also dissatisfied.

The following day, Tony and Helen indicated that they did not talk to one another. Helen felt only moderately good about the relationship, not very empowered and rather constrained. She felt that she put more into the relationship than Tony. Tony felt happy overall, praised the relationship and felt that he contributed more to it than Helen. On this day he also reported having taken an autonomous decision to buy the guitar, costing 1000 Euro, without Helen's agreement.

A day later, the topic of the guitar purchase was raised alongside topics of housework, personal feelings, and the relationship. Although the partners felt good during the discussions and indicated that there was agreement, the mood worsened during the argument about the guitar. The conflict took place with the children present, while Helen was doing housework and Tony indicated he was arranging a leisure activity. The conversation lasted for around five to seven minutes. Helen began the discussion about the guitar, although she still indicated that the topic was not important to her.

On this occasion she discussed less objectively than he did, and more emotionally. According to both partners' records, Helen had 10% of the influence and Tony 90%. Whereas Tony felt that the decision-making process and the result were extremely fair, Helen felt that the outcome was unfair and the process itself only moderately fair. She had no benefit from the decision and felt that he had all the benefit. He felt that Helen had at least 10% of the benefit from the outcome, although he indicated the same distribution of benefit in the final decision.

The dynamics of the discussion, as revealed through the record of tactics employed, were as follows: Helen began the discussion with negative emotions, to which Tony reacted by being more insistent. She then attempted to form a coalition with the children against her partner. The disagreement, which both described as a value conflict, ended with Tony insisting on his opinion. Whereas he was very satisfied with the outcome of the conversation, Helen was not at all satisfied.

Not until two months later, on 11 October 1996, did the topic of the guitar reappear in the notes recorded by the couple. Tony recorded that he had carried out his autonomously reached decision. He had bought a guitar costing 910 Euro. Next day, Helen initiated a discussion about the purchase. Although she discussed more objectively and he more emotionally, she indicated that she became very annoyed. By contrast, Tony appeared to have been completely satisfied: The decision had come out in his favour.

A few days later, the couple recorded having a five-minute conversation. They talked about their children's schoolwork and how Tony was feeling. Both indicated they felt good about their relationship. In the subsequent days and weeks there was no further mention of the purchase of the guitar in the diary records. The topic appeared to be closed. Tony, who was indicated by both partners to have less power in the relationship, had carried out his egoistic desire to buy a guitar and carried out the decision taken over two months earlier. He had sought, but not obtained, the agreement of his wife. The guitar was important enough to him to complete the purchase despite Helen's dominance advantage and her opposition to the decision.

This case reveals processes leading ultimately to an autonomous decision. In contrast to an individual, fully autonomous decision, Tony sought to take the opinion of his partner into consideration and to win her approval. In this instance, however, he did not succeed in this. The benefit from this decision clearly lay with the active partner, in this case Tony, who wanted to fulfil a wish he had. Whilst the records indicate that the clarity and strength of his wish were apparent, the active partner was not able to assert himself at first and even at a later stage he was not able to secure the agreement of his partner. Tony chose to ignore the fact that his partner was not in agreement with the purchase and was not satisfied with the outcome of the numerous discussions, and bought what he wanted.

FROM DESIRES, DISCUSSIONS, AND DISAGREEMENTS TO DECISIONS

The three decision-making processes selected from the recordings in the Vienna Diary Study show clearly that, in private households, partners do not sit round a table together to reach a decision, thereby freeing themselves up from other tasks and weighing up objective arguments for or against a particular alternative. Decisions are taken, but it only becomes clear in retrospect that desires have led to discussions, and these have led to disagreements, which have finally ended with the taking of a decision. A clear awareness of the need to take a decision and a direct focus on desires, alternatives, and criteria would appear to be the exception rather than the rule, even for economic decisions taken in the home.

In one instance it is apparent that decisions that are finally taken autonomously by one partner do not follow an autonomous pattern throughout: one partner repeatedly tried to get the agreement of the other, discussions were begun and then broken off, and only when no agreement could be reached did the partner make a decision to purchase autonomously. From another case it is clear that decision-makers may change their objectives over a period of time: whilst at the start of the discussion about a present for their son both partners were pursuing the same objective, the objective for the man changed during the period when alternatives for presents were being considered, so that in the end he was organising a present for himself and the original objective became lost. To sum up, these case studies are powerful evidence that decisions are not isolated incidents, but are instead woven into the complexity of everyday life: When an economic decision is being made, various other disagreements are brought out, and other everyday activities intrude repeatedly into the foreground. All three cases also show variations in the subjective description of the reality of what went on between the partners. Differences in perception and in recall lead to slightly different descriptions of joint experiences that are only a few hours old.

Social scientific methods applied to the study of decision-making must take account of these insights. These phenomena, so apparent from the case studies, cannot be captured in structured oral or written interviews.

To understand decision-making in private households, it is not only the research method that requires careful selection. We must also determine who the decision-makers are, and what kind of relationship they have. In romantic relationships, the goal of the partners when making a decision may not just lie in making the best possible choice from the given alternatives; promoting, or at least sustaining, the quality of the relationship can often be the overriding objective, leading to a position where not only the wishes of the individual, but also those of the partner must be taken into consideration. It therefore follows that the dynamics of decision-making depend to a large extent on the relationship between the partners.

Further definition is required to determine what is understood by decision-making. In private households a number of tasks crop up that are rarely tackled in a structured manner. What do the partners discuss, which problems lead to disagreements, and how can decisions be classified? Before decision-making in close relationships can be described, we must first address the issue of close relationships in general and the decision-making process in particular.

We start with an outline of what is understood by love, a summary of the psychology of money, and a description of everyday matters. What is love, which brings a partner to the point of setting up home with someone and jointly tackling everyday tasks over a number of years? What is money, and what is the significance of money in romantic relationships? And finally, what do we understand by everyday matters, those things that are ever-present and yet appear so unprepossessing, grey, and monotonous? Following this, we embark on an analysis of close relationships and offer a taxonomy of decision-making, before finally studying decision-making in close relationships.

CHAPTER TWO

Love, Money, and Everyday Matters

Close relationships are based on the love each partner has for the other. At the start of a relationship, this is most often reciprocal love. We aspire to a relationship built on love. If the relationship lasts, life "in a shared home" often comes about as a matter of course, punctuated with smaller and sometimes greater periods of excitement and often without particular incidents over long periods of time, resulting in correspondingly little attention being paid to what is actually happening.

Many activities and goals will be experienced and valued similarly by the partners. Some of their wishes and intentions, on the other hand, result in disagreements, which need to be settled and so lead to decision-making. If partners more or less consciously take decisions together, then they not only have to clarify their current egoistic goals and identify what the available alternative options might be, but they also have to take account of their partner's ideas and find a satisfactory solution together.

This book is concerned with disagreements and decisions in private households, mainly but not exclusively concerning financial matters. Financial matters are often the source of disagreements and of intense conflicts, which can call the whole relationship into question. Decisions regarding the joint budget in private households attract the attention not only of the clinically orientated family psychologist and the social psychologist, but also of the economist, because private households hold sway over a significant amount of a country's national income. Non-rational, or sub-optimal, decisions can significantly affect the whole of the economy.

The aim of this work is to understand how partners in close relationships shape their everyday life together, and particularly how they handle money. Love, money, and everyday matters are key concepts that pervade the whole of this book.

LOVE

Definition of Love

Much has been written about the loved one and about love itself: in distressed, mesmerised, mournful, ironic, and wholly cynical tones, and in tones that are objective and rational. Whenever this most highly sung emotion is put into words, the descriptions offered fail to capture that feeling which can make one blind and which is stronger than reason, disdaining to do battle with it. Whenever reason seeks to get a grip on love, love escapes like a brightly coloured bird which alights, wanting nothing to do with rights, law or power, and flies off if someone tries to catch hold of it.

At one time it fell to the grandfather to find a suitable marriage partner for his grandson, and his choice of bride was guided by economic considerations. Nowadays the choice of partner is freely made by the partner him- or herself, and love has become the basis for the partnership. Love has thereby become the basis for the most elemental of society's micro-systems. It is that condition which is most intensively sought after as we escape into the private sphere, and which seems to last for ever shorter periods of time (Duck, 1986; Hinde, 1997; Hyde, 1993; Piel, 1983).

What follows is an overview of the scientific focus on one of the most glittering phenomena of social psychology, love. No differentiation is made between love and being in love, although it is clear that the two phenomena are different even if the boundaries between the two are often blurred.

First, it seems prudent to draw together various findings and theories from social psychology and economics. This area has already been acknowledged by the awarding of the Nobel Prize for Economics to Gary S. Becker, in recognition of his work on the private household, the marriage market, and love as an economic good. In social psychology, the language used to describe love is scientific and objective, and in economics it is highly formal. Here we seek to substitute this often abstract formulaic language with a more discursive style, but nevertheless to provide a picture of the scientific preoccupation with love that is largely in contrast to the picture of love drawn by writers and poets.

The phenomenon of "love" has been addressed by various branches of science. Sociologists, psychologists, anthropologists, and economists have tried to relate love to their particular "market". In particular, Becker's writings (1974, 1981, 1982; see Bolle, 1987, 1992) on family economics and his conception of altruism or love have provoked much sober and spirited discussion. Here love is defined as a resource, with which business can be concluded after periods of consideration that have been as rational as possible. The economically orientated construct of exchange theory is at the root of even the most well-known social psychological theories about interpersonal interaction, and therefore also at the heart of theories about the interplay between lovers or loving partners (Blau, 1964; Homans, 1961/1974; Thibaut & Kelley, 1959). Put briefly, individuals sustain and intensify interactions with those people where the interaction brings a reward. Material and non-material resources are offered to those people who guarantee a similar pay-back, and ultimately love is bestowed on the "partnership option" that offers more benefits than the others.

Some people express concern that love is seen as an economic force (Fromm, 1977); others see this as an opportunity in longer-term relationships (Lederer & Jackson, 1972). Fromm (1977, p. 17 ff.) writes: "In a culture where the sales mentality is dominant and where material success is given exaggerated value, there is little reason to be surprised if human love relationships operate on the same principles which govern the market in goods and the labour market." Reducing love to a business transaction is, however, seen to be a major mistake by Fromm. By contrast, Lederer and Jackson (1972, p. 203 ff.) write that "dealings (between partners) form an essential part of a well-functioning marriage". Pleasing actions that one partner carries out must be responded to immediately. In an ideal arrangement, the response may not need to be demanded immediately, but this deferment can carry with it "the seeds of self-destruction".

From a medical point of view, love is interesting because it is said to have a preventative and therapeutic effect in respect of various illnesses. The loss of love can lead to depression and can bring on physical illnesses in the organs, sometimes causing the patient deadly torment and even in some instances bringing about death. The Italian weekly magazine *Europeo* has dedicated a front cover and several pages to this theme, which is an indication that everyone is aware of the power of love to act as a therapeutic and dangerous drug (Ferreiri, 1991; Rosso 1991; Vertone, 1991). Love, attachment, and intimacy contribute to mental health (Reis & Patrick, 1996). Being in love correlates with neurochemical changes in the brain (Liebowitz, 1983) and has a positive effect on the immune system of lovers (Siegel, 1986). People who have never been in love and those whose love relationships have been unsuccessful complain more often than those in love of minor physical ailments, colds, and flu symptoms (Duck, 1986). Love and intimacy affect the self, and people who experience love are affirmed in their self-esteem (Shaver & Hazan, 1993). Health risks related to loss of love have been researched by Verbrugge (1979) and discussed by Raschke (1987). Cobb and Jones (1984) discuss the connection between loving relationships and social awareness, as well as love, intimacy, and health. Lynch (1977) proved that emotional attachment and the stroking of patients with heart disease can reduce the incidence of irregular heart-beats. In Stroebe and Stroebe (1983) we read that separation from a partner through death or other causes can bring about health problems, particularly in men.

But what is this thing called love that can be used in the market-place, can charm the senses and can disturb the everyday chemical balance? Loving is not the same as liking. The people we love are a small portion of those whom we like (Mayers & Berscheid, 1997). Fehr and Russel (1991) collected associations for love and found over 90 different types of love that occur to people when prompted with that keyword. Kövecses (1991) analysed everyday expressions about love and found a system of metaphors that link love to the physical and psychic entity of the loved person, or describe it as a valuable resource which is hungered after. Love is an emotion that burns like fire, breaks like a storm, or acts like a force of nature outside man's control, a magic that charms and hypnotises. It can be the cause of increased pulse-rate, rising body temperature, physical weakness and blind devotion, sweaty hands, an inability to think rationally, the sex drive, and joyful experiences and behaviour in general. The social representation of the ideal of love understands it to be a "maximum of feeling". Love is spontaneous, directed in a particularist fashion towards one specific person, correlates with the highest feelings of joy and happiness, and is experienced jointly in intimate self-abandon to the other. Regan, Kocan, and Whitlock (1998) researched the characteristics of prototypical romantic relationships and identified the key features as fidelity and trust, honesty, blissfulness, commitment and friendship, respect, communication, and caring. Fletcher, Simpson, Thomas, and Giles (1999) report that ideal partners in romantic relationships are honest, loyal, and attractive; they feel committed to and care for one another, act respectfully towards each other, listen to and understand one another.

Witte (1986, p. 446) takes as his starting-point Simmel (1921) and Nedelmann (1983), and offers a definition of love that incorporates many of these characteristics: "Love is an emotion which generates a very close relationship with another person over a short period of time, but which at the same time is highly precarious." Love leads to an idealisation of the other, because all the happiness that is experienced is attributed to the other person. It leads, too, to a certain loss of one's own identity. As the personal identity of the lovers gradually comes to the fore once more, love can lead to a lasting commitment, which is no longer exclusively distinguished by intense emotions, but which exists as a balanced relationship between the partners.

In scientific models love appears in various guises, which range from romantic feelings of being in love to cold calculation (Bierhoff & Grau, 1999, offer an overview of theories and studies on love and romanticism). Sternberg and Grajek (1984) speak of love as a one-dimensional quality (see also Rubin, 1973), identifiable in intimate and close relationships of the most varied kinds. Accordingly there is a general factor of love that arises from the need for intimacy and finds expression in types of interpersonal communication, togetherness, and mutual support. This general factor is reflected equally in the way someone relates to the loved partner, parents, children, or close friends. Sternberg's triangular theory of love (1987) envisages love as composed of three components—intimacy, passion, and a decision to commit. Intimacy is understood as attachment to the other person, a bonding with them, and the desire that the other person should be happy. Passion is the descriptor for romantic emotions and physical attraction, and the desire for physical closeness and sexuality. The decision to commit is a decision to love the other and to commit oneself to them. Relationships with other people vary depending on whether all three elements are present, one element predominates, or a combination of two elements is developed. In total, eight qualities of love are identified by Sternberg:

(a)   Liking, if only the element of intimacy is developed.
(b)   Infatuated love, where only passion is developed.
(c)   Empty love, where only the decision to commit is developed.
(d)   Romantic love, which is a combination of intimacy and passion.
(e)   Companionate love, which combines intimacy and the decision to commit.
(f)   Fatuous love, which combines passion and the decision to commit.
(g)   Consummate love, where all three elements are present.
(h)   Non-love, a relationship concept where none of these elements appear.

Hatfield and Walster (1978) distinguish between "being in love" (defined as an intense desire to be together with the loved person) and romantic love (passionate love) on the one hand, and companionate love on the other. Companionate love encompasses all those feelings that are directed towards someone who has shared many common experiences and whose life is closely bound up with one's own. Reciprocated love is associated with feelings of satisfaction and ecstasy. Unreciprocated love leads to feelings of emptiness, fear, and despair. Similar distinctions between impassioned "being in love" and consolidated love are made by Burgess (1921; romantic and married love), Kelley (1983; love and commitment), and McClelland (1986; right-hemisphere and left-hemisphere love, or irrational–romantic and reflective–calculating love).

Mention should also be made of Lee's (1973) "rainbow" of love, a much-quoted concept which Hendrick and Hendrick (1986) successfully operationalized and verified empirically. Lee (1973) started from the knowledge of the ancient Greeks, particularly Plato, and drew on Freud, Lessing, and Paulus to specify six styles of love:

(a) Eros—romantic, sexually orientated, sensual love.
(b) Ludus—possessive desire, playful and challenging love.
(c) Storge—companionate love, love without feverish passion.
(d) Mania—a style of love combining aspects of Eros and Ludus, finding expression in desperate desire for the loved person, self-tormenting disquiet and jealousy.
(e) Pragma—a rational form of love combining aspects of Ludus and Storge and seeking or avoiding attachment on the basis of pragmatic calculation.
(f) Agape—a combination of Eros and Storge, finding expression as altruistic, selfless love which seeks to do anything to make the other person happy.

Bierhoff (1991) arrives at a similar division of styles of love as Lee (1973), following a comparison of characteristics of love in various theoretical models.

Shaver and Hazan (1988) identify three categories of styles of love, which depend upon the type of attachment to the other person. Style (a), "secure attachment types", accounts for over half the population, who find it easy to form and maintain close contacts with another person and are not worried about being left. Style (b), "avoidant types", accounts for around a quarter of all people, who feel uncomfortable if someone becomes too emotionally close to them. These people develop little confidence in other people and often complain that their lovers ask more of them than they are ready to give. Style (c), which covers the remaining fifth of all people, are "anxious/ambivalent" lovers. They seek attachment to the other person, often feel themselves to be not properly loved, want even closer attachment and notice with disappointment that their partner may then withdraw in fright. Shaver and Hazan (1988) attempted to integrate Lee's "wheel of love" (1973) and other concepts into their attachment theory and argue that not only does this fit well with the theory, but that their theory also explains the origins of the qualities of love. Levy and Davis (1988) also attempted to bring together the models put forward by Lee (1973), Sternberg (1996), and Shaver and Hazan (1988), and found that there was significant overlap between all the concepts, although each also contained some original and unique aspects.

Many attempts have been made to operationalise the various theoretical constructs about love and make it measurable by questionnaire. Hendrick and Hendrick (1989), Shaver and Hazan (1988), and Sternberg and Barnes (1988) offer an overview. Rubin (1973) established a scale for measuring liking and loving; Hendrick and Hendrick (1990) devised the Love Attitudes Scale and a questionnaire to measure Lee's (1973) love styles. Sternberg (1996) published an instrument to measure love as conceptualised in his theory of love, the Triangular Love Scale.

Apart from the usefulness of these scales in measuring various facets of love, we should mention that some surprising results have been obtained which indicate gender-specific differences (Bierhoff, 1991; Duck, 1986; Hinde, 1997). Women appear to be more pragmatic and less romantic than men. They rarely fall "head over heels in love", and treat close relationships not as a game, but with more seriousness than men. Women are reported as being less ready to enter into a loving relationship, and more willing to get out of a relationship than men.

Gender-specific orientation towards love may be explainable from the historical development of gender roles. A woman had to choose a partner who would be able to provide for her, as she was traditionally expected to perform the housework and to bring up the children—as is often still the case today. Men did not need to be driven by material considerations because of their role in society. The social recognition and the financial remuneration for their work meant men could afford to look for romance and, like "princes", choose their partners even from amongst the poor Cinderellas of the world. This also explains why men often think more about what they can give to their partner when considering a loving relationship; a woman spontaneously thinks about the possibilities open to her and her partner (Kirchler, 1989).

Women were and still are aware of material and non-material resources in close relationships because they were dependent on having a responsible and caring partner, at least for those times during pregnancy and in the early years following the birth of children. From an evolutionary perspective, a woman had to consider a prospective partner's status and the associated guarantee of chances of material protection when making her choice. Men, at least in the past, would choose a partner to guarantee healthy offspring; they focus, or focused, on health, which in lay consciousness is associated with appearance, attractiveness, and youth (Regan, 1998; Trivers, 1972).

Despite conditions for women and men differing in social and historical developmental terms, with different implications for love and partner choice, Regan (1998) emphasises that both men and women are looking for intelligent, honest, emotionally stable partners who are attractive and have a "good" personality. This search for a partner is not always successful, and sometimes significant compromises on this ideal have to be made. Pennebaker et al. (1979) conducted an original study on this point: Evening guests at a university campus bar were asked at various times about the attractiveness of people present, of the same and the opposite sex. As closing time approached, the perceived attractiveness of people of the opposite sex increased significantly, whilst those of the same sex were rated at the same level as before. Regan (1998) clarified gender-specific readiness to compromise over partner choice in short affairs and in long-term attachments. Whereas women are generally less ready than men to accept compromises on their ideal, it was shown that, for a love affair, both partners must at least be attractive; for long-term relationships, the partner's sense of interpersonal responsibility becomes an indispensable element.

Love and Close Relationships

If love is such a pleasant amalgamation of perceptions, emotions, motives, and behavioural tendencies, how does it come about? Freud (1920) considered the energy force that he called libido, and the sublimation of the sexual drive, to be the causes of love. Maslow (1954) sees love as arising from the need for security and belonging on the one hand, and the need for growth on the other. Fromm (1977) views love as the result of the capacity for sympathy with the other, respect, caring, and a sense of responsibility for the partner.

Probably the best-known theory concerning the development of love is the two-component model of Walster and Berscheid (1974). This model also offers the easiest means for producing love: It indicates that love can be brought about if a subject is brought to a state of excitement, which can be demonstrated at the electrophysiological and biochemical level, and if certain situational stimuli are offered at the same time, thereby suggesting that the excitement is linked to attraction and feelings of love. Ovid observed that the passion of a woman for her husband can be heightened during a particularly exciting gladiatorial contest (quoted in Rubin, 1973). Walster and Berscheid (1974), building on the theory of emotions propounded by Schachter and Singer (1962), argue that love is that emotion which a person feels if he or she is in a state of non-specific physiological excitement and the situation is so structured that this person is encouraged to think that this level of excitement is created through stimuli linked to interpersonal attraction, physical desire etc. Should a man find himself on a vertigo-inducing high bridge and meet an attractive woman who speaks to him, then he experiences an emotion that is love, or is associated with love. Empirical studies on this point have been conducted by Byrne and Murnen (1988), Cantor, Zillmann, and Bryant (1975), Dutton and Aron (1974), Istvan, Griffitt, and Weidner (1983) and others.

Walster and Berscheid (1974) relate their two-component theory to passionate love and passion or romantic feelings, but not to those emotions that bind together long-term partners who live in shared homes. To progress from passion about romantic love and intimacy at the start of a relationship to a sustainable, fulfilling partnership, bridges must be built. When lovers take off their "rose colored glasses" (Hendrick & Hendrick, 1988), they find themselves again and defend their personal identity. At this point, determinants other than physiological excitement and cognitive elements are more important for love. When the honeymoon is over, the serious business begins, for it seems to be marriage that brings the lovers back to reality and brings love to its senses. In the words of the cynic, marriage is the medicine to cure love. In the first year following the wedding, the relationship between the partners changes and has to be reshaped in order to be sustainable. Couples who are in love have positive illusions about their partners; and partners in harmonious relationships like to exaggerate when they are talking about their partner's qualities (Murray & Holmes, 1977). Huston, McHale, and Crouter (1986) found that a shift is usually required to move from being in love to having an enduring long-term loving relationship, and that the relationship work done in the first year of marriage is particularly important regardless of whether the partners lived together before the marriage, already had children together or whether the period of being in love led directly to marriage.

Foa and Foa (1974) describe love as a resource exchanged by partners in the same way as goods, services, information, status, or money. Kelley (1983; also Adams, 1965; Homans, 1961/1974; Thibaut & Kelley, 1959) considers loving relationships to be stable if the expenditure laid out to maintain the relationship is balanced by the pleasures offered in return. The greater the rewards in comparison to the costs and the less attractive alternative partners are, the greater the stability in the relationship. For Kelley (1983) a decision process that is often rational underlies long-term commitments. Sternberg (1986) also suspects a cognitive basis for long-term commitments when considering the decision to commit. In their interdependence theory, Kelley and Thibaut (1978) place emphasis on the mutual dependence of partners on each other, alongside the exchange of resources and the evaluation of possible alternative partners and the pleasures that are passed up in rejecting them. Emotional as well as behavioural dependence is essential to a declaration of love and stability in the relationship.

Adams (1965) presented resources and their exchange between partners as the basis for a loving relationship, as did Homans (1961/1974), and Thibaut and Kelley (1959). Adams (1965), however, emphasises that the partners must perceive the exchange of resources to be fair, in order to develop a stable relationship and to sustain it over time. Assessments of fairness derive from processes of comparison between the expenditure that one person lays out and the pleasures they experience, together with a comparison against the comparable expenditure and pleasure enjoyed by their partner. If there is a balance of cost and benefits, a harmonious and stable relationship probably exists (Sprecher, 1986; Walster, Walster, & Traupmann, 1978).

Rusbult (1980) and Rusbult and Buunk (1993) extended the interdependence theory into an investment model which seeks to clarify satisfaction with the relationship, commitment to the partner, and the stability of the relationship. Under this model, partners in loving relationships assess their partnership in relation to their past relationships, their relationships with relevant others and with regard to the pleasures that result for themselves and the other partner. Satisfaction is achieved if the individual processes of comparison lead to a positive result. The commitment of one person to their partner depends on the level of satisfaction, on possible alternative partners and the denial of pleasure from them, and on the investments (e.g. of time, emotions, shared friends, shared "secrets") that are bound up in a relationship.

Whereas exchange and equity theory seek to interpret loving relationships on the basis of resource exchange, learning theory views close relationships and satisfaction with them as the result of conditioning processes. Under classical and operant conditioning theory, a long-term relationship is possible and love between the partners is guaranteed if the presence of the partner is felt to be enriching, if pleasant associations are bound up with the presence of the partner or if the partners themselves serve as the reward (much as is assumed by exchange theorists). Byrne (1971) devised a theory to explain interpersonal attractiveness as a learning process. If love is understood as the result of a classical conditioning process, then it also offers an explanation for the "sobering-up period" that often follows a wedding and is particularly commented upon by women: In a study on well-being Brandstätter (1983) found that housewives felt worse when doing housework if their husband was at home resting than when he was absent. On the other hand, the man feels good if he returns home to find his wife there. This interaction makes sense, in that the woman's work often starts as he returns home and begins his leisure time, but it also forms the basis of a conditioning process that has negative effects on the relationship, at least from the woman's point of view.

Bowlby (1969, 1973), Ainsworth, Blehar, Waters, & Wall (1978), Shaver and Hazan (1988) and others locate the roots of various types of love in early childhood development, in contrast to the exchange and conditioning models. Early childhood experiences regarding availability, approachability, and affection for relevant significant others are internalised and represented in internal attachment models. The "internal working models" contain illusions and convictions about interaction with other people and the self, and determine behaviour when meeting other people. Ainsworth et al. (1978) differentiate between three different attachment types or styles, which can be traced back to early childhood experiences: secure, ambivalent, and avoidant types. People who have a secure attachment style are said to have parents who were supportive and empathetic, open, tolerant, and warm-hearted. People with ambivalent attachment styles describe their parents as often being unfair, unpredictable, suddenly emotionally forthcoming and then equally suddenly reticent. Avoidant types grew up in families that were critical, placed high demands on them, gave little warmth, and showed no respect for individual weaknesses and desires. Research by Mikula and Leitner (1998) demonstrates how an individual's attachment style can make relationships in later life, particularly close relationships, resilient or easily broken. These factors also affect the degree of trust or anxiety experienced by partners, the dynamics of conflict between the partners, and whether the level of attachment between partners is appropriate. A secure attachment style is a better guarantee of well-functioning relationships than an ambivalent or avoidant style. Secure types are more able to develop confidence than others, and also recall events that generate confidence more easily (Mikulincer, 1998). Ambivalent and avoidant types come before the divorce courts more often than secure types (Shaver & Hazan, 1988; see also Reis & Patrick, 1996).

MONEY

Definition of Money

Money and its attributes are known to all: "Money makes the world go round", but love of money is also "the root of all evil". Money is a resource that is exchanged between partners in close relationships alongside goods, services, information, status, and love. Money can buy many things, even emotions and sometimes love, it is said. But what is money, so doggedly sought-after but ultimately no more than a promise printed on metal or paper, which is worthless in itself, or even just a "virtual" commodity?

How is "money" to be defined? Snelders, Hussein, Lea, and Webley (1992) stress that "money" is a polymorphic concept, that is to say a concept that has no clear definition but is understood from experience and described using applied terms and examples. In an English study, 1- and 20-pound notes and 10-pence pieces were given as typical examples of money; 90% of those surveyed described a cheque as a typical example, 72% named a savings book and as many as 68% agreed that diamonds were typical of money. Banknotes and coins appear to be prototypes of money, while credit cards, cheques, foreign currency etc. lie at varying distances from the centre of the definitional field. Rumiati and Lotto (1996) came to similar conclusions in a study conducted on Italian students and bank employees: Coins and banknotes were seen as prototypes of money; "bank-related" forms such as cheques, postal orders, and pre-paid telephone tokens (jetons) were also seen as money. Less prototypical forms were credit cards, telephone cards, food tokens, vouchers indicating that road tolls had been pre-paid, etc.

In Old High German, the term for money ("Geld") means "recompense" ("Vergütung"). Money is a means of recompense for a resource received. Since around the fourteenth century money has been used as a universal means of exchange.

Money plays a central role, particularly in economics. The functions of money are of the utmost importance in a society based on the principle of the division of labour; money serves as the organising principle for exchange processes, and is a symbol for corresponding exchange values in the economy. Money is universally recognised as a means of payment and it serves as an accounting unit, since monetary units are a common measure for the value of different goods. Monetary units are an objective orientation measure (Brandstätter & Brandstätter, 1996). Money also serves as a means of storing value. Whereas many goods cannot be stockpiled, or only stockpiled with difficulty, money can be hoarded with ease and translated into goods again at any time (Burghardt, 1977). Private households and businesses, and states too, all act for different reasons to fuel the demand for money. Henrichsmeyer, Gans, and Evers (1982) adduce motivations that are principally transactional, precautionary, and speculative. Money is a universal means of exchange and makes transactions easier because the person offering a particular product no longer needs to find a partner who wants to trade and who is offering a product of comparable value in exchange. Money is a useful tool for saving, and makes it possible to offer and take up credit. Money can be hoarded and saved up in order to buy a particular item some time in the future. Money is also a good that can be used for speculation.

From the psychological point of view, money performs several central functions. In a materialistic world, money is part of the identity of the person who owns it, and it represents security, power, and consumer freedom. Money offers opportunities to trade. Where the identity of a person is measured by what they do and what they have, the self too is defined by the money at a person's disposal. Belk (1988) and Dittmar (1992) see money and material possessions as an extension of the self or as a means to acquire or do things that are an expression of self. Furnham (1984) developed a questionnaire about the meaning of money and identified several factors: money is experienced as an expression of power; money is used to win the liking of others; money offers security; money is a reward for and an expression of achievement; money can drive some people (as evidenced from psychoanalysis) to exercise obsessive control over it, to hoard it avariciously or to lust after it. Money can also be the cause of feelings of jealousy.

The significance of money varies from person to person. Women believe that they handle money with less care than men do. They see money in less functional terms than men do; for them, it is less associated with the self, but seen more as a symbol for comparing themselves to other people. Men view money mainly as an expression of power and status; women use money more to satisfy pragmatic needs and hedonistic desires, and it leads to feelings of envy if the person to whom they are comparing themselves has more financial resources than themselves (Prince, 1993). How money is handled also varies from person to person. Furnham (1996) and Forman (1987) differentiate between people who have an exaggerated drive to hoard (misers), people who spend money unchecked and without regard (spend-thrifts), people who make money to gain status and power ("tycoons"), people who use money to buy an item when they can negotiate the price down below the original asking price (bargain hunters), and hopeful gamers who are drawn to high-risk gambles but often lose (gamblers). People are influenced towards a particular form of spending behaviour by their religious beliefs, work ethic, political views or personal characteristics (Furnham, 1994, 1996).

The significance of money, at the theoretical level, is revealed in psycho-analysis and is explained by learning theories. Developmental psychology is exploring the knowledge and significance of money among children. Money is also defined in the social exchange theories of Foa and Foa (1974) as a universal exchange good, and studied in relation to other exchange resources: love, information, status, goods, and services.

In the language of psychoanalysis, the significance of money is explained as the symbolic displacement of the significance of excreta. In a short treatise in the early 1900s, Sigmund Freud sought a connection between experiences during the anal phase and how people later handled money. The development of sexual functions went through several stages, according to Freud's discoveries: until about 18 months, the mouth, tongue and lips are the main pleasure organs of the child. Desires and their satisfaction are primarily determined orally. Gradually the mouth loses its importance as a source of desire. The end of the alimentary canal, the anus, becomes the most important place for sexual enquiry. Until the third year of life, retention and expulsion of excreta produce sexual excitement, and playing with the excrement itself becomes interesting. Toilet training begins, and success is usually praised by the parents. Because excreta can be seen as the child's first product, its first present, at this age the development of a personal style for the future handling of material things, above all money, is begun. The drive for order, compulsiveness, and the desire for economy all have their roots in these developmental stages. The path from excreta to money proceeds via the child's play with marbles and other toys. The later developmental stages are less important for the development of the signi-ficance accorded by the individual to money (Bornemann, 1976; Freud, 1908), moving as they do through the phallic phase characterised by a fascination with genitalia (which extends up to the sixth year of life) and on to the genital stage in puberty. The attraction of money reminds us of the attraction of faeces, and from the psychoanalytical point of view it origi-nates in the period of play where faeces are saved up, or expelled ("spent"), or given as a present. Depending on whether the retention or expulsion of excreta is experienced as being pleasurable and rewarding or not, the individual develops their style of handling material goods, which can be described as avaricious, spendthrift, envious, or generous.

A further theoretical explanation of the significance of money is derived from learning theory, which views money as a secondary reinforcer in operant conditioning. In terms of the theory of operant conditioning, a reinforcer is understood to be a stimulus which leads to repetition of a specific behaviour that precedes it, with a greater degree of probability. Reinforcers are therefore pleasant stimuli which influence the probability of a particular type of behaviour if they occur immediately after that behaviour. Some stimuli relate directly to the satisfaction of needs, thereby having a reinforcing quality and are described as primary reinforcers. Primary reinforcers are experienced spontaneously as being pleasant. Other stimuli are experienced as neutral, but can acquire reinforcing qualities through the learning process and are then described as secondary reinforcers.

Money is a typical example of a secondary reinforcer. Neutral stimuli like money acquire reinforcing qualities through the following process: if, over a short period of time, a primary reinforcer repeatedly follows closely on a neutral stimulus, then this stimulus becomes a secondary reinforcer which can then be applied in operant learning processes without the primary reinforcer (Herkner, 1993). Wolfe (1936; cited in Herkner 1993, p. 55) conducted an experiment to simulate the way in which money acquires the properties of a secondary reinforcer. He allowed chimpanzees to put coins into a machine that released grapes. The grapes acted as a primary reinforcer and encouraged the chimpanzees to keep feeding coins into the machine. Eventually the chimpanzees learned that the coins were in themselves "valuable", because they could be used to "buy" grapes. Once their value had been established, the next step was to use the coins to encourage certain patterns of behaviour. The coins became what money is to adult humans.

Money is an important universal secondary reinforcer because it can be used to satisfy various needs. It can be used to satisfy primary needs such as the need for food, protection from the cold, or safety; it can also satisfy higher needs, such as the need for power, recognition or success, or offer the possibility of controlling the environment. The greater the emphasis placed on the acquisition and the hoarding of money in the past, the higher the value that the individual places on money.

What is the value of money? Economists define the value of money using the monetary value printed on the coins and bank-notes. The psychologist believes the value of money is subjectively defined and varies from individual to individual. Money is worth what can be bought with it. The purchasing power of money relates to the amount of goods that can be obtained for a unit of currency. The more money circulating in a national economy, the greater the demand for goods, and the higher the price that can be asked as a result. If goods are sold at higher prices than in the past, then the purchasing power of money decreases. The value of money and the rate of monetary circulation are directly allied to the amount of goods available: more money and a faster rate of circulation equate to higher prices for goods and more and more transactions exchanging goods for money. If the purchasing power of money falls, then the exchange value also changes over time. Changes in the value of money (inflation and deflation) not only lead directly to economic changes, but also unsettle individuals and shake their confidence in the economy.

The subjective value of money has been researched in several different ways. As a person's absolute wealth increases, the subjective value of an additional unit of money diminishes, in accordance with the economic law of diminishing marginal utility and the psychophysical laws of Weber and Fechner (see, for example, Sixtl, 1967). Whereas people with little money experience even a small increase in income as an improvement in their financial position, rich people may only notice a change from their original financial position if a larger additional sum, in absolute terms, is added.

The subjective value of money has been measured particularly using estimations of the value of coins. A classical experiment of this kind was conducted by Bruner and Goodman (1947). Conforming to the hypothesis, children from rich families underestimated the size of the coins shown, whereas children from poor families tended to overestimate their size and thus their value.

The more money an individual has, the lower the subjective value of an additional unit of money. Over time, satiation effects may become evident. Theoretically, it is possible to imagine that people would attribute increasingly less importance to money as their deficit needs have been satisfied and they seek to satisfy higher needs, such as the drive to self-development. Brandstätter and Brandstätter (1996; see also Brandstätter, 1998) found that the value of a unit of money reduces as income increases. Individual attitudes also proved to be significant determinants of the subjective value of money: Where someone believes that money influences the character of a person for the worse, or where someone prefers spending money to saving it, they will value money less highly than other people.

In everyday life, however, it is often noticed that rich people do not lose interest in money, despite the economic law of satiation and its psychological equivalent. Indeed, one often notices expansion effects: money seems to lose its function as a means to an end, transcending that instrumentality to become an independent, intrinsically powerful motivation (Wiswede, 1995).

Is the value of hard-earned money perhaps greater than the value of money obtained without effort, such as inherited or gifted money? It may be that people who bring income into a private household weigh up purchases more and are more inclined to save than those who help to allocate the money. If this is the case, then men in particular should be especially involved in deliberations over purchases, since in western industrialised countries it is still the case that men are wage-earners more often than women. However, if non-earners with financial resources at their disposal spend money only after having regard for the laborious work that has earned it, and sometimes with feelings of guilt, then we would expect in particular to see non-working women who share homes with working men to be frugal with their housekeeping money. As yet there is no empirical study of these hypotheses.

Money in Close Relationships

What is the significance of money in close relationships? Coria (1994) writes that money is of such central importance in the private household that a study of it ultimately reaches into all aspects of close relationships. She also states that the way money is handled reflects the complex power relations between the partners and their children. Discussion of money issues touches on a taboo area: Men are easily offended if the conversation turns to money, and women often feel guilty if they are asked to justify their everyday expenditure. Wilson (1987) also stresses the difficulties encountered in studying financial matters in private households. Few households have sufficient financial resources to satisfy all the desires of the family members. For that reason partners often see themselves as being in competition with each other when financial matters are discussed. Money is a source of conflicts of interest which people do not like discussing.

Some social scientists claim (Coria, 1994; Wilson, 1987) that the person who has money at their disposal in close relationships possesses a powerful weapon, allowing the user to exercise control over everyday events and power over others through that control. By contrast, the person who is dependent on money earned by another has to fit in with that person. It is often the woman who is dependent on the income of the man. In low-income households, money matters are often an issue that women have to confront because whilst they are responsible for setting standards in the home, they have little or no control over financial resources (Wilson, 1987).

Many scientific studies of money and close relationships have been conducted from a sociological perspective. These have looked at the incomes of men and women, their experience of fairness and satisfaction with the relationship (e.g. Jasso, 1988), and gender-specific power relations and the significance of money to women and men. Pahl (1989, 1995) and Vogler and Pahl (1994) have presented studies from England offering a detailed look at money and partnerships. They interviewed many women and men about how they organised their finances. One finding related to the significance of the money that women and men bring into the home. The man's income is usually defined as household income and spent on family members. He is the traditional breadwinner, enjoying the power of that role, in Pahl's opinion (1995), whereas women who bring additional income into the home provide what seems to be "extra money" for additional desires. Almost all the men who were interviewed (93%) believed that their income was at the disposal of the partnership or family; 76% of the women interviewed agreed with this; 7% of the men and 24% of the women said that the man's income was his money. By contrast, income earned by women at work was seen as the woman's own money by 53% of men, and 35% of women.

Pahl (1995) also researched how money was handled within the relationship. She identified different types of arrangement, as follows: joint accounts managed equally by both partners, found in 18% of all partnerships interviewed; joint accounts managed by the man (15%) or the woman (15%); accounts managed solely by the woman (27%), or solely by the man (10%); and in a further 13% of cases there was mention of separate accounts for various areas of expenditure segregated along gender-specific lines. In 2% of cases, partners operated completely separate accounts, and even when an expense was a shared one they rarely had access to their partner's financial resources. The probability of separate accounts is high in instances of remarriage, significantly higher than for couples in their first marriage (Burgoyne & Morrison, 1997). It was noticeable that the accounts operated by women were often empty, or with low credit balances. In relationships where income was low, the woman managed all the money, whereas in high-earning households the man managed the finances (Table 2.1; Vogler & Pahl, 1994).

Money bestows power. Vogler and Pahl (1994) investigated relative power in decision-making situations, also exploring whether the man or the woman had the final say in important matters, and who usually took important decisions. Their research clearly showed that the relative power of a partner correlates with their power over money (Table 2.1). Overall the man's power is greater than that of the woman, but especially if he alone disposes of the household income. A further finding was that women can more easily do without certain luxuries than men in difficult times. They asked who goes without what when money is tight, and drew up an index of relative deprivation based on the difference between the total number of luxuries given up by the woman as against the total number given up by the man. A positive deprivation value indicated a greater readiness to go without on the part of the woman, with a negative value indicating that the man was more prepared to make sacrifices. Table 2.1 shows that, overall, women were more prepared not to spend money on themselves than men, particularly when the woman alone managed the family finances. Women therefore viewed neither their own income, nor the household income, as "extra money" for their egoistic desires. Vogler and Pahl (1994) also found

TABLE 2.1
Management of accounts, household income, and the relative power of partners

Type of account management	Income in Euro (monthly)	Relative power of partners			Financial deprivation	Personal money		
		man > woman	man = woman	man < woman		man > woman	man = woman	man < woman
Woman manages the household income	967	7	61	33	.52	34	50	15
Woman mainly manages joint income	1020	21	69	9	.55	24	61	15
Woman and man manage joint income	1114	26	69	5	.07	18	67	15
Man mainly manages joint income	1128	41	56	2	.11	20	70	11
Man manages the household income	1170	53	45	2	.15	26	55	20
Separate accounts for specific areas	1052	61	37	2	.44	42	47	13

Source: adapted from Vogler and Pahl (1994).

Note: The figures for relative power and personal money are percentages. The index of relative deprivation expresses the difference between luxuries the woman is prepared to go without in times of economic hardship and those the man is prepared to go without.

that money for personal expenses varied depending on who managed the money: Men had more personal money at their disposal than women, even in cases where the woman managed the household accounts.

Pahl (1995), summarising the results of various studies, writes that money matters in private households are often viewed through an ideological filter. Men are usually seen as breadwinners, making their income available for joint expenses, whereas the woman's income is her own, for her extra expenses. In fact women make their income available as household income, often doing so more than men. Brannen and Moss (1987) also reached this conclusion, following their research into how money was organised in households with children and both partners working. The women's income was more often spent on the children and the daily running of the household, whilst the men's income was allocated to the house, telephone bills, and the car.

There are many myths circulating about money management in close relationships, which serve to sustain current social stereotypes in countries where women are working increasingly frequently and not prepared to go without a career. However, despite all indications that money matters are still a taboo subject and that some scientists continue to cling to fixed and outdated ideas, gradual progress made by social scientists in establishing the facts of the matter indicates that the true picture is unlike the traditional, if enduring, stereotype.

EVERYDAY MATTERS

Definition of Everyday Matters

What do we understand by "everyday"? Although "everyday" is a common expression, many people struggle to define it when asked, and perhaps doubt the sense of the question. Laermann (1975, p. 88; quoted in Pulver 1991, p. 16) concluded after going through several dictionaries that "everyday" did not exist. Yet it is there all the time. On the one hand it is blatantly obvious what is meant by "everyday", until someone is asked what they understand by it. On the other hand everything that is not extraordinary is everyday. The concept appears limitless, defying every attempt of definition and therefore ultimately unusable. The everyday is universally grey, not just monotonous, and it may be of no practical use to science.

For a long time, psychology forgot about the everyday, which is unremarkably ever-present; this despite the fact that Sir Arthur Conan Doyle (quoted in Pulver, 1991, p. v), writing over a hundred years ago, had Sherlock Holmes say to his friend Dr Watson, "Believe me: nothing can be as extraordinary as what is called ordinary!" The everyday is the basis that defines all special elements of human experience and behaviour.

Even if routine matters appear monotonous, they still put every theory to a stern test.

The everyday is the opposite of Sundays, holidays or festivals and the exception to the rule; it is the unremarkable and the usual which is set against the sensational (Elias, 1978; Pulver, 1991, p. 19). Wagner (1994, p. 51ff.) offers a definition for the social psychologist: everyday knowledge is to be understood as "the sphere of natural, spontaneous, more or less unreflective experience and thought which relates to the area of experience of daily life and forms the cognitive and affective basis of everyday routines". Wagner (1994) relates his definition to everyday knowledge, subsuming lay knowledge of sensational events under this heading, and differentiating this knowledge particularly from scientific thought and the usual formulation of theory. However, his definition can also be applied to the description of everyday events. These mainly rely on automated sequences of actions, resulting in events that require little thought and mainly disappear unnoticed into the flow of time. They appear monotonous because they lack sensation or challenge and, in retrospect, give the impression of "empty" time. This may give the impression that the everyday is exclusively "grey" in colour. Clearly non-automated actions and unexpected events are also part of everyday events, although little attention is paid to routine events and attention is instead focused on unexpected events and special incidents. In retrospect, days without distinctive events appear "empty", and those events that are rare and special serve as a contrast to the "everyday". Here we use the word "every-day" to refer to the stream of usual activities, from which unexpected events repeatedly rise to the surface and attract attention as they "go with the flow".

What is the importance of everyday matters to partners who are looking after their children, doing the shopping, enjoying their leisure time, and planning their next holiday together? Is it a chronology of monotony: up in the morning, bathroom mayhem, preparing breakfast, shared conversation over breakfast with the news on the radio, a goodbye kiss as usual before driving off to the office, the hours at work, lunch in the canteen, the permanent tiredness brought on by the weather in the afternoon, the telephone call to check that one partner is doing the shopping while the other picks up the kids, then back home, preparing dinner and so on before filling several hours of leisure with television, and then off to bed?

In an extensive work, Pulver (1991) offers a minutely observed study of the building-blocks of the everyday. Over a period of several years he recorded his actions at work and for some of the time at home too, finally establishing that no day was like another and that no day could be identified as being an average day. His attention to the many events and the details of them made every day special. In the working life of the author around 1500 topics came up—a topic being a matter with which someone engages one or more times over a given period of time, or intends to engage with, and which is considered to have a cohesive content distinct from other topics. A large number of these topics were interrupted by other topics. "This degree of 'chopping and changing' sometimes came close to (or even exceeded) the threshold of P's tolerance . . . The . . . desired concentration on important and urgent topics (and the continuity of work or thinking on those topics) was rarely achievable; firstly because the day became swamped in a tide of smaller matters, and secondly because the working conditions led to an animated jumble of topics and occasionally to a wild 'flight' from topic to topic" (Pulver, 1991, p. 728). Regardless of the work the author wanted to pursue during the period of the recording, and of the fact that the records relate to his working life rather than his private life, it seems possible to establish that in general terms the everyday is marked by a wealth of routine tasks that pass unnoticed by the active person, becoming repeatedly stopped or sidelined by new topics, only to reappear and perhaps be dealt with later. The individual topics neither attract great attention in themselves, nor present themselves as isolated units which can be seen through from beginning to end. If this is true of the world of work, it must be much more true of the private sphere where there are no performance standards, time pressures or competition in planning one's own actions and executing those plans in an economically sensible fashion.

Everyday Matters in Close Relationships

When partners discuss matters such as how to spend their leisure time, the purchase of a car or the daily shopping and then reach a decision, these are processes embedded in a complex background that are difficult to comprehend in their entirety. The everyday life of a couple in a shared home is not simply the sum of the actions and reactions of two people in varying socio-physical contexts. A couple with children form a unit and, as such, a social system, whose dynamics are defined by the structure of the relationship, the characteristics of the individuals and a social and physical context that is determining to a greater or lesser extent.

According to Dörner (1989), complex social systems are generally characterised by a series of features which should be taken into consideration when analysis is focused on parts of a whole system:

(a)   The various system components have a reciprocal effect on one another. Variables are linked in a kind of matrix, so that a change in one variable causes changes that are visible to a greater or lesser extent in other variables. The net-like matrix of variables results in great complexity.

(b)   The net-like matrix of variables means that, in looking at these complex systems, the overall pattern must be understood. Individual parts cannot be separated out from the whole.

(c)   Because the systems are complex, researchers should gather information on a range of levels. However, it is usually not possible to gather all the information required, and often interactions at a higher level cannot be recorded. Moreover, it is sometimes difficult to separate individual variables from the overall context and to analyse, operationalise and measure them in isolation. Where there is insufficient data collected, aspects of a system remain opaque, and ultimately some processes remain impenetrable and unpredictable.

(d)   Systems such as those of couples with children in close relationships are subject to constant change. Because social systems undergo continuous development, a freeze-frame snapshot of events is not adequate for analysis, as it is, by definition, already locked in the past at the point where an interpretation of the picture is begun. Snapshots are only of value if transformation rules can also be discovered to explain changes over time.

(e)   Using the system features that have been identified, short-term predictions about system developments can sometimes be given successfully. Medium- or long-term predictions are rarely undertaken with any great success, because they mostly do not follow linear models and can be influenced by variables and connections that do not appear to be relevant.

(f)   Changes in social systems are also difficult to predict because goals are unclear. Members of complex systems often do not set their sights on differentiated goals, but instead try to avoid serious problems by "muddling through". They focus on those aspects in the process that "stick out" from the stream of events. Interventions result in changes to the whole system, to new developments (and new problems) which demand action. This action again results in new, unforeseen circumstances. Goals may not have been set at all, or may change in the course of actions, developing and then disappearing once more.

(g)   Apart from the lack of clarity over the setting of goals, it is also possible for a variety of goals or minimum demands to exist simultaneously, some of which may contradict each other. In close relationships diffuse goals are pursued one after another; partners may attempt to satisfy many needs at the same time, all at once, and a variety of dangerous developments are fought off should they appear on the horizon.

In normative models, it is assumed that everyday processes even within the private household can be marked out as having a precisely definable start and a clearly recognisable end. Decisions in the economic sphere in particular are presumed to follow this normative pattern, according to which the decision-makers move through several specific phases (stages of desiring, information-gathering, and evaluation) before arriving ultimately at the end of a decision-making process, where an alternative—the optimal choice—is selected from the range of available options. However, if partnerships are understood as complex systems, then it cannot be assumed that the decision-making dynamic will follow a normative pattern.

Weick (1971) has little doubt that decision-making and other processes in everyday situations deviate markedly from the pattern of normative models: people in private households solve their problems at times when everyone is either still tired or tired again, in the morning or in the evening after a day at work. Economic decisions are embedded in the everyday of a relationship, which is scattered about with a variety of different types of problem. These often do not land in one's lap one after another but instead require solving simultaneously. Is it any wonder that a large number of problems remain unresolved under such circumstances, where household members "jump" from one problem to the next without having resolved the previous issue?

The view of economic and non-economic decision-making in private households put forward by Weick (1971) calls for a holistic perspective. Decisions are not activities that can be isolated, removed from everyday events and analysed separately. To arrive at an adequate understanding of the dynamics involved, decisions have to be studied in the stream of activities that are unfolding at the same time. In addition, it is necessary to take into account the time-frame surrounding that stream of activities and events that follow one after another. Present patterns of interaction are partly a result of earlier experiences, and the structure and logic of past and current experiences are the basis of expectations, intentions, and plans for the future.

Research into everyday processes between partners in the private household is not only made difficult on account of the large number of variables that influence each other and determine the events of the present. It is also made particularly problematic because those people who are being asked to provide information about their behaviour and its consequences do not usually pay close attention to their actions and reactions. More or less often they allow themselves to be "driven" to a particular outcome (i.e. a decision) rather than actively influencing the course taken. For that reason, particular importance attaches not only to the manner in which the complexities of studying everyday life in partnerships are acknowledged, but also to the methods used to collect information and to select the subjects of the study.

In a work devoted to theory (Kirchler, 1989), a model for the study of purchasing decisions in private households was put forward which provides a framework for the analysis of decision-making processes. Under this model, it is necessary to describe structural characteristics of the partnership and the interaction processes between the partners and to be precise about the various types of decision being made. Equally importantly, the course of decision-making in general within the partnership should be sketched out. Before presenting the range of relationship structures and theories of interaction, we firstly offer a brief sketch to define the social unit that forms the main focus of attention in the present work.

CHAPTER THREE

Close Relationships

UNIQUENESS OF CLOSE RELATIONSHIPS

When love between two people leads to their sharing a life together, then they enter into a close relationship. "Close relationship" means a "partnership", which the dictionary defines as a "social principle for collaboration (based on trust) between individuals (e.g. between a woman and a man, between sexual partners) or organizations with different goals, who can only realize these goals jointly through a reciprocal readiness to compromise. In organizations, this usually involves the introduction of appropriate institutional measures to regulate conflicts and compromise" (*Meyers Großes Taschenlexikon*, 1987, Vol. 16, p. 286). It seems to be essential that the people involved in the partnership seek to realise joint or individual goals through collaboration, which is to a greater or lesser extent based on trust or regulated by a series of rules.

If the situation of couples living together as man and wife is recognised by the law, then the partnership is accorded the status of being a family unit by the state. Whilst it is true that the classical concept of the family, which is also reflected in everyday use, includes children alongside adults (traditionally one boy and one girl), it is well known that families can be constituted differently, maybe with one parent and one child, or with parents, grandparents and children living together. In some countries same-sex couples can also have the legal status of being a partnership and a family.

In the present work, we study decisions between partners of different sexes, some with and some without children, in shared homes. Married and unmarried couples with children are studied because they represent the most frequent "group" in private households. Duck, West, and Acitelli (1996, p. 7) observe that "research is implicitly or explicitly restricted to openly conducted, able-bodied, heterosexual relationships", since these relationships are most easily approached by researchers. Children are included as people additionally present in the joint household, although they are rarely participants in the relevant studies. Now that it is common for women and men to live as partners in a shared home without being married, whether or not they have children of their own or of one partner living with them, we can no longer say that studies such as the present one are exclusively concerned with decisions between married couples. Instead we talk of decisions between men and women in shared households, or close relationships for short.

"Close relationships" are often analysed with the aim of understanding the system dynamics, both by those studying everyday matters and by those watching from a clinical-therapeutic viewpoint (Cox & Paley, 1997). Close relationships are more than the sum of the people involved and their various interactions, and for that reason they cannot be adequately understood if parts of those relationships are studied in isolation and then added together. The system consists of dyads or pairs of people (the partners, one parent and one child, etc), which function as sub-systems of the whole system. It is important to understand that the people are interdependent, that the sub-systems are similarly interdependent, and that they exist within a hierarchical structure. Close relationships are also open systems, embedded in a social context, which can take in information, react to it and adapt to changes or become "fixed" in a position which is traditional for that relationship. The system and its sub-systems are certainly defined by boundaries, but these allow information to pass through in both directions. Rules of interaction within and between the sub-systems, within the system itself and between the system and its social environment define the exchange of information (Cox & Paley, 1997).

Couples living in close relationships must overcome everyday problems together. The essential feature of partnership is that the partners have developed a close relationship with one another through joint experience and resolution of everyday problems, and are generally committed to preserve this relationship into the future (Schneewind, 1993). If children are also present in the shared home, then the social make-up can be described as a group (König, 1974, p. 98) which "[binds together] its members through feelings of intimacy, cooperation and reciprocal help, and where the (mutual) relationships . . . have the characteristics of intimacy and of community within the group".

Close relationships are different from relationships in ad hoc groups, circles of friends and relationships at work through a variety of characteristics (Kirchler, 1989). Over time, people in close relationships change more and more to become a group rather than a collection of individuals. This group can best be described in terms of its network of relationships, rather than as the sum of its individual members. After examining a series of studies, Burgess and Huston (1979, p. 8) summarise the particular group characteristics of a close relationship as follows: An individual's personality traits become less important as a determinant of patterns of interaction. In a close relationship, crystallised personality traits are much less influential over behaviour than is the case in ad hoc groups. The density of interactions and the variety of activities shared by members of the group is different from other types of groups. There is a desire to remain together forever, or at least for a long time, a high degree of intimacy, and emotional inter-dependence. The individuals involved cannot be simply exchanged for another, and the relationship itself is irreplaceable. Close relationships operate differently in their treatment of differences in status in the dyad or group, and handle socially determined instrumental and emotional role concepts in a different way. There is a different emotional interaction style and different rigidity of interaction processes; synchronisation of goals, interests, and desires is different, contributing to efficient problem-solving, and a different way of handling information.

These findings on close relationships are repeatedly confirmed and supported by the scientific studies referred to in what follows.

Kurt Lewin (1953, p. 133) had identified important characteristics of life in community in a familial context as early as 1940. The partners form a group in which the social distance between the members is kept small and which touches on "key personal areas": "Marriage is bound up with the important problems of life and with the central core of the individual—their values, their dreams, their social and economic status. In contrast to other groups, marriage must work not only with one or other of the aspects of an individual, but with their whole physical and social being." The group members bring their strengths and weaknesses to the group. Unlike any other group, partners in close relationships both expect and demand that they should be able to act according to their personality, free from all pressure as to what may be considered socially desirable, and to express their innermost desires. In functioning relationships, partners not only express themselves, but have an intuitive understanding of each other.

Partners in close relationships are dependent on each other. Wish, Deutsch, and Kaplan (1976) found that relationships between life partners are particularly intimate, marked by a high degree of socio-emotionality, structured in a relatively egalitarian way, and functioning in a cooperative and person-orientated style. Kelley et al. (1983b) stress that the behaviour of life partners is not only experienced as being highly interdependent, but that a high degree of interdependence is observable. This contrasts with behaviour patterns in groups of friends, work colleagues, or acquaintances.

Interdependence, intensity, and intimacy in the emotional sphere, self-disclosure and a dense network of shared activities all develop over time. Close relationships last; ad hoc groups, however, are usually formed to solve short-term problems or to make decisions and are not intended to preserve or to intensify relationships between members after the task is successfully completed. Because partners in close relationships spend a long time together, their relationship becomes unique (McGrath, 1984).

In close relationships, each individual is of special importance. Grieving partners do not easily overcome the loss of a partner, whereas in ad hoc groups or working groups an individual can be replaced by another and friendship groups survive the loss of a member. The loss of a (family) member through death or divorce leads to negative feelings and can even induce lasting depression (Argyle & Henderson, 1985; Stroebe & Stroebe, 1987).

In the private sphere, as opposed to ad hoc groups, many phenomena can have an entirely different meaning. Walters (1982) concluded that differentiation of status and role, and characteristics of interaction, had a fundamentally different significance in close relationships. Research into the influence of status differences in discussion groups demonstrated that people with the highest status (whether for reasons of gender, age or ability) have the greatest influence on a group decision (Blood & Wolfe, 1960; Rubin & Brown, 1975). In order to counter the pressure for conformity from the high-status partner, weaker group members may form a coalition. Coalitions are also common in close relationships, but here the isolated members receive far greater support than in ad hoc groups (Scott, 1962).

Parsons and Bales (1955) found that group members take on different roles; they distinguish between instrumental and emotional ones. The task-orientated, or instrumental, person is interested in solving tasks; the people-orientated, expressive or emotional person is more focused on interpersonal needs. According to traditional gender stereotypes, the man performs the instrumental role. He assumes responsibility for performing specific econ-omic tasks within the family and is the "public face" of the relationship. The woman stereotypically assumes the emotional role, and her responsibilities cover the private side of the relationship, especially the emotional climate. Kenkel (1957) observed this role differentiation in young couples asked under laboratory conditions to discuss how they would spend an imaginary sum of money, and found that traditional role differentiation could be identified in many instances. Where the interaction takes place in their home environment, however, stereotypical role models are less in evidence (Losh-Hesselbart, 1987). It appears that social prejudices and standards are less effective in determining actions in the private sphere than in the public arena.

Partners in close relationships also differ from members of other groups in that they behave more negatively towards each other and offer positive reinforcement less often than members of ad hoc groups. Negative behav-iours are observable in harmonious close relationships as well as in non-harmonious relationships. Birchler, Weiss, and Vincent (1975) compared the behaviour of happily and unhappily married couples towards each other, and of interaction by couples who did not know each other. In problem-solving situations as well as in free conversation, happy couples displayed more positive and fewer negative behaviours than unhappy couples. In comparison with the ad hoc groups, however, even happily married couples exchanged more negative and fewer positive behaviours.

Sequences of interactions between partners in close relationships are less fixed than those between strangers. In close relationships, conversation sequences are less structured and speakers are more likely to interrupt each other, cutting across the speaker and breaking the strict rules governing interactions (McGrath, 1984). In other groups, the member who is speaking is allowed more time to "monopolise" the conversation.

Life partners are more likely than people who do not know each other to have similar desires and values when presented with a decision-making situation. If they are presented with the same problem separately, they make the same decision as their partner more often. Winter, Ferreira, and Bowers (1973) described seven neutral situations and ten possible reactions to couples, who then had to choose the most desirable option. Partners in close relationships chose the same option more often than couples who did not know each other. They seem to have values that are more similar than those of strangers, and to handle discussions on controversial matters more effectively.

Another indicator of the uniqueness of close relationships comes from the fact that the dynamics of decision-making and problem-solving are influenced by different variables than in ad hoc groups. Sorrels and Myers (1983) believe that problem-solving is generally problematic if group members are intolerant, voice negative criticisms, and fail to express their expectations whilst at the same time experiencing a strong pressure to conform. Concentration on the details of a problem, dominance, rigid differences in status, and suppression of interpersonal feelings all prove to be less disruptive if a problem is to be solved by romantic partners rather than strangers.

Because close relationships are unique, extrapolating from findings in ad hoc groups or laboratory groups is problematic. Phenomena in close relationships cannot be described satisfactorily using theories conceived for ad hoc groups or tested in the laboratory, since the specific private atmosphere cannot be recreated there. The study of everyday decisions in the home therefore has to be carried out in the private home, and to involve people who have a suitably close relationship with each other (Bradbury & Fincham, 1990).

Close relationships change over time, and it is possible to speak of a life cycle of such relationships. This is generally assumed to begin with shared management of a home, moving through the arrival of one or more children, until the children move out of the family home and finally the relationship ends with the death of one, or both, of the partners.

The death of a partner certainly signifies the end of a close relationship, but it is increasingly rare for partners to see through the theoretical model of the relationship life cycle up to that point. Divorce rates are on the increase in western industrialised countries, and the current figure for the USA is around 60%. In the 1990s, remarried couples are even more likely to separate, according to statistics from the United Census Bureau in the USA (Castro-Martin & Bumpass, 1989; Cherlin, 1992; Gelles, 1995).

Research into the family life cycle, or into the life cycle of private households, distinguishes between various stages of development in private households. Earlier models operated with a classification using the following categories: single-person households; households with a married couple and no children; couples with children under 6; couples with dependent children over 6; couples with children no longer living with them; and households with a widowed partner. Murphy and Staples (1979) and Gilly and Enis (1982) developed models that take contemporary types of households into account; these are summarised in a study of spending behaviours by Wilkes (1995). In addition to the traditional life-cycle stages, the authors distinguish between: singles who are divorced and have no children; singles who are young and have one or more children; singles of middle age who are divorced and have one or more children; and singles of middle age who are divorced and have one or more adult children.

Of those recorded as families by the United Census Bureau in the USA, the largest group of close relationships was defined as being married couples without children (around 29%); 26% of families consist of parents living with children. Around 5% of relationships are defined as being unmarried adults; 7% are in a unit resembling a family where there are no children, and 9% in a unit resembling a family where there are children. Twenty-five per cent of adults live in single-person households. Between 1960 and 1990 the proportion of married couples with children fell from 44% to 26%, whilst the proportion of women living alone rose from 9% to 15% and the proportion of men living alone rose from 4% to 10% (Gelles, 1995). Similar developments have been observed in Europe: Eurostat reports that the percentage of single-person households increased from 16% to 28% in the period from 1950 to 1991 in Belgium; in Germany the respective figures are 12% to 35%, and in the UK the changes were from 11% to 26%.

The increase of single households mirrors preferences for having fewer children than in the past or no children at all, and also increased opportunity for individuals to make family-related choices freely (Sorensen, 1998). Nevertheless, satisfaction with partnership has declined over the past decades. Gelles (1995) reports the results of representative opinion surveys

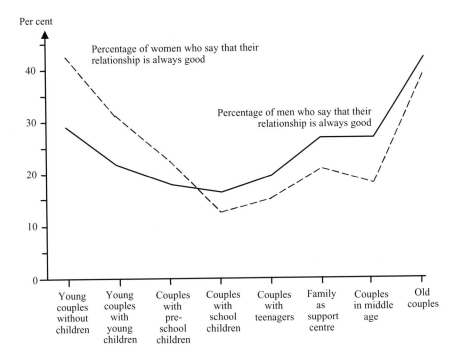

Figure 3.1 Satisfaction with the relationship over the course of the relationship life cycle (adapted from Gelles, 1995, p. 247).

in America, according to which around 68% of those interviewed (in the period 1972–1974) were satisfied with their close relationship. In the years from 1975 to 1979, satisfaction with the relationship fell to 66%, and this figure fell by a further 2% by 1984. Between 1985 and 1988, only slightly over 60% of interviewees were recorded as being happy.

There is evidence that couples' reports on marital happiness vary across the life cycle following a curvilinear path. The most frequent explanation for a deterioration of relationship quality in young families concerns parents' responsibility for young children. Partners report themselves as being most unhappy with the relationship during those phases of the relationship life cycle where children are infants or of school age (Fig. 3.1). The obligations at home increase when children are infants, and autonomy in deciding how to spend leisure time decreases. For the woman, housework may represent an additional source of strain over and above her career work, in those cases where she does not have to forgo her career completely for a number of years. Rogen and Amato (1997) emphasise also increased financial strain during these stages. However, these observations and explanations are not shared by all researchers in the field: Karney and Bradbury (1997), for instance, criticise cross-sectional research designs. Feeney, Noller, and Ward (1997) stress multi-dimensionality of relationship quality and support the idea that communication, compatibility, mutual respect, and intimacy suffer during the period of children in the joint household, but not necessarily other aspects of relationship quality.

PARTNERS' AIMS AND OBLIGATIONS

The relationship between two people lasts as long as the partners cooperate with one another. Cooperation is taken to mean the joint effort to reach specific goals. These goals are the concrete expression of desires, needs, motives or intentions of at least one of the partners, but generally of both partners. Where children are also present in the shared home, then these goals are usually shared by all family members.

The goals of partnerships and of shared households lie in generating resources, such as money obtained through employment, or all kinds of services provided in the home, and also in the resources themselves (Winch & Gordon, 1974). Provision and distribution of resources is a further aim in the shared household. Resources of various types need to be made available to satisfy the needs of the partners.

According to Foa and Foa (1980) resources are all forms of rewards that people can exchange in social interactions, regardless of whether these rewards are material or non-material. Six categories are offered to classify these resources: love, status, information, money, goods, and services. The category of "love" incorporates emotional caring, intimacy, liking, emotional warmth, and emotional support. The category of "status" subsumes recognition, respect, praise, and prestige. The category of "information" contains enlightenment, instruction, expressing one's own opinion, and advice. The category of "money" brings together all recognised standard methods of payment. The category of "goods" covers material resources or objects, and the category of "services" covers personal services that are mostly associated with work for other people.

These six types of resource can be described using a two-dimensional model: an axis between the concrete and the abstract, and one between the universal and the particular. The first dimension ranges from the symbolic-abstract (e.g. information) to the concrete (resources such as goods), and reflects the "degree of materialisation". The second dimension relates to the degree to which a resource is connected to a particular person. As an example, goods or services are concrete resources, whereas status and information are symbolic resources. Love and money are both in the mid-range of the concrete–abstract axis, but they are on opposite ends of the scale on the universal–particular axis. Love is a particular resource—that is to say, the loved partner with whom interactions are shared cannot be exchanged for another partner. A partner with whom only money transactions are conducted is replaceable at any time. Money, unlike love, is a universal resource.

A goal perspective in household studies provides a useful framework for the understanding of close relationships. Such a perspective is, however, rarely taken by social scientists (Berscheid, 1994; Fincham & Beach, 1999). Partners in the private household are concerned to initiate activities that will enable them to obtain a desired end state; these activities aim at generating and distributing material resources and may also represent goals in themselves, such as caring, readiness to help, emotional, instrumental, and social support.

Unlike working groups or committees, where a major goal can be determined (e.g. to obtain information or money, or to carry out services), partners in close relationships address several goals at the same time. In decision-making situations, partners are motivated by a desire to use the available financial resources optimally, to make decisions based on rational arguments, and to obtain information and to select products carefully. At the same time, they want to make the atmosphere in which the decision is taken as pleasant as possible for all members of the group. Where several goals are operating at the same time, it is possible that in seeking to come as close as possible to one goal, a sub-optimal solution is accepted with respect to a second goal.

In decision-making, optimal use of the limited resources available is sought, i.e. solutions that are sound in objective terms, and at the same time intensify or maintain the quality of the relationship. These simultaneous goals can, however, be in competition with each other. Can partners in close relationships be efficient agents in problem-solving? Jehn and Shah (1997) found that people who were friends with each other achieved better results than acquaintances in problem-solving situations. This research was conducted on students in the laboratory, who solved isolated problems after having been either "made" friends or not. But what happens if multiple goals are pursued?

Partners in close relationships address several goals at the same time. Because emotional goals, such as the lasting value of the relationship, seem particularly relevant, they can compete with the goals of economic decision-making and serve to diminish the urgency of such goals. If two goals are being addressed and a satisfactory solution for both goals is sought, then the isolated study of the solution of one goal may appear to indicate a sub-optimal decision. However, a sub-optimal solution that does not optimise one's own utility but benefits the relationship may be preferred to an economically sensible decision.

RELATIONSHIP STRUCTURES

If the dynamic between partners could be "frozen" at a particular point in time (e.g. by capturing a segment of an interaction), and then recaptured at similar points at other times, then the observer could see whether the same people act in the same or similar fashion each time, and whether the reactions of the other partner equally follow the same pattern. In this way it would be possible to discover at least part of the structure of the relationship (Fraser, 1978, p. 183).

The structure is a picture of invariables from past interaction processes or, as Luhmann (1984, p. 383) puts it, "the systematic relating of elements over time". The structure is a result of interaction processes and creates the basis for future interaction processes.

The concept of structure suggests something rigid. Structure and process are often considered as central objects of research, which by their nature contrast with each other. Structure is seen as fixed, process as fluid. Luhmann (1984, p. 73) criticises the contrasting of structure and process using metaphors of stasis and dynamics, or permanence and change, as a misleading polarisation: "It would be wrong simply to conceive structure as being timeless and process as temporal." Structures come into being, are repeatedly redefined and decay over time.

The structure of close relationships can be described using two fundamental dimensions (Kirchler, 1989). One dimension measures emotional aspects (the structure of emotions, friendliness or harmony within the relationship); the other measures dominance relations (the structure of power or dominance). Hinde (1997) suggests that the involvement of the partners represents a further dimension, which is frequently ignored when the structure of close relationships is being described.

The horizontal and vertical structural dimensions "harmony" and "power" help us to understand and to make predictions about decision-making processes. Because the structure of the relationship is on the one hand a variable in the causes of interaction processes, but on the other hand can also be understood to be the result of interaction processes, there is a danger of arriving at little more than tautological conclusions if we attempt to predict behaviours on the basis of the known structural dimensions. If we predict that happy couples will relate in a different way from unhappy couples, or that egalitarian partnerships will develop different processes from patriarchal or matriarchal partnerships, these predictions may appear trivial precisely because the structure of the partnership reflects past interaction processes and therefore predictions should be confined purely to future interaction processes. For example, if harmony is defined as the result of the frequency of interactions between the partners, along with mutual consideration and accurate understanding of the emotional and motivational position of the other partner, etc., then a prediction is tautological if it simply restates what is already contained in that definition.

One possibility of countering the charge of offering little more than tautologies consists in offering a counter-definition of harmony as a compacted accumulation of the experiences of the partners. Past experiences and the feelings associated with them are remembered by the partners and their emotional value is accumulated. Self-reflection enables partners to provide information about their shared, subjectively reconstituted experiences in interviews or via questionnaires. The evaluation of a reconstituted past is a measure of harmony. Predictions about the effects of harmony, liking, and relationship quality are effectively predictions about the effect of history on the present pattern of interactions. In relation to decision-making, alongside the question of historical continuity (the temporal dimension) there is also an issue concerning generalising from common everyday experiences to specific decision-making situations (the dimension of content and context). Harmony is based on emotional experiences in a variety of situations and is measured as such. The overall evaluation of the relationship then has implications for a specific situation. This conceptualisation of harmony, liking, and relationship quality and the similar understanding of the dominance structure recall the trait concept in the psychology of personality. This is where genetically predisposed potentials and past learning experiences are fused together, providing a basis for predictions about certain patterns of behaviour in particular situations which place demands on the individual. Instruments for the measurement of personality also record how people generally act, and postulate that a certain person will behave in accordance with that pattern when faced with a specific future situation.

Horizontal Relationship Structure: Harmony

The emotional climate in a partnership is described in various ways. Love, affection, emotional quality, empathy, satisfaction, harmony, success in the marriage, marital happiness, relationship quality, cohesion, and liking are just some of the terms that can be found in the literature, mostly with no explicit field of definition and quite often being used interchangeably. Hendrick and Hendrick (1997, p. 57) write that "satisfaction is only one of several terms employed to describe some sort of summative judgement about an intimate relationship". These diverse terms are applied to phenomena that are largely overlapping, and to the overarching concept of satisfaction with the relationship. Whilst the various terms may emphasise different aspects, there is significant overlap even when an attempt at differentiation is made, e.g. between love and commitment (Kelley, 1983; Fletcher, Simpson, & Thomas, 2000). It is clear that the whole represents a single, fundamental dimension, which is here referred to as relationship harmony or satisfaction.

If we choose to write about satisfaction, and to interpret various concepts as overlapping and synonymous in use, then this is because relationship quality is understood to be the moderating variable of the dynamics of joint decision-making. It is of course self-evident that concepts such as satisfaction, cohesion, or love differ greatly from one another if the focus of scientific study is on precisely those differences between the concepts (e.g. Weigel & Ballard-Reisch, 1999).

Satisfaction with a relationship is a function of the sum of positive and negative emotions, and the intensity of positive and negative emotions, which have been experienced together with the partner and attributed to them (Clore & Byrne, 1974; Clore & Itkin, 1977; Lott & Lott, 1960). Where partners are able and ready to come together, expectations and needs are met, the relationship is harmonious and the level of satisfaction high. The reverse is also true: Misunderstandings, causing frustration of needs and reluctance to work together, lead to disharmony and dissatisfaction.

Interaction between partners can be viewed as a conditioning process (see Fehr, 1996). Conditioning theory suggests that the essential precondition for satisfaction is the association between pleasant stimuli and the partner. Initially the partner is a neutral stimulus, experienced as positive if in his presence positive feelings increase and negative feelings diminish, with the result that finally the partner himself personally obtains the status of a reward. Learning theory suggests that positive experiences with the partner correlate positively with satisfaction, whilst negative experiences correlate negatively with satisfaction. The higher the reward or penalty value of the partner, the higher the level of satisfaction or dissatisfaction experienced.

Whereas conditioning models do not take conditions extrinsic to the relationship into account, exchange theorists concentrate especially on the comparison between the attractiveness of a current relationship and possible alternative relationships (e.g. Thibaut & Kelley, 1959). Equity theories (Walster, Walster, & Berscheid, 1978) draw attention to the fair distribution of the results of interactions between the partners. If rewards and sacrifices are borne equally and distributed fairly between partners, the relationship is judged to be satisfactory. Balance models understand satisfaction to be the result of a cognitive process. Heider (1958) and Newcomb (1971) consider a relationship between two people to be harmonious if these people have developed consistent attitudes towards relevant attitudinal stimuli.

The different views of learning theory, exchange theory, equity theory and balance theory can be subsumed under the learning theory approach. Affection between partners is high if joint experiences are pleasant rather than unpleasant. The higher the level of reward from these experiences, the higher the level of satisfaction. In addition to this general statement, exchange and equity theories add that experiences are positive if interaction with the partner throws up high levels of profit, and if this is shared fairly.

Balance theory confirms the assertion of learning theory that attitudinal conflicts lead to negative feelings, and that this results in dissatisfaction.

Numerous empirical studies reinforce the predictions of learning theory, exchange theory, equity theory, and balance theory (e.g. Berscheid & Lopes, 1997; Gilmour & Duck, 1986; Hinde, 1979; Kelley et al., 1983a; Kurdek & Schmitt, 1986; Lewis & Spanier, 1979; Noller, 1984; Perlman & Duck, 1987; Sternberg & Hojjat, 1997; Weigel & Ballard-Reisch, 1999). Partners who are often together and who plan many activities together feel better when their partner is present, communicate positively with one another non-verbally, have an accurate awareness of the needs of their partner and are open towards their partner. Although they report having as many conflicts as other couples, these are resolved far more efficiently, and the partners have trust in each other and are happy with each other (Koski & Shaver, 1997; Stinnett & DeFrain, 1985; Swensen, 1972). Meeks, Hendrick, and Hendrick (1998) report close links between satisfaction with the relationship and self-expression, perception of that expression by the partner, the frequency of integrative bargaining during discussions, and passion and altruistic love from the partner. Shackelford and Buss (1997) believe that satisfaction with a partner depends on whether the partners allow each other time and space to pursue their own interests, whether they are loyal to each other and sanction disloyalty where necessary, and whether they manipulate each other emotionally, i.e. by forcing them to act in a certain way through using intense emotions. Harvey and Omarzu (1997) use the term "minding" to refer to the variables that promote satisfaction with the partner, which are a collection of actions and thoughts that have the aim of furthering the relationship. The key element in this process of minding are behaviours that enable one to express one's own feelings, uncertainties and fears, thoughts and opinions to one's partner. Despite the risk of possible upset by the partner, opportunities are provided to get to know and understand the characteristics of the individuals involved. This involves attribution processes: partners who are able to imagine themselves in the position of their partner and to empathise with them tend to attribute positive behaviours to their partner and to explain negative behaviours as being conditioned by the situation. As was demonstrated by Murray and Holmes (1997), happy partners exaggerate the positive characteristics of their partner and play down negative behaviours. Harvey and Omarzu (1997) talk of acceptance and respect for the partner, as well as the mutual nature of selfless actions taken with regard to the partner. Satisfaction is ultimately also dependent on the orientation of the partners being committed to maintaining a close relationship over a longer period of time.[1]

---

[1] A highly informative summary of research on close relationships and satisfaction is presented by Holmes (2000) from an inter-dependence theory approach.

Whereas learning theory defines satisfaction as the association of good feelings with the partner, exchange theorists and the later models based on that theory explain the conditions that bring about that state of well-being and therefore of satisfaction, which is then associated with the partner and the relationship. A detailed overview of the development of these theories can be found in Hinde (1997).

If a couple moves from initial attraction and the "rose coloured glasses" of falling in love to develop a lasting, loving relationship, which endures over time to become a long-term close relationship, then they are good subjects for a study of relationship harmony and its determinants. Hinde (1997) believes that self-expression and privacy are most important in the development of close relationships. Self-expression can enable the subjective attitudes and interests of the partners, and their values and their way of seeing things, to be integrated into a coherent whole. Reciprocal trust is an essential determining factor for self-expression. Trust can only be developed over time, where partners assess the risk of being upset by the other partner to be sufficiently low, since risk increases with increasing self-disclosure. If the partner reacts to private and intimate information with encouraging responses and with sensitivity, then the other partner is helped to take further steps in self-disclosure and to develop increasing trust. Communication with their partner, adequate encoding and decoding of information, and the ability to imagine oneself in the position of the other are essential. Communication and constructive conflict resolution where there are disagreements offer the possibility of understanding the partner; they also serve as essential determinants of satisfaction with the partnership (Feeney, Noller, & Ward, 1997; Hinde, 1997).

Satisfaction with one's own relationship is viewed as linked to the stability of the relationship. Karney and Bradbury (1997) believe that the guarantee of stability lies not in a high degree of satisfaction being achieved, but in the speed with which changes in satisfaction levels occur over time. Satisfaction with one's own relationship, the commitment of the partners to each other and the stability of the relationship are explained in Rusbult's (1980) "investment model". Based on the interdependence theory of Kelley and Thibaut (1978) and Kelley (1979), which stresses the mutual dependence of the partners on each other, Rusbult also assumes that satisfaction with the relationship is dependent on the costs and rewards that are experienced through the relationship. The expectations of partners are most important in this process. Satisfaction, investment in the relationship, and the availability and quality of alternative partners determine the commitment of the partners to one another; increasing commitment stabilises the relationship and makes it a lasting unit. The investment model emphasises the differences between satisfaction with the relationship and the dependence of the partners on the partnership. Satisfaction is dependent on processes of comparison with earlier relationships, on observation of other relationships, and on subjective costs and rewards. Commitment to a relationship is partially defined by satisfaction, but also depends on the possibility of pursuing alternative relationships and on the material and non-material resources invested in the existing relationship, as well as on the relevance of a relationship for the identity of a person.

The investment model has been investigated empirically on many occasions, and has been largely confirmed. In a long-term study by Bui, Peplau, and Hill (1996), the stability of a relationship proved to be dependent on the commitment of the partners, which was in turn dependent on satisfaction, investments in the relationship and quality of alternatives. Satisfaction was mainly determined by the perceived rewards and to a small extent by the experienced costs of the relationship.

It is stressed that any idea of a unidirectional causal connection between satisfaction and commitment, and the clear differentiation between the two constructs, can be called into question. On the one hand, there are repeated findings of a high correlation between satisfaction and commitment (between $r = .50$ and $.80$; Rusbult, 1991). Lydon, Pierce, and O'Regan (1997) state, on the other hand, that there is an important distinction between "enthusiastic commitment" and "moral commitment". The authors take "enthusiastic commitment" to be mostly what would be termed satisfaction, whereas "moral commitment" comprises normative obligations experienced by someone wanting to preserve a relationship over a period of time. Normative–moral feelings of commitment especially allow one to predict the stability of a relationship.

It is interesting to note that costs appear to have little significance for satisfaction with the relationship. Bui et al. (1996) admittedly believe that costs were perhaps not recorded as such in their study. This criticism does not appear to be justified, given that rewards and costs were in fact measured in similar ways. Satisfaction proved to be significantly more dependent on rewards than on costs. Costs are actually ambivalent: if interaction between the partners is not simply an exchange transaction of material or non-material resources, in order to achieve a profit, then costs could also correspond to the desire of the partners to prepare pleasures for the other person. Costs could then be experienced as positive if they are incurred by one partner in the course of preparing something pleasant for the other partner. If the preferences of the partners do not correspond in a decision-making situation, then it is not improbable that in harmonious relationships one partner will willingly surrender their wishes to the wishes of their partner and meet the needs of their partner. In a harmonious relationship, the denial of realisation of one's own desires and other costs can be understood as denial of a short-term goal in favour of a long-term, lasting one—the consolidation of the partnership.

Clark and Grote (1998) also draw attention to the ambivalent signifi-cance of costs. Costs can be incurred if one partner initiates poor behaviour, if inadvertent behaviour by one partner causes negative things that become associated with the relationship, or if one partner behaves in a certain way to comply with the needs of the other. If the costs relate to the first two categories, it is likely that dissatisfaction will result, whereas costs that fall into the final category correlate positively with satisfaction, according to their findings.

Van Lange et al. (1997) found, in several empirical studies on the "willingness to sacrifice" in close relationships, that the readiness to deny one's own preferences and the associated readiness to carry the cost depended above all on the degree of commitment to the partnership. If Rusbult's investment model is understood to operate in a circular fashion, then individual commitment is determined by satisfaction and other vari-ables, but commitment to the relationship also influences the significance of the resources exchanged, the rewards and costs and also the significance of selective and enduring goals. This circular construction would suggest that pleasures reinforce satisfaction, but costs do not have negative effects. The readiness to sacrifice can be understood as an altruistic act, as an investment in the relationship, or it can quite possibly also be seen as an economically sensible investment against future decision-making dilemmas, where past sacrifices can be used to assert one's own point of view in the future.

If costs are experienced as being a willingly made sacrifice in favour of one's partner or as investments for the future in lasting harmonious relationships, then it can be assumed that partners in harmonious relationships to which they feel committed will interact differently from partners in disharmonious relationships whose future is uncertain. Happy partners develop a different dynamic of interactions to unhappy partners. Holmes (1981, p. 279) writes: "Distressed couples regress in the sense that they tend to behave in a manner more similar to that of casual friends." Many parallels can be drawn between disharmonious partners and people who have an economic relationship with one another. If the quality of a relationship diminishes, the partners tend increasingly to behave towards each other as if they had an economic relationship and were aiming to maximise their own individual benefits. In happy partnerships, such a profit-orientated basis for exchanges in everyday interactions and in decision-making situations is unlikely.

Vertical Relationship Structure: Power Relationships

Alongside the emotional characteristics, an understanding of the interaction processes, and especially of decision-making processes, also relies on an appreciation of reciprocal power relations between the partners. Concepts such as power, control, dominance, influence, and authority are sometimes used as synonyms in social science, but on other occasions they are strongly differentiated from one another. We find the possibility of control is the intended meaning at one point, and at another a distinction is being drawn between potential and manifest control. McDonald (1980) believes that definitions of reciprocal dependence and power have to take the following aspects into consideration: Power is the potential (latent) or current (manifest) ability to achieve desired goals, both by influencing the behaviour of the other partner or by realising desired goals against the resistance of the other partner. It is a characteristic of the system, and not a subjective attribute of a person. Power is not static, but dynamic, i.e. there are reciprocal processes of influence between partners. It is a phenomenon that encompasses both activities and the perception of an imbalance in power, and it relates to asymmetrical relationships. Even if the imbalance in power is asymmetrical, this simply means that one person has the say in certain areas; in other areas the imbalance of power can be shifted in favour of the other partner. Power is a multidimensional concept, which incorporates socio-cultural, interactional, and outcome components.

Given that power can be understood as a manifest and/or potential control over the behaviour of others, as intentional or unintentional actions, as a process or an outcome of social interactions, Olson and Cromwell (1975) apply three categories to the power relations in private households: the bases or sources of power; the power processes; and the outcomes of power.

The sources of power are all the conditions that make it possible for a person to exercise power. French and Raven (1959), Collins and Raven (1969), and Raven and Kruglanski (1970) define six types of power based on different sources:

(a) Reward power: this is based on the possibility of one partner providing pleasures for the other by making available material or non-material resources. The dependence on rewards from one partner makes the other dependent on the desires of the powerful partner.

(b) Coercive power: this is based on the possibility of one partner providing displeasure for the other. This can be done by introducing unpleasant stimuli or by withdrawing pleasures. It is generally assumed that the exercise of power is easier to achieve using pleasures rather than punishments, which can lead to resistance and aggression. According to conditioning theory, both rewards and punishments are effective means of influencing behaviours.

(c) Legitimate power: this refers to contexts where one person is allowed to decide the facts of a matter and to presume the acceptance and the licence to exercise power on the part of the other partner. Age, and the breadth of experience associated with it, are the usual sources of legitimate power. In traditional societies the man is accorded responsibility and power in matters relating to the outside world, while women are expected to exercise power and responsibility in internal family matters.

(d) Referent power: this is based on the attraction that one partner exercises over the other. Love, admiration, and attraction can lead to one partner viewing the other as an idol and a model, and therefore coming to meet their needs. The tendency to imitate the other partner leads to changes in behaviour even before the attractive partner actively exerts this power.

(e) Expert power: this depends on the specific knowledge and abilities of the individual. If one partner possesses expert knowledge and both are interested in the objective solution of a problem, then there is a high probability that the partner with less expert knowledge and fewer abilities in a particular area will shift position to meet the needs of the other.

(f) Informational power: this is similar to expert power, and is specific to a particular subject area. If a partner has gathered information about a problem or about an area where a decision is to be made, he can influence the other partner to shift position to meet his needs by exerting his information power and passing on less, or diffuse, information.

Later work by Raven (1993, 1999) has extended the concept of the six sources of power, and identifies a total of 11 different sources. He differentiates between reward power and coercive power, which are either directed towards people or not directed towards people; formal legal power and legal power based on patterns of reciprocity, exchange rules or dependence; positive and negative expert power or information power, and direct and indirect information power.

In decision-making situations, the partners' relative interest is also a factor alongside the bases of power. The interested partner usually gathers information about the problem being addressed and assimilates it. The lower the level of interest in a decision, the lower the readiness to divert available time away from other problems to devote it to the current problem. The interested partner establishes a basis of power by virtue of the time he commits to the problem and the level of competence he can acquire in a short time; the other partner is unlikely to be able to overcome this position in a decision-making situation. The reciprocal attraction of the partners also represents a basis for power, i.e. referent power, which means that the partner who is less in love is stronger than the other.

Whether a person actually exploits their power advantage and influences their partner in what they do remains an open question, even where they are aware of the power advantage. In harmonious relationships, it is assumed that the imbalance of power only exists to a small degree in favour of one or other partner, or that the uneven power distribution between the partners is not used by them to obtain advantages in decision-making.

If a relationship is harmonious, the partners often report having egalitarian power relationships. It may be that the dimensions of power and dominance on the one hand, and of harmony in the relationship on the other, are not dependent on one another. In well-functioning harmonious relationships, power advantages for one or other partner may not be of any further significance because they are not used to move one partner into meeting the needs of the powerful partner (e.g. Cromwell & Olson, 1975; Safilios-Rothschild, 1970; Sprey, 1972). In disharmonious relationships, it may be assumed that the powerful partner uses his or her advantage to realise his or her own wishes.

Power processes encompass those strategies that partners bring to bear in decision-making, negotiation, and problem-solving situations in order to bring the other partner round. These are strategies and tactics that are used in order to make the other partner give way.

Finally, power outcomes are concerned with the relative influence actually manifested by partners in decision-making situations. Studies of decisions in private households, particularly those on purchasing decisions, have in the past often concentrated on the power outcomes, and equally on the determinants of these outcomes.

MODELS OF INTERACTION

The basis of interaction between two or more people are the primary events, the actions and reactions of those involved (conative component), their emotions (affective component), and their thoughts (cognitive component), all of which occur sequentially. Interaction refers to the processes as they occur, in other words to transactions between people. Interaction processes can be recorded at the micro or macro level. Whilst the micro level is concerned with the sequence of actions and reactions, the macro level sketches out a model of the course of the interaction and attempts to capture it in its entirety. Exchange theories formulated in the 1950s and 1960s are particularly concerned with interaction processes at the macro level (Blau, 1964; Homans, 1961/1974; Thibaut & Kelley, 1959).

Unlike analysis of the micro level, which starts with sequences of actions and reactions (Gottman, 1979), exchange theories describe interaction episodes and rules that people use to shape their contacts with other people. A particular feature of exchange theories is the assumption that social actions follow an economic cost–benefit analysis. Accordingly a repeated theme in social interaction is the goal of maximising one's own or one's joint benefit, minimising costs and achieving the highest possible level of profit.

Nye (1979), extrapolating from the various exchange theories, offers the following ideas about behaviour in social interactions. People take rational decisions, and people also evaluate social relationships for the profit that they bring, on the basis of the available body of information and the abilities of the individuals involved. This is compared with the profit which possible alternative relationships would offer. Apart from the rewards or the relationship income, the costs or outgoings of the relationship are also taken into account. If in the past a particular pattern of behaviour has been rewarded or punished in a certain situation, then a person will in future be more or less likely to repeat that behaviour if the new situation closely resembles the past one. Social contacts are based on the principle of reciprocity (Gouldner, 1960), which means that costs and benefits received from a partner are answered by either punishing or rewarding the partner.

The model of humans underlying exchange theories is that of the "homo oeconomicus", or "economic man". There has been much criticism of the notion that even loving relationships are understood to follow the principles of the market economy (e.g. Huston & Burgess, 1979; Willer, 1985). Can exchange theories adequately explain interaction processes in functioning romantic relationships where, unlike interactions between acquaintances or people in economically orientated groups, there is far more frequent communication, on a more intimate level, conducted over a longer period of time and as part of discussions over a wider range of different problems? If one assumes that social interaction in general is a process of give and take, and that in interactions in close relationships there is also an exchange of material values, feelings, and ideas, then it may be appropriate to consider which rules of exchange are developed in close groups.

Maccoby (1986) differentiates between various types of relationship and argues that the economic rules of exchange theory are not applied in functioning and satisfactory partnerships. Transactions in ad hoc relationships and in economic relationships can be accurately described using exchange theory and the equity principle, as can transactions in close relationships characterised by a hierarchical imbalance of power or reciprocal antagonism. On the other hand, interactions in relationships between friends and in satisfactory close relationships do not follow principles of maximising profit.

It is generally assumed that relationships between happy partners and between friends resemble each other. Partners in unhappy relationships, on the other hand, are inclined to view themselves as acquaintances or economic partners and to calculate what return they can get from the other partner and what they have to contribute to the other partner (Holmes,

1981). Depending on the structural characteristics of the relationship, the behaviour of the partners can range along a continuum reaching from exchange transactions to spontaneously altruistic behaviour. Moreover, it can be hypothesised that, in harmonious relationships, power advantages that exist to the benefit of one or other partner are not exploited, out of consideration for the wishes of the other person. In disharmonious relationships, it can be hypothesised that potentially stronger partners seek to assert their wishes in decision-making situations.

According to Maccoby's (1986) classification, close relationships can be ordered into different types of relationship, based on their structural characteristics. Partners in disharmonious relationships seek to make egoistic profits, even at the expense of the other partner. If the partners become increasingly uninterested in the continuance of the relationship, the relationship mutates into an economic relationship and can be adequately described using the equity rule. Depending on whether there is a hierarchical imbalance of power or an egalitarian distribution of power, the dominant partner determines the exchange transactions. The relationship is at best sustained because the partners can gain egoistic advantages from it. The more harmonious the relationship, the more the individual interests play a lesser role and become overlaid with interests that serve the relationship as a whole.

Partners in harmonious relationships act in accordance with a model that has been called the "love principle", regardless of whether or not one partner holds a power advantage over the other. The lower the level of emotional attachment to each other, the more the love principle mutates towards a "credit principle". The partners then still seek to offer pleasures to each other, and look after one another, but they are waiting for a similar effort to be made in return and, at best, they offer the other partner a kind of long-term credit. If the relationship quality diminishes further, then the pattern of interactions no longer follows the credit model, but instead mirrors the "equity principle". The partners act increasingly like two business partners. The lower the quality of the relationship, the more important the power differences between the partners. Whereas the power relations in harmonious relationships are unimportant, in "cooled-off" relationships the partner who possesses more power will also use the opportunity to control exchange transactions with the other person. In such instances, we can speak of an "egoism principle" (Fig. 3.2).

The interaction process in close relationships that operate according to the love principle, the credit principle, the equity principle or the egoism principle, whether or not there is an imbalance of power between the partners, can be described using the following characteristics:

Interdependence versus independence of partners.   People in relationships that can be described using the love principle are dependent upon one

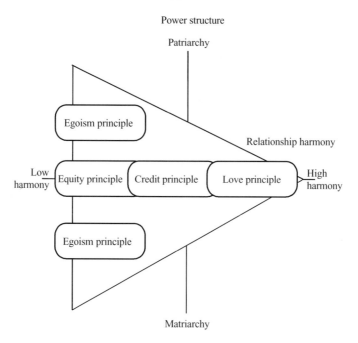

Figure 3.2   Principles of interaction in close relationships (Kirchler, 1989, p. 119).

another in their feelings, thoughts, and actions. Being dependent means that they are affected by the behaviour of the other person and are at the same time aware that their own actions can affect the other person. According to Kelley and Thibaut (1978) mutual dependence is based on the opportunity for partners to prepare pleasures for each other and to generate costs. The closer and the more harmonious the relationship, the greater the mutual concern and consideration.

Brandstätter and his colleagues conducted a series of studies on the interdependence of partners in relation to harmony and to imbalance of power in the relationship. The research design they used resembles the interaction matrix of Kelley and Thibaut (1978). Wagner, Kirchler, and Brandstätter (1984) and Brandstätter, Kirchler, and Wagner (1987) asked partners about how they felt if they wanted to buy a product which is solely of use to themselves (an egoistic purchasing desire), whether their partner would agree to the purchase or oppose it, and whether they would finally buy the product or go without it. They also asked interviewees to imagine that their partner wanted to buy a product and that they would either agree with or oppose the desired purchase. The studies show that men and women assessed the presented purchase situation in different ways, depending on the harmony in the relationship. There was a high correlation between the feelings of partners where the partnership was happy and patriarchal. The lowest correlation was in egalitarian relationships. In harmonious, patriarchal partnerships the partners took each other into consideration and felt uncomfortable if they satisfied an egoistic desire to purchase something against the wishes of their partner. "Taking into consideration" was defined as acknowledging the difference between feelings in the conflict situation (that situation, in which one partner buys something against the wishes of the other) and feelings in other situations.

Long-term versus short-term credit.   In ad hoc groups or economic relationships, give and take are directly linked. If people hand over a part of their resources, then they expect a corresponding share in rewards from the other person in return, and the other person feels obligated under the principle of reciprocity. The direct recompense is expected in an exchange relationship is not expected in happy close relationships (Levinger, 1979). If the relationship is good and the future seems assured, then—as Axelrod (1984) found—there is no requirement for an immediate return for a pleasure that has been given; he writes of the length of the "shadow of the future" and describes how a short shadow indicates that the end of the relationship is close by. In a good relationship, there is no need for a short-term response to an advantage, a positive outcome of an interaction process or a profit for one partner at a certain point in time. Although Levinger (1979) believes that interactions in close relationships are always governed by exchange principles, he agrees that partners can apply these principles differently in the course of the development of the relationship. At the outset, when the relationship is still young and there is no basis for reciprocal trust, there is a strong need for reciprocity. When the partners trust one another, they look for experiences that satisfy both partners and distribute the available resources according to needs. Balance is sought over the long term. If the relationship progresses harmoniously, then in the end "book-keeping"—to use a banking analogy—is no longer necessary.

Joint maximisation of profits versus cost–benefit analysis.   Unhappy partners whose relationship has become an economic relationship seek to exploit their opportunities for profit to the full. The more harmonious the relationship, the less interest the partner has in concluding a trade with their partner. The relationship in itself acquires a value. As the partnership intensifies, the economic interest in the relationship gives way to interest in the relationship itself. In order to realise the goal of confirming the harmonious relationship, partners are often inclined to forgo short-term, current goals and are prepared to make sacrifices that benefit their partner (Van Lange et al., 1997). Instead of seeking to draw advantages for themselves from the relationship, the partners seek shared advantages (Kelley &

Schenitzki, 1972). The original goal of partners who have no shared history, to maximise their individual advantage, gives way in longer-lasting relationships to the goal of seeking shared advantages (Holmes, 1981). Hinde (1979, p. 248ff.) writes: "were each participant to be concerned merely with maximizing his own rewards and minimizing his cost, with no thought for his partner, that partner might soon find a better option elsewhere. He must, therefore, consider not only his own probable rewards and costs, but also those of his partner." In negotiations, participants are increasingly able to put themselves in the position of their partner as their appreciation of the partner increases, and they then want to show their "good side" and move position to meet that of their partner "even before the negotiation really gets going" (Rubin, 1983). Scanzoni (1979a, b) writes of joint maximisation of benefit in this context: the more harmonious the relationship between the partners, the more something that one partner perceives as a reward is also considered as such by the other partner. Competitive patterns of behaviour, which offer the best chances for the highest individual profit, are passed over in favour of cooperative behaviour, which maximises joint benefit. Disharmonious relationships are marked by an egoistic focus on profit, where the powerful partner is more likely than the weaker partner to satisfy his desires.

The distribution of rewards using rules of need, as opposed to equity rules.   Criticism of exchange theories refers particularly to the rule of distributive justice which was postulated by Homans (1961/1974) and subsequently elaborated further. According to this rule, every member is compensated in proportion to their contributions (the equity rule). In close relationships equity rules cause upset. Good friends and happy partners offer one another pleasures as spontaneous acts, unlike what happens in other types of relationship. In business relationships and relationships between strangers or between unhappy partners, it is more likely that pleasures will be arranged if the partner has been the source of positive experiences in the past (Clark & Mills, 1979) or if such experiences can be expected in future (e.g. Kelley, 1979). In harmonious relationships, resources are not distributed in proportion to individual contributions, but according to individual need. In lasting love relationships and harmonious partnerships the principle of reciprocity gives way to the principle of responsibility, according to which resources should be distributed according to the individual's needs. Lujansky and Mikula (1983) found that relationships where equity rules were applied were not qualitatively better and more stable than other relationships. In their study, the absolute level of pleasures offered by the partners to each other was decisive for a satisfactory relationship. Similar results were found by Michaels, Acock, and Edwards (1986) and Michaels, Edwards, and Acock (1984). Similarly, Hays (1985) found that the best predictor of the success of a relationship was not the difference between rewards and costs—in other words, individual profit measured by the subjective contributions of the partners—but the total sum of rewards and costs. Clark and Reis (1988) interpret this finding as an expression of need orientation.

Abundance versus scarcity of resources.   In economic relationships, only certain types of resources are traded, which are mainly universalistic in terms of the concept of Foa and Foa (1974). In close relationships, the main resources traded are particularistic, although universalistic resources are also exchanged (Berg & McQuinn, 1986). The increasing abundance of resources in close relationships was also confirmed from the study by Kirchler and Hölzl (1996), which investigated profit orientation and altruism in three different types of relationship. A total of 71 students were asked to imagine relationships with "romantic partners", with same-sex friends and with work colleagues, and to indicate what they receive from or what they might give to the corresponding person in each case. The abundance of resources exchanged proved to be significantly conditioned by the relationship: while over 60 different types of resources were named for loving relationships, participants could also name over 46 types of resources for relationships with friends, but only around 30 types of resources for relationships with work colleagues. The types of resources listed could be divided into universalistic resources such as politeness and friendliness, and particularistic resources such as love, tenderness, and sympathy. In addition, emotional resources (e.g. love, eroticism) were differentiated from informational resources (e.g. ideas, exchange of opinions). In loving relationships it is assumed that it is mostly emotional and particularistic resources that are exchanged. In relationships with work colleagues, a variety of informational and universalistic resources are exchanged. In relationships between friends, men perceive their same-sex friends as sources of information and as partners for discussions and exchanges of opinion; women appear to be closer to their women friends, sharing personal and relationship problems with them and seeing their attributes as trust, openness, reliability, and helpfulness. Whereas men differentiate clearly between partners in romantic relationships and partners in friendships, women make less of a distinction between them.

In economic relationships, resources of one kind are paid back by pleasures of the same or of a similar kind. For example, goods are exchanged for goods, and money is exchanged for goods or for information. In close relationships, it is not only a few resources, but instead a wide variety of resources that are exchanged. Hatfield, Utne, and Traupmann (1979) report that it is not only the number and type of resources that change with the increasing intensity of the relationship. The "value" of pleasures and the "costs" of unpleasant things are experienced more strongly.

Spontaneous altruism versus control of demands and obligations.   Happy partners do not seek to keep an account of demands and obligations. They act spontaneously in a partner-orientated manner (Clark & Chrisman, 1994; Van Ypern & Buunk, 1994). In a series of experiments Clark and her colleagues demonstrated that no account was kept of emotional income and expenditure if the partners are disposed towards each other in a friendly manner (e.g. Clark, 1984; Clark, Mills, & Powell, 1986). Clark and Waddell (1985) found that a friend is not expected to offer a favour in return when they ask for something, whereas that was expected of partners in exchange relationships. Clark, Ouelette, Powell, and Milberg (1987) report that friends are more helpful the more their partner is needy, unlike partners in exchange relationships. Exchange relationships work on the basis of mutually profitable taking, whereas friendships operate on the basis of mutual giving, where no book-keeping is necessary.

In a series of experiments, Clark (1984) allowed her participants to perform a task together with another person. She used two different experimental situations: in one, an economic exchange situation was investigated, and in the other a friendship relationship was investigated. A test volunteer was asked to begin the task of crossing off certain numbers on a matrix of figures using either a red or a black pen. After this, the partner was asked to continue with the task. The partner could choose to continue with the same coloured pen or use the other pen. The study investigated which colour pen was chosen by the second person. It was found that significantly more than 50% of those tested used the differently coloured pen in economic relationships, in order to distinguish their effort from that of the other person; in the friendship relationship, the work was continued using the same-colour pen in a significant majority of cases.

"Keeping track of inputs is necessary in order to allocate benefits in proportion to inputs—something that is called for in exchange relationships. However, in communal relationships such record keeping is unnecessary because benefits are distributed according to needs or to demonstrate concern for the other", conclude Clark et al. (1986, p. 333) after a similar study. People in an exchange relationship were more prepared to help their partner in solving a task in the laboratory if the partner later had the opportunity to return that help. Friends acted according to the needs of the other person and helped them, regardless of whether or not there was the possibility of later returning that help.

In a resumé of their studies, Mills and Clark (1986) summarise briefly those situations that were felt to be causes of conflict in economic relationships and contrast these with the conditions that have negative consequences amongst friends. In exchange relationships, conflicts result above all from situations where the equity rule is broken. This occurs, for example, if one partner underestimates the contributions made by the other, overestimates their own contribution, and regards the partner's costs as too low and their own costs as too high. Between friends, all those exchange constellations experienced as exploitative in economic relationships can equally be experienced as sources of conflict. However, there are many further conditions that can lead to differences: if a family member exaggerates his needs and underestimates the needs of others, or if the value of something offered by the other person is underestimated, or if one partner misunderstands the actual intensity of the relationship, then it becomes more likely that the interaction partners experience the relationship as being out of balance and therefore unsatisfactory.

Because the studies of Clark and her colleagues demonstrate the difference between various types of relationship so impressively, it is surprising that the premises identified for a loss of quality in these relationship types are so similar, again lending force to the validity of exchange theory. If the expectations of actors in exchange relationships are placed on a par with the needs of friends, the differences are largely resolved: For example, in an exchange relationship the attempt to minimise the costs to a partner in order to lower his expectations of a corresponding reward is strikingly similar to the attempt made not to overestimate the needs of the friend in order to keep the cost to oneself as low as possible. If an actor in an exchange relationship overestimates the value of his contributions for the other person, then this is a parallel to the overestimation of an individual's own contributions as a source of satisfying needs between friends. Equally congruent are the causes of conflict adduced by Mills and Clark (1986): If an actor in an exchange relationship mistakenly assumes that a friendship relationship exists and his expectations of the other person are correspondingly high, then the starting-point is the same as for a relationship between friends where one partner overestimates the intensity of the relationship and has correspondingly high expectations of the other as a result.

Whereas partners in disharmonious relationships keep account of their demands and obligations and immediately seek to achieve a balance between the two, partners in happy relationships orientate themselves above all by the needs of the other person and show consideration. "Care plays a more important role than need in judgements of love", is Kelley's (1983, p. 273) appropriate comment on the matter. The partner who cares for the other person is more loving than the needy partner. Family members who have a good, loving relationship act spontaneously in a pro-social manner, without weighing up the subjective costs (Montada, Dabert, & Schmitt, 1988). Caring means giving, whilst assurance that the other is needed is a form of taking. Happy partners are not put off by the costs involved in satisfying each other's needs. That is why it is not the difference between the costs and the pleasures partners prepare for each other, but the sum of those costs and pleasures that is an indicator of the success of the relationship (see the interpretation by Clark and Reis (1988) of the findings of Hays, 1985; see also Lujansky and Mikula, 1983).

If partners in economic relationships maximise their benefit and wish to act in accordance with the principle of reciprocity, they must record their outgoings (claims), but also record how many pleasures have been provided by the partner (liabilities). Partners in loving relationships orientate themselves by the needs of the other person, in order to please them. In extremely altruistic love relationships there would be no demand for reciprocity. The high intrinsic satisfaction resulting from the selfless favour would be sufficient attraction to keep on preparing pleasures for the partner. The receiving partner would similarly be prepared to dedicate themselves selflessly in order to satisfy their partner. Although neither partner thinks in terms of keeping accounts, both would prepare the maximum reward for each other. The observer of the interaction process who was expecting to see an exchange transaction could still find that the analogy of the shop was appropriate even in the absence of any book-keeping: if both parties selflessly give each other pleasures and receive pleasures, the observer might falsely assume that such pleasures were being offered with reference to or in response to pleasures offered by the other person. The observer would miss the point that motivation in this instance is intrinsic, not extrinsic.

If the process of interactions is analysed, especially the relationship between the reciprocally offered (although not necessarily exchanged) resources, then often a balance between give and take can be identified, both between acquaintances as well as in loving relationships. What one person offers is taken by the other. If in happy relationships both partners orientate themselves to the needs of the other person and no balance is sought, they nevertheless achieve a balance even though this may not have been set as a goal, if they remain aware of both claims and liabilities.

In the study by Kirchler and Hölzl (1996), investigations were conducted into profit orientation derived from exchange theory versus the altruistic orientation of partners in three types of relationship. It was predicted that altruism would be more marked in close relationships, and that in absolute terms more and more varied types of resources would be exchanged. The hypothesis ran that, when thinking about close relationships, people would find it easier to suggest ideas about resources that could be given than about ones that could be received. When imagining close relationships, participants would be more orientated towards altruistic behaviour, whilst as the degree of closeness reduced in the imagined relationship a more even balance between give and take was anticipated. The hypothesis was only confirmed in men: Male participants named more resources that could be given to their partner than ones that they could receive when imagining a romantic relationship. When they imagined a relationship with a work colleague, the situation was reversed and they named more resources that they could receive than give. In the female sample the hypothesis was not confirmed. It appears that men could afford the romance of giving "more easily" than women. Perhaps gender-specific differences in the results, and the more pragmatic loving style identified in the literature (Bierhoff, 1991; Hinde, 1997), can be traced back to socio-political necessities that are historically conditioned. Gender-specific differences in naming resources for a work relationship could be explained by the opportunities men and women enjoy in the employment market, where women still have to give more than men in order to be seen as being capable, whereas it is often automatically assumed that a man possesses the necessary skills and is capable (Kirchler, Buchleitner, & Wagner, 1996).

In summary, much research appears to indicate that the process of interaction in close relationships follows different rules from these in economic relationships. The more happy the partners are, the more likely it is that they will spontaneously act to please each other, and the less likely they are to subject their joint actions to the principles of doing business and to consider the costs of their actions. Egoistic desires diminish and are superseded by shared desires. Egoistic maximisation of benefits, which is taken as the "dominant strategy" of "homo oeconomicus"—economic man—is the exception rather than the rule.

CHAPTER FOUR

Decision-making

DISAGREEMENTS VERSUS DECISION-MAKING PROCESSES

Partners in close relationships are confronted with a variety of tasks. Alongside the everyday routine of activities at home and at work, and the regular routine of leisure activities, which do not require much conscious thought because they have become routine, decisions need to be taken which may be more or less complex. Partners have to choose between alternatives and to take decisions that require in-depth analysis, maintaining their viewpoint in deliberations and raising doubts before finally taking action. Alongside other tasks, economic and non-economic decisions mark out everyday life at home. Decision-making does not always happen without conflict. Opinions between the partners often differ at the start of a decision-making situation, and are a frequent source of arguments and sometimes of stressful conflicts.

If conflicts are to be recorded, we need to remind ourselves of the definition of conflict as more or less serious disagreements. In order to understand the dynamic of disagreements and "heated" conflicts which may finally lead to decisions, it is necessary to consider the relationship between the partners. Appreciation of the quality of the relationship is a precondition for proper understanding of the course and the development of controversial discussions. However, knowledge of the specific dynamic of conflict resolution is a necessary precondition for understanding the relationship between two people.

Conflicts can be understood as more or less clearly conscious disagreements or as discussions about partners' incongruent desires (for an overview of research into conflicts in close relationships, see Fincham and Beach, 1999). Whilst conflicts about the same topic can repeatedly attract the attention of the partners, be explored and then postponed, a disagreement is concluded by a decision. A decision that is conflict-rich can be drawn out of the stream of events on several occasions before a joint decision is eventually taken.

The intensity of conflicts can range from slight differences in the viewpoints of the partners to serious divergence over different goals and values, dissent from the wishes of one's partner, and determination to implement one's own point of view. Conflicts are unavoidable in close relationships. The focus of this study is the frequency of such conflicts, how intense they are, and how they are resolved. It is likely that in retrospective reports the frequency of conflicts is underestimated, because positive experiences are more desirable than negative ones, conflicts are experienced as being dissonant with the preservation of the relationship, and because conflict is socially undesirable and therefore is more likely to be omitted altogether than described in detail to an interviewer or in a questionnaire.

McGonagle, Kessler, and Schilling (1992) report that unpleasant disagreements are rare, occurring perhaps two or three times a month. Straus and Sweet (1992) found that conflicts were similarly rare. Against that, Burgess (1981) concludes that conflicts can occur daily, but depending on the quality of the relationship will occur at least once a week. Conflicts, understood as being non-corresponding opinions between partners, are also found to be frequent by Gottman (1994), Holmes (1989), Kelley et al. (1983b) and Surra and Longstreth (1990).

Statements about the frequency of conflicts in close relationships vary widely. In the literature about purchasing decisions in private households, it is assumed that most joint purchasing decisions are preceded by disagreements (Spiro, 1983), although there is no indication of how often purchasing decisions are taken together. If partners at home only talk with each other for somewhere between a few minutes to a maximum average of an hour a day (Kirchler, 1988a, c), then perhaps one should not expect, in absolute terms, a high number of conflicts to be recorded over a period of days, weeks or even months; the frequency of conflicts will only be high relative to the amount of time spent together.

Partners say different things about conflicts and often report the conflict situation completely differently, as was found by Klein and Milardo (1993). In 98% of cases, partners were found to have reported a shared conflict situation in such a way that it seemed that there had been no "dispute" between them. If partners have different opinions but are pursuing the same goals, they are often not aware of any conflict. They discuss their points of view, objectively as far as possible, and in the most favourable case they reach their shared goal. If asked, it is probable that couples would not describe this situation as a conflict. However, if different goals are being pursued and there are value conflicts, with partners wanting to convince each other or seeking to negotiate some advantage for themselves, then it is more likely that they will be aware of the conflict. At the start of a relationship, one might expect goal conflicts and value conflicts to arise more often than in relationships that have lasted for some years and have given the partners the opportunity to adapt their expectations and their preferences to each other. It is the case that young couples report more conflicts than older couples (Hinde, 1997).

TYPES OF DECISION-MAKING

Ferber (1973) starts his classification of decision-making in private households by looking at the content of the decision, and distinguishes in principle between financial or economic decisions and ones that are primarily non-financial. Financial decisions concern money management (budgeting for the available money, paying outstanding bills, etc.), savings (the proportion of money to be saved or spent), capital and investment management and expenditure. All other decisions (e.g. about the number of children, the division of leisure and work time, visits to friends and acquaintances) are primarily non-financial and concern work in the home and for a career, matters to do with the children, leisure activities and the relationship between the partners. In what follows, we shall focus mainly on economic decisions.

Although there is much research into expenditure, empirical studies have largely ignored management of capital and assets. For example, Hempel and Tucker (1980) make the criticism that all available information about the interaction behaviour of partners when solving problems of asset management was in the form of answers to simple questions, such as who handled outstanding bills and who arranged insurance. It may be an important finding that the level of joint income is a significant determinant in such questions; however, to date little research has been conducted into the role of men and women in handling these tasks (see Meier, Kirchler, & Hubert, 1999).

There is also a need for information about money management. Ferber and Lee (1974) report that at the start of a close relationship both partners decide jointly about payment of outstanding bills and how saved money is used. After a while the pattern of decision-making moves increasingly from being egalitarian to being matriarchal, with the woman being responsible for money management. This result was established over two decades ago. Nowadays it is thought that joint accounts are set up far less often, and that if two people do this, it is questionable whether both have the same level of access to the money earned. Schaninger and Buss (1986) demonstrate that in lasting partnerships the woman is accorded more say over decisions than in partnerships that later fall apart. Rosen and Granbois (1983) report that women in traditional partnerships had the final say. However, Heinemann (1987) found that unemployed women who reluctantly took on the role of home-maker surrendered control and the say over income and financial matters to their partner.

To date, there are also few psychological studies of savings in private households, or about use of loans and debt. The University of Tilburg in the

Netherlands is conducting a wide-ranging research project looking at savings behaviour. There are some results available which look at savings and life cycle (Wärneryd, 1995, 1999) and savings and debt (Webley, 1994).

Readiness to take out loans is on the increase generally. Engel, Blackwell, and Miniard (1993, p. 249) report on American statistics showing that 82% of the population think it is acceptable to borrow money to buy a car or to settle medical bills; 79% are in favour of taking out a loan to finance education and training; 19% are prepared to use credit to finance a hobby, and 5% believe that "the bank could pay" first even for the purchase of jewellery or furs. Young people in particular were relatively positive about the use of loans to finance new purchases. Looking at nine different areas of expenditure (buying a car, spending on hobbies, medical expenses, training, furniture, holidays, living expenses, paying gas, electricity or telephone bills, and jewellery or furs), 57% of those under 25 thought it was acceptable to take out a loan to fund expenditure. As age increased, the percentage of those positively disposed to taking out a loan fell: Calculated for age groups with a 10-year spread (25–34, 35–44, 45–54, 55–64, 65 and over), the percentages fell from 53% through 50%, 47%, and 45% down to 35%.

Taking out a loan, for example to buy a property, is completely sensible and desirable from an economic point of view. However, a loan is simply a different form of debt, which can lead to serious problems in the private household. In a study by Lea, Webley, and Levine (1993) involving three groups of people—those with no debts, those with small debts, and those with serious debts—it was found that personal debt correlated with the financial poverty of the person affected. People with low incomes are more likely to be in serious debt than those who earn more. Reasons for indebtedness were given as poverty and, less often, irresponsible purchases, inadequate budgeting of income, and other personal causes that were specific to the individual. Livingstone and Lunt (1992) researched differences between people without loan debts and those who were having to make loan repayments and found that older people were far less likely to be in debt than younger people, as well as people with a positive attitude towards taking out a loan, and also people who experienced consumption as a form of reward. The level of debt was dependent on financial, socio-demographic, and psychological variables, but was above all dependent on the level of income of the indebted person. Studies of attitudes to poverty show that lay opinion about financial debts rates individual reasons as the principal cause, so that being in debt is often seen as the result of irresponsible purchasing behaviour on the part of the person concerned (e.g. Roland-Lévy & Viaud, 1994; Walker, 1994).

The majority of empirical studies of financial decisions in multiple-person private households have been devoted to purchasing decisions. Detailed classification schemes have been put forward for the purpose. In economics, decisions about expenditure are most often divided up according to the nature of the goods being purchased. For example, Davis (1976) distinguishes between purchasing decisions for frequently needed goods and services, consumer durables, and other economic decisions. Tschammer-Osten (1979) distinguishes between purchases of: (a) products (e.g. food, heating fuel); (b) services (e.g. doctor or lawyer); (c) opportunities (stamps, entry tickets, shares); and (d) object systems (which are combinations of the first three categories). Kotler (1982) takes as his starting-point the period of use of the good in question and the purchasing habits of the consumer, which allows him to distinguish between the purchase of everyday consumer goods (daily items), consumer durables (items that satisfy higher needs), and services. Decisions about everyday items relate to goods in the form of objects, which are usually purchased regularly and consumed within a short period of time (e.g. food); decision-making in such instances is often brief and often automatic, from a psychological point of view. The purchase of these goods is directed by routine programmes. Consumer durables, satisfying higher needs, are similarly objects or material goods. However, they can be used repeatedly, are more expensive and are bought correspondingly less often (e.g. electrical products, a flat, or a car). When rarely used goods are bought, the family generally has no routine programme to direct the decision-making process, and often lengthy decision-making processes are required before a sensible choice can be made and existing disagreements between the family members are resolved "in a manner which does not harm the relationship". Decisions about the ordering of services refer to the purchase of activities or advantages (e.g. a taxi ride, or car repair). Such goods are not objects, but non-material values which often require a thorough examination of the quality and the reliability of the service provider.

Economic practitioners may be interested in a classification of purchasing decisions by goods acquired. However, the goods acquired cannot explain why decision-making processes take different courses. A psychologically usable classification must start from the different characteristics of those decisions. The basic psychological characteristics of decisions are: (a) the availability of cognitive scripts that direct the course of the decision; (b) the financial commitment; (c) the social visibility of the product or service; and (d) the changes that the decision implies for the people in the shared household (Kirchler, 1988b; Ruhfus, 1976). The more often a good is purchased and the less information needed to make a satisfactory choice, the more likely it is that cognitive scripts are available. Expensive goods are usually more thoroughly considered than cheaper goods; differentiated cognitive scripts are less often available and all those involved take part in the decision because it involves committing a considerable part of the joint financial budget. Where goods have a high additional use (such as having a high significance for the status of the household) alongside the principal use, their purchase affects all family members. The more people within the shared household who are affected by the decision, the more likely it is that they will join in the decision-making process and put forward their own interests.

There are different types of purchase—impulse buys, habitual purchases, and "genuine" purchasing decisions which have been arrived at by one person autonomously or by several people together. Which type of decision is made depends on whether or not there are cognitive scripts available, whether the financial outlay is large or small, whether the good available for selection is socially unimportant or carries symbolic value, and whether one or more family members are affected by the purchase (Katona, 1951; Ruhfus, 1976). Impulsive actions and habitual decisions may be observed frequently in the private household, particularly over the issue of expenditure on bills. Because these are usually dealt with by one person and require action in a compressed space of time, they are less informative than genuine purchasing decisions in the context of an analysis of decision-making processes.

When genuine decisions are being taken collectively and are not automatic, it is mostly implicitly assumed that the people involved in the private household will have different preferences, resulting in a conflict as defined by Deutsch (1973). Partners are concerned to discuss competing preferences, to think through the viewpoints, and to assert their view or to reach a compromise. According to Spiro (1983), around 88% of partners did in fact record considerable disagreements over the purchase of a durable good. It is, however, possible for decisions in private households to be reached without conflict. This is true above all for decisions about consumer durables, and for those products that belong to the domain of one or other partner in relationships with traditional gender roles.

Genuine decision-making situations can be divided up according to whether there is a conflict or whether the partners' goals and desires are in accord with each other (Davis, 1976). March and Simon (1958) distinguish between three different levels of conflict: (a) if both partners reconstruct reality in a similar way, so that they reach the same view as to the utility functions and they prefer the same goods, then there is no conflict; (b) if the partners perceive the attributes of the different goods available differently, then there is a probability issue which needs to be resolved; (c) if the partners have different views of what the goals are, then there is a genuine conflict. This conflict is more or less serious, depending on whether the disagreements are (d) confined to sub-goals or (e) concern the basic value concepts. Madden (1982) develops the models offered by Davis (1976) and March and Simon (1958) and arrives at a division on the basis of the awareness of conflict. If neither partner is aware of a conflict, then different

TABLE 4.1
Examples of different types of conflict

Probability conflict: You and your partner must finally buy a new car. You will use the car roughly equally often and you are already both agreed that it should not be too big, it should have low fuel consumption and it should be comfortable to drive. Two types of car are on the short-list: One of you prefers type A; this model has 55 brake horsepower, a top speed of 150 km/hour and uses little petrol. The other prefers type B; this car costs a little more than type A, but has a better performance (67 brake horsepower). Petrol consumption is comparable to type A.

Distributional conflict: You and your partner have jointly filled out a lottery ticket and have won a certain sum of money. With this money each of you would like to buy a luxury item. One of you would like to buy a particular item of clothing, e.g. a stylish jacket. The other would like to buy some sports equipment for themselves, maybe a new tennis racket or a pair of expensive running shoes. The amount won is not enough to buy both items.

Value conflict: You and your partner are planning your joint holiday and are looking through a brochure from a tour operator. Each of you has a preference, but in the course of the conversation it comes out that your wishes do not coincide. One of you would like to spend the holiday at the seaside, lying in the sun and lazing. The other would like to go into the mountains. He or she would be bored doing nothing, and would prefer an activity holiday. Although your travel goals are completely different, you are agreed that you want to spend the holiday together whatever happens.

Sources: Brandstätter, 1987; Kirchler, 1993a.

processes are set in motion than in those instances where one or both partners are aware of the extent of the conflict.

The classifications offered by Davis (1976), March and Simon (1958), and particularly Madden (1982) remind one of systems that are familiar from group research in social psychology, where a distinction is often drawn between tasks with a single correct solution (intellectual tasks or problems) and those with no verifiably correct solution (decisions). Brandstätter (1987) describes types of conflict with a single correct solution as probability conflicts and those with no verifiably correct solution as value conflicts; he contrasts these with tasks that generate dissent or helplessness in the group because of their pressures on distribution (distributional conflicts). This division seems applicable to decisions about expenditure as well as all other economic and non-economic decisions in the private household. Examples of the three types of conflict are shown in Table 4.1.

Value conflicts exist if there are fundamental differences in goals between the partners. Here the concern is not so much the resolution of probability issues, but of value concepts. Purchasing decisions present a value conflict if, for example, one partner wishes to buy certain fashionable items whilst the other rejects the purchase, not on the grounds of the quality of the product but because they have fundamental doubts, e.g. about the power of the consumer industry to promote illusions. In this instance the partners have fundamental differences with regard to the symbolic power of the product. Value conflicts are genuine conflict situations, in which partners try to convince each other of the advantages of their own point of view, using tactics to convince and influence each other.

Probability conflicts relate to judgements about true objective contents and possibilities for making something happen. A judgement as to the probabilities or the material facts is necessary if partners agree about the social significance of an item and, for example, are agreed that they want a fashionable item but are finding the decision difficult because they rate the various alternative products differently in terms of quality, or because they have different views on the price–utility relationship. In this situation, it is not really possible to speak of a conflict in the negative sense of the word. The partners are not seeking to influence each other, but are having an objective disagreement in which the crucial elements are items of information, and normative pressure is kept to the background.

A distributional conflict exists if the discussion revolves around the division of costs and benefits. Even if both partners are convinced that a particular product represents the optimal alternative and is desirable, so that there is no value conflict, one partner may still argue against the purchase on the grounds that the product largely benefits the other partner or would mainly be used by them. There is a distributional problem if the costs and benefits of a decision are distributed asymmetrically. The partners will then try to reach a compromise using their negotiating skills.

In the same way as has been indicated for types of conflict, it is possible to categorise decision-making in private households according to the diagram in Fig. 4.1. Apart from the fact that decisions hardly ever fall wholly within one type of conflict, but instead contain aspects of two or all three conflict types to varying degrees, it should also be remembered that decisions are of course processes. This implies that a conflict of one type can shift into a different type of conflict in the course of the problem being worked through. If, for example, discussions initially revolve around value issues and a solution is found, then the decision-making process may still continue; the partners may negotiate over asymmetrical distribution of benefits, for example. Both partners may, for example, agree over a purchasing decision to buy a particular item of clothing even though it only benefits one partner. In subsequent decisions this overriding benefit for one partner could represent a kind of benefit debt towards the other partner. The benefit debts that are due could represent a kind of outstanding loan taken out by one partner, so that this loan could be "repaid" by moving towards the views of the other partner in a subsequent decision. In this instance the decision-making would have mutated from an initial value conflict into a distributional conflict, if the discussion had moved on from the purchase of the item

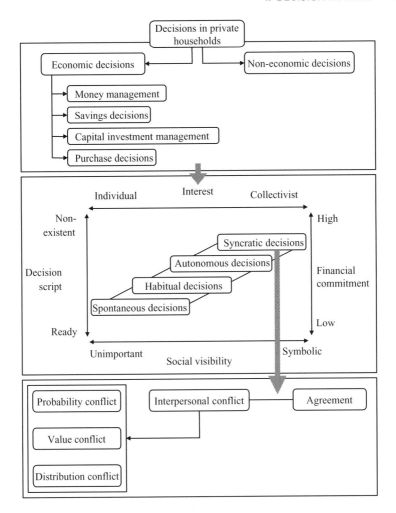

Figure 4.1 Classification of decisions and disagreements (Kirchler, 1989).

of clothing to revolve around the distribution of benefit and the benefit debt it created.

Depending on the type of task and the characteristics of the relationship, different patterns of decision-making are to be expected. In happy partnerships, where the partners often share the same values, there may be just as many conflict situations as in disharmonious relationships, but these will more often be probability issues rather than value issues. Happy partners will discuss objectively with each other more often than unhappy partners, and will try to influence each other or to persuade each other less often.

Moreover, happy partners involved in distributional conflicts will seek to maximise the shared interest, whilst unhappy partners will try to extend their own egoistic advantage (Kirchler, 1993a, b).

MODELS OF DECISION-MAKING

Decision-making processes are described according to various models which vary from context to context, being usually either normative or descriptive. Normative models map out a logical-rational decision-making process, whereas descriptive models try to describe how decisions taken by individuals or groups are actually arrived at.

In economics, and later in psychology and other social sciences, choice situations and decision-making situations are researched from the perspective of rationality and the maximisation of utility. In this field, the leading model is that of "homo oeconomicus"—economic man—which assumes that people are informed about the possible options available to them, perceive differences between those options and can evaluate their preferences accordingly before finally deciding on the option that offers the greatest personal utility. This model is a maximisation model, which simulates how an idealised individual makes, or should make, optimal decisions.

Decisions have to be made if a discrepancy is identified between a current state of affairs and a desired state, and if there are various ways of moving from one to the other. Normative decision-making models break down the decision-making process into a series of steps that follow on from one another, before finally arriving inevitably at a desired decision outcome. Those making a decision have a clear goal in mind, not two or more possibly incompatible goals. The route from the current state of affairs to the goal proceeds via logically ordered steps, from perception of a critical situation, via definition of criteria for making the decision, prioritising of the criteria and evaluation of the available options, to making a selection. Those making the decision proceed sequentially along this route. They have clear and stable preferences, have complete knowledge about the available alternatives, and are able to isolate all relevant criteria for making the decision. Normative decision-making models relate to the rationality of the process which, however, does not always need to lead to the optimal solution.

Although normative decision-making models appear rational and applicable in many situations, individual decisions and group decisions in everyday situations deviate from this pattern. Decisions are often taken over-quickly, because people are short of time, and in retrospect the decision-makers justify their actions, "rationalising" after the event. Decision-making situations are often complex, with the amount of information being more than one person is capable of dealing with, and the pressure of time calling for quick decisions on the basis of few criteria.

Normative decision-making models attempt to describe decisions in close relationships, working groups and organisations in such a way as to match what is actually observable. March and his colleagues (e.g. March & Shapira, 1992, p. 279) describe decisions in organisations as a more or less chance succession of problems and solutions. This model, and also the model of Braybrooke and Lindblom (1963; Lindblom, 1959, 1979), can also be applied to decision-making in private households. Braybrooke and Lindblom describe decisions in politics as step-by-step, incremental processes or as "muddling through". The more complex the task, the less likely it is that rational strategies and the so-called "root-method" will be applied. Political decisions, and also decisions in commercial businesses and in the private household, are all much more comparable with each other than with well-controlled, simply structured tasks in clearly defined work settings. Because several other tasks are being dealt with at the same time as a decision is made, the situation in which the decision is made is often in itself complex. In complex situations where time is essential, inappropriate (i.e. non-rational) efforts are often made to overcome the issue: for example, comprehensive analysis might be dispensed with, or there may be a readiness to experiment with unsystematic and illogical attempts at a solution, to restrict the focus to smaller problems that are more easily solved, to concentrate on a few aspects of the overall task, or to imitate past solutions and seek to operate within a known framework.

In politics, and in private households too (as shown by Park, 1982), the process of arriving at a decision can be described as incremental, and may be compared to walking through a swamp where there is a danger that the next step may be fatal. In complex situations, small steps forward are taken and, "if the ground holds", the next step forward is taken. If the consequences of an action are negative, if the ground does not hold, then a step is taken to the right or the left. Sometimes it may even be necessary to take a step backwards. The complex interactions of various variables, whether changed or unchanged, cannot always be foreseen because consequences often cannot be predicted: this is why an incremental approach is adopted. The direction of the altered course is pursued until such time as a negative consequence arises. The decision-making teams feel their way from one "bank of the swamp" to the other, eventually arriving at the solution to the problem via a series of small steps.

Park (1982) demonstrates that partners in a shared home do not pursue rational models that aim to maximise utility, because their limited capacity to process information means that they are not in a position to isolate the most important and the most prominent dimensions of the product alternatives on offer for both themselves and their partner. They would be hopelessly over-stretched if they had to judge their partner's preferences and know their selection criteria. Partners may be aware of some attributes that the other considers relevant, but they can hardly know the value and the benefit that is attached to the relevant attributes. They would find it difficult to register and to process correctly the changes in value in the course of the decision-making process, and they cannot understand the rules by which attributes are added together and composed into an index of benefits. Since it is questionable whether individuals apply strategies to maximise utility in everyday decision-making, it is far more debatable whether partners can put themselves in the position of the other partner so as to arrive at a partially correct understanding of their analysis and synthesis of the information available, and then reach a joint decision.

For his study, Park (1982) interviewed 48 couples who were intending to buy a house and for each interviewee he constructed a decision matrix, following Bettman's (1979) model. The matrix map represents a decision-making structure based on attributes that are subjectively relevant, and those of lesser importance. For example, an interviewee might put forward the following considerations: He or she is looking for a house that costs less than one million Euro and is in a particular area. It must have at least five bedrooms and a cellar, although four bedrooms would be adequate if the house possesses several other desirable attributes. The cellar is not essential if the house has a garage. The interviewee would like to have a garden, but this is not a critical factor and other attributes could compensate for the absence of a garden. Once the criteria for the decision have been established, attributes are assessed as to whether they meet the basic criteria for a purchase (the rejection-inducing dimension), whether they offer an advantage (the relative preference dimension) or whether they can be compensated for by other attributes (the trade-off dimension). This process gives rise to a decision matrix.

Every interviewee was asked about their plans regarding the decision before they collected information, immediately after they had collected information, and again once the house had been bought. Although the partners themselves thought that they had realised plans that had been largely identical, there was little congruence between plans. "Perfect congruence", defined as a high-proportion match between the total number of attributes that appeared in the matrices and the number of relevant and exchangeable attributes named by both partners, was actually at the level of 25% during the phase of searching for information. Partial congruence, defined as a proportional match between the total number of attributes indicated by the partners and the number of elements indicated as relevant in both plans, stood at 41%. Even after the phase of collecting information and after the decision to purchase was made, congruence levels were low (between 30% and 47%). The plans agreed most closely when the dimensions considered were objectively measurable, such as price, size, etc. When sub-jective dimensions were compared, such as aesthetic appearance, interior furnishing, resale value, etc., the congruence levels were low.

Apart from the difference in decision matrices, Park (1982) also found that partners could not reliably provide information as to who had influenced whom with regard to particular attributes. In 49% of cases, interviewees indicated that they did not know who had influenced whom. Where differences of influence were reported, then these conformed to con-ventional clichés regarding gender roles. This evidence points to rational-isation in retrospect rather than a conscious processing of information and rational choices.

How did the partners reach a decision if they were neither agreed about what had happened during their conversations, nor were able to adapt their decision matrices to each other in the course of the interactions? Because rational decision-making models presuppose that those making the decision know how they arrive at an order of preferences, in actual decision-making processes criteria other than rational criteria must come into play. In summary, Park (1982) believes that these results go against the "synoptic ideal" or the theory of rationality, and they suggest that close partners "muddle through" decisions rather than proceeding with them analytically, rationally, and seeking to maximise utility.

In the literature on purchasing decisions in private households, it is sometimes assumed that decisions have a clearly definable beginning and an identifiable end, and that the decision-making process runs its course step-by-step along the way. A series of models for purchasing decisions that follow these assumptions has been published in the literature. It was certainly not assumed that these models reliably described reality, but they proved useful in the study of decisions within the family. Their advantage lies in the fact that they offer a starting-point for scientific research, and a variety of questions for empirical study can be derived from them.

Starting from these purchasing decision models, what follows is a comprehensive model for economic and non-economic decisions between two people. This model is based on a purchasing decision model developed by Kirchler (1989) on the basis of models by Corfman (1985), Pollay (1968), Sheth (1974), and Scanzoni and Polonko (1980). Fig. 4.2 shows the com-plete model, which should serve as a framework for the formulation of various research questions.

The starting-point for decisions is the wishes or needs of one or both partners, which are prompted by stimuli in the personal sphere. Decisions about the purchase or the non-purchase of a particular good are often provoked by what is being offered in the market. If particular needs require satisfying, the information is collected about the available alternatives that promise to satisfy those needs. A desire can either be satisfied immediately,

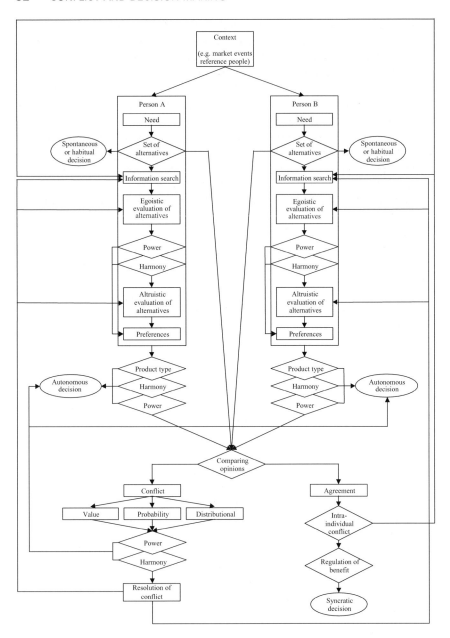

Figure 4.2 Descriptive model of joint decision-making (Kirchler, 1989).

without information being collected and without a lengthy decision-making process (a spontaneous purchasing decision), or can take place routinely with the decision-making following a habitual pattern (a habitual decision). Other factors affecting the speed with which the desire is satisfied are: the level of costs involved; whether one or more people are affected; whether the decision has consequences in terms of social visibility; and whether it involves short-term or longer-term changes.

If a rarely activated desire is involved, a genuine decision-making process is set in train. The partner who has the desire, for example for a particular good, can immediately communicate that desire to the other partner to gauge their attitude and to seek their help in searching for information and making the choice. The desire can also be expressed once information has been collected about the various alternatives and an individual has already made their pre-selection. The active partner—the person who is expressing the desire—can gather information about alternatives and then either share this information with their partner, or can autonomously decide without prior discussion with their partner.

Autonomous decisions, unlike individual decisions, do not occur completely independently of the passive partner—the partner who does not have the desire. The active partner will evaluate the benefit of the decision for their partner and their level of agreement with the decision (perhaps the purchase of a good), and will take account of this in reaching the decision.

Whether a spontaneous, habitual, autonomous or joint decision comes about is largely dependent on the clarity and the strength of the desire, on the goal that is to be realised by the decision, on the power relationships in the partnership and on the quality of the relationship. The less expensive, the less socially noticeable, the more mundane and the simpler the set of alternatives from which a choice is to be made, the less likely it is that a joint decision will be taken. There is a similarly low probability of a joint decision if the active partner wields the greater power in the relationship and if the quality of the relationship is poor, or if a decision is being taken in a traditionally orientated relationship with a strict gender role division and the decision relates to an area that is controlled by the active partner.

If no impulsive or habitual or autonomous decision is taken, then a decision process between the partners begins which starts with the desire phase if a need is identified, or with the information-gathering or the choice phase. If one or both partners have gathered information about possible alternatives and the alternatives have been evaluated to see how well they will meet the needs, then satisfaction with the alternatives is assessed and a choice is made. The interests and the level of information of the partners may be different during this process, and conflict results.

In conflict situations, most often two goals are presented simultaneously. On the one hand it can be assumed that people would want to satisfy their egoistic needs, but on the other the quality of the relationship should not suffer as a result. Subjective preferences are not simply the result of individual desires. In harmonious relationships in particular, the partners do not "do their sums" on their own. When considering the realisation of a desire, they take into account the consequences for the other partner and seek to maximise the joint benefit. The subjective preferences of one partner are thus essentially dependent to a greater or lesser degree on the assumed preferences of the other partner. If loose ties exist between the interaction partners, then the benefits for the other partner are often ignored when a partner calculates his or her own preferences.

The higher the satisfaction with the relationship, the more likely it will be that partners in the interaction processes will be guided by the love principle and will give equal, if not greater weight to the anticipated satisfaction of their partner with the product than to their own satisfaction. In credit or exchange relationships, weight is given either to one's own satisfaction or to that of the partner, depending on whether the partner is owed or owes something. In egoistic relationships only one's own satisfaction is considered.

For partners to know what each other's preferences are, they have to discuss the matter. In arduous, often stubborn discussions an attempt is made to influence the divergent viewpoints of the other side and thus arrive at a joint decision. The influence tactics for swaying the other's preferences vary according to whether the conflict involves an assessment of probabilities (objective judgements), value issues, or the distribution of pleasures. They can entail normative or objective techniques, attempting to persuade the partner to give way through promises, or intimidating the partner through threats. The influence tactics employed vary according to the type of conflict, the quality of the relationship and the imbalance of power between the two (Kirchler, 1993a, b).

If the partners manage to resolve the conflict and reach agreement, the decision-making process is still not over; at this point, a check is made to see whether the realisation of a decision implies asymmetries of influence or of benefits. If one partner has dominated the decision, then that partner incurs influence debts and the pressure on that partner increases to give way to the other partner in the next decision-making situation. If one partner benefits more from an action than the other, then benefit debts can arise. If, for example, one partner wants to buy an expensive item of clothing, he or she will seek the consent of the other partner. If the choice of the partner coincides with the taste of the other and the latter agrees to the purchase, the purchase is made. Although both partners have decided on the same alternative from the range of clothing on offer, this purchase results in benefit debts for the partner who will wear the item of clothing. Depending on the internal rules within the relationship for regulating differences in overall benefit, the other partner can then expect to enjoy the agreement of his or her partner when they next want to make a purchase, or in another decision-making situation. A decision is not complete until the partners have agreed on whether it results in an asymmetrical distribution of benefits, and how this should be dealt with.

The concept of benefit debts, or "utility debts", plays a central role in Pollay's (1968) model of purchasing decisions. He assumes that the utility or benefit of a good is a function of the strength of need for that good experienced by a partner, and of the frequency of use and the anticipated degree of satisfaction. In well-functioning relationships, the presumed satisfaction of the partner is also part of the calculations. If there are differences of opinion, the situation is dominated by the partner who enjoys higher status, who is more affected by the decision and its consequences, and who has the higher benefit debt. By introducing the concept of benefit debt, Pollay emphasises the temporal matrix of decisions and encourages us to view decisions as a matrix of events. The partner who has gained a concession in the past from the other partner has incurred a benefit debt which he or she will have to repay. The egoistic benefit from a decision and the concessions made in a decision-making situation must be repaid at a later stage, fully in accordance with exchange theory. Thus, for example, if one partner has asserted his will in one situation, it is to be expected that he will give way to his partner in a future decision. If one time he decides where they will go on holiday, it is fair that she makes the next decision about holidays, or about some other matter.

Influence debts and benefit debts may often form the basis for arguments in negotiations: if one partner is pursuing a specific goal whilst the other prefers a different alternative, then one partner can assert the right to take a decision because the other partner has had the final say in previous decision-making situations. Alternatively, one partner might offer to accept the agreement of the other partner in the current situation in return for a concession to be made in a future situation.

Influence debts and benefit debts are recorded in an "imaginary account". In theory, the way in which the debt is recorded is entirely dependent on the quality of the relationship and the balance of power within it. Depending on whether interaction processes are regulated according to the egoism principle, the equity principle, the credit principle, or the love principle, influence debts and benefit debts will be treated differently:

(a)   If the partnership resembles a relationship between acquaintances and there is a dominance imbalance towards the man or the woman, so that the relationship can be said to operate according to the egoism model, then he or she will decide when and how influence debts and benefit debts are settled. The stronger partner can override the imaginary account of influence and benefit debts, and the weaker partner must give in. Reflecting the power structure, the dominant partner has influence both over decisions and over regulation of the account of influence and benefit debts.

(b) If the quality of the relationship is poor, but there is an equal power distribution, then interaction with the partner takes place along the lines set out in exchange theory (the equity principle). The benefit that the other partner receives in a particular decision-making situation must be repaid directly. If one partner has had the say in one decision or benefited from the decision, then it will be the other partner's turn in the next conflict situation.

(c) If the relationship is like that between two trusting business partners or friends, then the partners operate according to the credit principle. Once the partners have interacted with each other over a long period of time and trust one another, differences in influence and benefit can continue to exist over a long period. In the course of time a balance is sought.

(d) The closer and more harmonious the relationship, the more altruistically the partners behave towards each other. Individual maximisation of profit gives way to altruistic profit maximisation. Each partner seeks to offer pleasures to the other, without expecting a reciprocal gesture. No account is taken of the balance of benefit in a conflict situation, because the pleasure enjoyed by the partner carries more weight than the satisfaction that would result if one's own most preferred option were chosen in making the decision. Demands, similarly, are not "entered into the accounts" either. There is no requirement to ensure an immediate or an eventual balance of influence or benefit debts which could theoretically be established. The more the exchange model mutates via the credit model into the love model, the more a win–win situation develops where a benefit for one partner is also a benefit for the other. In this situation the concept of a "benefit account" serves little purpose, since both partners achieve benefits and there is no asymmetry.

If there is agreement over influence debts and benefit debts, then there are no further obstacles to a final decision and the decision-making process can be considered at an end, apart from a post-decision phase—where often considerable effort is expended on gathering further information about the alternative decisions in order to clear up cognitive dissonance. Following a decision, once a choice has been made, individuals or groups are no longer in conflict over a decision. In order to reduce any doubts about the decision or the opportunity costs that have been incurred through the rejection of other alternatives, partners may deploy various mechanisms. Dissonance effects are marked to varying degrees, depending on the number of possible alternatives from which a choice was made, the similarities between the alternatives, the importance of the decision and the relative differences between the alternatives. According to Festinger (1957), dissonance following a decision can be reduced if the decision taken is cancelled or if the advantages of the alternative selected and the disadvantages of the other alternatives are particularly emphasised. The latter course is often followed.

CHAPTER FIVE

Methods for Studying Decision-making

In the social sciences, various methods are employed to record the phenomena that are the focus of study. Von Rosenstiel (1992) divides the known procedural methods on the basis of the activities of the researcher, the strategy employed, and the research location. The activities of researchers could be to record introspectively their own experiences, or involve oral or written questioning of participants in studies, or observation of behaviour or behavioural outcomes of participants. Research strategies range from experimental test projects through quasi-experimental designs to unsystematic recording of events that appear interesting or relevant. Research can be conducted either in the laboratory or in the natural environment. Depending on the problem being investigated, either the controllable environment of the laboratory setting with its artificial triggers will be chosen as the research location, or if ecological validity (Brunswick, 1949) is required, the natural life context will be preferred.

If decisions taken by two or more people are being studied, either as processes or as outcomes of decision-making processes, then all the above procedures could be applied, especially the techniques that relate to group research. Research methods such as experimental and quasi-experimental designs could be developed and observational studies conducted with couples and children in the laboratory, or observational procedures and interview techniques could be applied in the natural environment. Because it is not always easy to involve couples and their children in research projects, attempts could be made to go beyond the usual research techniques of social science. Results from experimental small group research should be examined for their validity for family or family-like settings, so that, if appropriate, these findings could be extrapolated for people in close relationships and in the private household. Interviewing all members of a close group can be demanding, so it may be considered adequate to let one person in the group provide information about the whole group.

Critical worries about traditional techniques lead smoothly into the discussions of a group of well-known researchers into decisions within households. In a workshop of the Association for Consumer Research in 1989, the limits of traditional procedures were criticised. The researchers called for longitudinal studies in which all people living in a shared household were researched while decision-making processes took place or immediately afterwards, so that the memories of events were still fresh (Burns & Gentry, 1990). As a further example, Corfman (1990) criticises the practice of interviewing only one partner about events in the home. It has long been confirmed that people misinterpret the position taken by the other partner to a considerable degree and that they would rather speak about themselves than their partner. Experimental studies looking at the behaviour of groups of people in the laboratory have found that it is mostly quite different from the behavioural dynamic that develops in the private home. Although laboratory research enables close analysis of phenomena, these do not reflect the true focus of study—which is decision-making processes in the private sphere—for several reasons: the time in which the decision is taken, the isolation of the problem from the other tasks that are ongoing at the same time, the assumption that problems would be solved at home whereas in actual fact they often "swim past" in the stream of everyday events without anyone "fishing them out", the pressure to give a good impression that is generated by the presence of an external observer, and other characteristics of the laboratory context. Tansuhaj and Foxman (1990) bemoan the way children are left out of research into families. Having moved from the study of one person to the interviewing and observation of dyads or pairs, research must now take the next step and acknowledge triads. Gentry, Stoltman, and Coulson (1990) present simulation games for research into events in the home, although even simulations are not free from the charge of the unnaturalness of the situation. Shanteau and Troutman (1990) demand that more attention should be paid to decision-making processes and put forward the argument that disputes between partners over a probability issue and the step-by-step change in their points of view can be studied using the tradition of Anderson's (1982) theory of information integration. Vankatesh (1990), whilst acknowledging the demands of a longitudinal study, calls for just such a study of decision-making in the family context with reference to changes over time.

At the workshop, issues of false sources and general problems were voiced which deserve consideration when seeking to study decision-making in close relationships and which are associated with observation in the laboratory or in the natural environment. The lack of interview techniques requiring the recall and evaluation of past experiences was noted, and diary research methods were presented, which offer a number of advantages over traditional procedures but which require a great deal of effort in keeping them.

OBSERVATION IN THE LABORATORY AND IN PRIVATE SETTINGS

Couples and their children can be observed in their natural life context or be invited into the laboratory for observation. However, it is extraordinarily difficult to persuade family groups to come into the laboratory to conduct an argument about how an imaginary sum of money is to be spent or to have a serious disagreement over some other matter. Some workers have therefore considered whether findings from small group research can be extrapolated to cover close relationships. A further argument in support of this approach is the fact that when partners are asked to produce natural everyday family life in front of the cameras in their home setting, the data that are recorded are often unproductively "smooth" and without incident.

Efforts to draw parallels between ad hoc small groups and partners in close relationships, which intensified throughout the 1970s, ultimately proved unsuccessful. In close relationships, processes develop that are unique. By contrast, the people in small groups acted fairly independently of one another. Typically, small groups were mainly observed in the laboratory, and were ad hoc acquaintances who had only recently met. These volunteers were asked to perform a task that was neither particularly interesting nor particularly challenging. Because these participants had neither a shared past nor the prospect of a shared future in front of them, there was no reason for them to show particular commitment to the joint task and the interactions were at best an ordered series of actions. By contrast, in close relationships complex patterns of interaction can develop over a short period of time which can be difficult for an external observer to decipher.

After the results obtained from ad hoc groups were shown to be only applicable to close relationships in exceptional instances, and faced with the fact that research into close relationships would require exceptionally expensive research, an attempt was made to create artificial or synthetic families and to observe them solving various tasks (Waxler & Mishler, 1970). Synthetic families are triads of strangers consisting of a man, a woman, and a younger person, and comparable with a traditional family in terms of age and gender. Although the structural characteristics of synthetic and natural families are similar, the artificial group lacks the most essential characteristics: the shared history and shared future, and all those characteristics that can develop over a period of time, such as trust, reciprocal dependence, and intimacy. Ad hoc groups and synthetic families are like a "good-looking car with no engine" (Kemp, 1970, p. 30) when compared to partners in close relationships. Because close relationships have little in common with ad hoc acquaintances, for several decades there has been a need for intensive scientific study of close or intimate relationships as groups.

This demand has not yet been satisfied, either by research into ad hoc groups or even by research that has "paired off" the participants into groups, mainly dyads. Often it is students, mostly drawn from the social science disciplines and needing to collect "credits" for their high school course, who are put into groups. By manipulating similarities in attitudes and sympathies between the participants, friendship groups are created whose behaviour is deemed to correspond to that of partners in close relationships. Aron et al. presented a new technique in 1997 that was designed to create close relationships under laboratory conditions. By manipulating similarities in attitudes and values, students were induced to like one another; for example, people who did not know one another were told that the laboratory partner had similar attitudes on student dress codes, similar smoking habits, etc. In fact, it has been proven that similarities can be used to generate sympathy and to influence the negotiating behaviour of partners (Cialdini, 1993), even if it is not likely that this would create the basis for even the rudiments of a long-term relationship. Aron et al. (1997) report that 75% of their synthetic couples had a further meeting outside the laboratory; 35% undertook an activity together and 37% sat together in class. However, caution is advised here, because—as the authors themselves note—the attachment between the partners, reciprocal dependence, loyalty, even a minimal shared history and attachment, were completely absent. Students are a wonderful source of data, but how far can their interaction patterns be applied to close relationships, even if they like each other? Even student couples who have been dating for several months hardly offer a suitable sample from which to generalise about long-term relationships. Nevertheless, psychological journals that devote themselves to close relationships are full of work based on findings from student groups. The theoretical concepts that are supposed to explain long-term relationships are, in an unacceptable fashion, tested either on experimentally created relationships or on student couples who have only been together for a few months. It is a simple enough matter to create sympathy under laboratory conditions and to find that the partners in these relationships like one another. In young partnerships the stage of being in love lasts for quite a while. However, long-term relationships are kept going not only by feelings of sympathy, liking, or being in love, but by a mature feeling of reciprocal love which guarantees the stability of the relationship even when there is a current conflict situation. It is this that allows the conflict to be played out with full force.

The study of close relationships cannot be satisfactorily concluded using findings from ad hoc groups or synthetic families, nor with the results of interviews with students who are in love or student couples who have been living together for a few months. If the main focus is to be on long-term relationships, then observational studies and interviews must be directed towards partners in such relationships.

The specific characteristics of close relationships demand the development of adequate procedures to study them. Account needs to be taken of the fact that even today many aspects of the intimate sphere are taboo areas (Baxter & Wilmot, 1985). The degree of emotional interdependence, the intensity of feelings, the intimacy between the partners and the secret codes of communication they have developed over the course of time are "protected data", which remain hidden from observers. On the one hand the techniques are lacking to uncover this hidden information, and on the other hand those being studied will themselves withhold or disguise information. The presence of strangers, be it inquisitive scientists or all-seeing cameras, can result in significant changes in the phenomenon being researched. The public nature of the research, apparent in the laboratory context but generated equally by cameras or researchers in the home, can lead to either a dulling or a simplification of emotions. As is put forward in the theory of objective self-awareness by Duval and Wicklund (1972), the presence of a mirror, cameras or even observers draws the attention of subjects onto themselves. Their behaviour becomes more compatible with current norms, is aimed at leaving a good impression, and they tend to behave in a consistent manner. In situations of objective self-awareness, people care about how they are seen by other people, conform more readily to social rules and exercise a strategic control over their interactions. For example, Gottman (1979) found that married couples at home communicate far more negatively with one another, with differences between happy and unhappy couples much more evident than in the laboratory, where people know that they are being observed, and so studiously control their behaviour and feel obliged to act politely towards each other in order to leave a good impression.

In the artificiality of the laboratory, the variables being studied can usually be controlled to a reasonably satisfactory degree. Laboratory experiments may be valuable in testing theoretical predictions. When seeking to describe decisions between partners in close relationships, however, the loss of ecological validity involved in a laboratory experiment is unacceptable. In everyday life, decision-making processes take a different course to those in the laboratory, where a task is presented to be solved. Observational studies must take into account that in the natural setting a variety of joint activities are going on between the partners, running at the same time and not in sequence, and that these are often interrupted by events that suddenly intrude. The isolation and observation of a limited aspect always involves a reduction in complexity and therefore a change in the reality of the private situation. In experimental small groups, and sometimes in groups within business organisations, members will exclusively discuss a particular problem. In the private household, this happens at best only as an exception: decisions, even those that are important and have long-term implications, are embedded in everyday matters and can only be properly understood if activities in the home are recorded in full.

Ecological validity is also required because partners tend to "jump" from one task to another, postponing difficult problems and hoping that solutions will "present themselves", because there are often a multiplicity of tasks which are rarely clearly formulated. Once started, discussions are broken off because another problem forces its way to the fore, are postponed, and are often continued at inappropriate times. The partner who is little affected by a particular matter may, for example, agree to the desire of the other partner in return for agreement with his preference in another matter. It would not be appropriate to study the one matter in isolation from the other (Weick, 1971).

When interaction processes are observed and analysed, the partners are often asked to perform a task in front of the cameras. In doing so, it is implicitly assumed that close relationships are principally task-orientated. Everyday experience shows us unmistakably, however, that alongside objective goals there is an attempt to preserve or to improve the existing emotional climate. In lasting close relationships, emotional costs carry more weight than rational–objective solutions. In the laboratory, or in the natural environment once it is opened up to public scrutiny, the situation is simplified: task orientation is brought to the fore, and feelings and their consequences for the quality of the relationship are suppressed.

The observation of interaction processes is set about with further deficiencies. The advantages, such allowing the dynamics to be recorded and external observers creating a common frame of reference for evaluation purposes, must be set against the disadvantages, which diminish the value of the findings. Apart from the fact that an isolated problem is discussed over an extremely short period of time, the task set often has minimal significance for those being observed. If the task is without significance, it would be surprising if the partners "put special effort" into it (Miller & Boster, 1988). What is important at home, and requires time, effort or money, can unfold only in a rudimentary fashion in front of the cameras.

There has been much criticism of observational techniques, but it would be inappropriate to condemn as wholly unusable all the procedures that have been applied to date to research close relationships. Some attempts are highly inventive and, at least in their planning, overcome problems of anonymity and ecological validity. However, they have not been realised successfully so far. Webb (1978) describes a procedure that invades the private sphere and could therefore offer a guarantee of ecological validity: tape and video recorders could be set up in different houses in such a way that the recording was triggered whenever someone close to the recorder began to speak or to move. If there were no observers in the private household to get in the way of these fragile spontaneous events, it would be possible to record conversations and to film people. But how, once the ethical questions involved have been answered, would one begin to evaluate the mass of data produced? And how could it be guaranteed that observers would correctly understand and interpret particular gestures and meaningful symbols, which partners in long-term relationships have developed and use to communicate with each other in interaction processes because they can be decoded by the receiver? Vetere and Gale (1987) believe that an observer could live for a period with the participating couple in the shared home and could make careful observations. After a period of acclimatising to the strange guest, who would then become "one of the family", the partners and their children would react spontaneously and naturally.

INTERVIEW TECHNIQUES

To study everyday events in close relationships, adequate methods of observation and interviewing are required. It is also necessary to study the appropriate group of people, i.e. partners living together in lasting relationships. Particularly in studies of purchasing behaviour in private households, mainly conducted by market research institutes, interviews are mainly conducted with one partner, occasionally with both and rarely also with children, asking about a specific area of expenditure. Events in the home have to be remembered and recounted. In researching shared everyday life, both observation procedures and interview techniques are often inadequate (e.g. Clark & Reis, 1988; Kirchler, 1989; Miller & Boster, 1988; Zelditch, 1971).

If partners are asked to recount their shared experiences, their accounts often differ markedly. The differences are partly caused by the difficulty of recalling and "reconstructing" mundane events, and partly because people distort their account to bolster their own self-esteem (e.g. de Dreu, Nauta, & Van de Vliert, 1995). Smith, Leffingwell, and Ptacek (1999) suspect that information recalled by people about their experiences is not valid because experiences are encoded in an incomplete or distorted fashion, details are forgotten and memory recall is affected by a tendency to portray oneself in a better light, a tendency to conform to notions of social desirability and social stereotypes, etc. They researched the congruence between memories of coping behaviours in stress situations and information that was recorded by participants on a daily basis, and found that less than a quarter of the information could be matched.

Schütz (1999) interviewed 25 couples separately about shared conflicts and found that in each case the other partner was blamed for initiating the conflict: Participants reported that the other partner began the argument and behaved in a negative manner. The partner who criticises the other often has the feeling that the argument is not over, whereas the partner who initiates the argument often believes that the problem has been solved once the conflict is resolved.

When devising sets of questions to be asked about the private household, consideration must be given as to who will be asked to provide information, which experiences should be reported and how reliable the interviewees may be. The form of the questions, and the suggested answers, may also influence the data obtained.

In earlier studies, it was common to ask one person to provide information about everyday events, and for interviews conducted in the home this was usually the woman. Their interpretation of shared activities was taken to be valid and reliable, based on the assumption either that all those involved (usually husband and wife in household surveys) shared the same attitudes towards the problem being raised, or that one partner both knows and can accurately report the views of the other partner. It is assumed that close relationships can be reduced to a single person providing information about everything that is going on in the shared home. A series of studies have shown that reconstruction of a shared reality varies considerably, both between adults and between adults and children. One partner can only offer their version of shared experiences, not the reality as perceived and reconstructed by all.

Kim and Lee (1997, p. 319) researched information from fathers, mothers, and children about joint purchases and found considerable differences in the information obtained. The authors attribute this to perceptual differences between individuals as well as chance and systematic measurement errors:

> Multiple-respondent single item data remain highly vulnerable to unreliability and invalidity due to frequent perceptual discrepancies among family members. This is because discrepancies in family members' perceptions of a family phenomenon reflect both random and systematic measurement errors: to present an unbiased depiction of family influence structure, measures ideally should incorporate views of all family members who are participants in the decision-making process. Furthermore, family-level measures must capture constructs of phenomena that are commonly perceived by all the informants.

Davis (1970) reports that the perceived pattern of influence of partners in discussions about purchasing a car or furniture is a near-perfect match if the information provided by men and women is taken across the sample as a whole. At the aggregated level, differences between individual couples' responses are balanced out; whereas at the level of individual couples there are clear differences in male and female perceptions.

Kirchler (1989) summarised the results of 16 studies looking at influence patterns in relationships, as reported by both partners, and found that in about 60% of cases overall there was congruence in reports. In over a third of cases the reports differed.

In the Vienna Diary Study (Kirchler et al., 1999), later described in detail, 40 couples recorded their disagreements and their decisions daily over a period of a year. Day by day, men and women separately recorded, amongst other things: (a) whether they had spoken with one another; (b) how long they were together; (c) how long they had spoken together; (d) what they had spoken about and whether they had had different opinions. If there was a conflict, they were also asked to indicate (e) how long the conversation about the issue had lasted; (f) where they were, what they were doing, and who else was present; (g) how much specialist knowledge each person had about the issue; (h) how important the issue was to both partners; the extent to which the conversation was (i) objective and (j) emotional; (k) how much influence each partner derived from the discussion; and (l) how much benefit each partner derived from the discussion. Respondents were also asked to record (m) whether the conflict was a value conflict, a probability conflict, or a distributional conflict, and finally (n) what tactics had been used by both partners to try to influence the other (see Table 7.5). Because both partners reported on the same situations independently, the degree of congruence between their answers could be calculated.

There was a complete match regarding whether partners had spoken with each other on a particular day, but the time that the partners had spent with each other (a daily average of around four hours) was underestimated by men in comparison with women by around 8%, and the time that they had spent in conversation (barely an hour) was overestimated by men by around 14%. Men in unhappy relationships overestimated this time by 19% and those in happy relationships by 9%. Information about disagreements in discussions about expenditure, money management, children and friends, work, the relationship etc. (using a scale from 1 = we did not agree at all, to 7 = we agreed completely) correlated on average with $r = .69$ (range of variation $.51 < r < .80$). The length of time during which topics of conflict were discussed, which on average lasted for barely 15 minutes, was also overestimated by men: compared to the women, their estimates were 26% longer. Again, men in unhappy relationships overestimated this time more (41%) than men in happy relationships (10%). With regard to economic decisions, men indicated the sum of money being argued about to be 10% higher than the figure given by the women. Again, men in unhappy relationships overestimated more (17%) than men in happy relationships (1%). Even the information about who had started a conversation and whether a decision had been taken differed in about 15% of cases. The question about influence and benefit derived from the discussion revealed that men systematically attributed themselves 1.31% higher influence and 3.71% higher benefit than the women gave them. Again, the differences were more marked in unhappy relationships than in happy relationships (divergence in influence: 3.48% and –0.98%; divergence in benefit: 4.22% and 3.17%). Differences between the information provided by men and women were found regarding the type of conflict recorded, again varying depending on the harmony in the relationship: unhappy partners agreed in 85% of cases over the type of conflict, but happy partners agreed in 91% of cases.

In the study, participants also indicated how much subject knowledge they and their partner had, how important the issue was to them and to their partner, and how objectively or emotionally they had both been in the discussion. The information from the women about the men correlated for expert knowledge, importance, objective argument and emotionality with $r = .63, .58, .56,$ and $.54$ respectively; the men's information about the women correlated with $r = .71, .80, .51,$ and $.57$.

Partners also indicated which of 15 suggested influence tactics (see Table 7.5) they and their partner had used during the disagreement. By comparing how frequently one partner recorded using a tactic, and seeing whether that tactic is also recorded by their partner as having been used in the discussion, it emerges that the couples agree in about 45% of cases. Women accurately recorded in 47% of cases that their partner had used a particular tactic, and men were accurate in 44% of cases.

These gender differences with regard to tactics employed seem of interest. Men generally accurately "discovered" that their partner was insisting over a particular issue (64%), was using negative emotions (60%) or engaged in integrative bargaining (60%). Women relatively frequently recognised withdrawal tactics (71%), physical force (65%), and negative emotions (60%). Men rarely acknowledged that the women had used physical force, the withdrawal of resources, or distorted information, although this was indicated by women (7%, 14%, and 25% respectively). Women rarely recorded helplessness of husbands as one of their tactics (indicated by men in 21% of cases).

Satisfied women and men were more likely to recognise integrative bargaining (64% and 67% respectively) than dissatisfied men and women (48% and 52%). Satisfied women also recorded more objective–rational discussions than dissatisfied women (64% against 47%), and more openness about the facts of the matter (59% against 46%). Men in happy relationships are similarly more aware of objective–rational discussions (60% against 45%) and the distorting of information (39% against 13%). Dissatisfied women were particularly able to recognise when their partner was trying to distort information (54% against 14%), or was seeking to form either direct coalitions (57% against 32%) or indirect coalitions (51% against 17%), and were also better able to recognise threats to withdraw resources (43% against 28%) or offers of trade-offs (54% against 32%). Dissatisfied men were more likely to recognise when women used helplessness (47% against

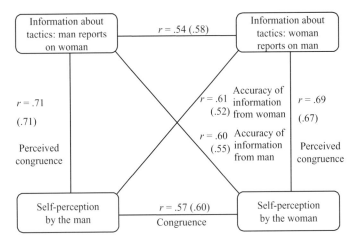

Figure 5.1 Correlation between self-perception and the partner perception (results of the Italian study are shown in brackets; Kirchler, 1999; Kirchler & Berti, 1996).

35%), offered resources (60% against 25%), withdrew from the argument (18% against 4%) or tried to form direct coalitions (52% against 23%). Tactics that conform to gender stereotypes appear to be more easily recognised than those that do not conform. In addition, satisfied partners seem more able than dissatisfied partners to recognise positive tactics, which promote a solution of the problem, when they are offered. Dissatisfied partners are more likely to record negative tactics if these are also confirmed by the partner as having been used.

The Vienna Diary Study analysed the tactics during a conflict with the partner on the day of the diary entry. In an Italian and Austrian questionnaire survey (Kirchler & Berti, 1996; Kirchler, 1999), a total of 402 couples were interviewed about their own tactics in decision-making situations and those usually used by their partner. Both partners were interviewed separately about how they and their partner might use any of 17 different tactics. Figure 5.1 shows the correlation between self-perception and partner perception. The average correlation between self-perception and partner perception in the Austrian study was $r = .60$ (women) and $r = .61$ (men); the figures for the Italian study were $r = .55$ and $r = .52$ respectively. The figures are statistically significant, but surprisingly they are lower than the correlation between self-perception and what was said about the partner. If the influence tactics mentioned in the self-descriptions were kept constant, then the partial correlation between the partner's self-image and the image of the partner reduced to $r = .33$ and $r = .35$ for the Austrian study, and $r = .19$ and $r = .24$ in the Italian study. The statements of those interviewed about their partner's behaviour appear to be based on knowledge of their own behaviour. Partners in close relationships view each other through the "filter" of their own behaviour and indicate that the tactics they would employ in a particular situation would also be employed by their partner (Fig. 5.1).

The difficulty of putting oneself in the position of one's partner is observed mainly in dissatisfied couples. However, it is not only a matter of satisfaction: Further analyses of the correlation between self-perception and partner perception have found that the degree of congruence in happy relationships is significantly higher than in unhappy relationships, but that this higher correlation cannot be attributed to better knowledge of the behaviour of the partner. If a person's own description of their behaviour is kept constant in calculating the correlation between the self-description and the suspected behaviour of the partner, then the degree of congruence in happy relationships and unhappy relationships falls to the same level (Kirchler & Berti, 1996; Kirchler, 1999). Satisfaction with the relationship does not necessarily mean, therefore, that partners can provide more valid information about their partner than dissatisfied partners; rather it indicates that they have, through frequent interaction and constructive disagreements, developed similar attitudes and similar patterns of behaviour, with the result that even when they talk about themselves much of what they say is also true of their partner. Dominance, the length of the relationship, and other variables had no effect on the correlation between self-perception and partner perception. In a study of romantic love and the readiness to commit to the relationship, Grau and Bierhoff (1998) found that actual similarity in attitudes was a better predictor of relationship quality than the similarities as perceived by the partners.

It could be objected that the experiences partners were asked to report on in previous studies were everyday events and would therefore be perceived without particular attentiveness, or would quickly fade from memory as a routine matter. If the matter being discussed is important, then partners perceive the situation accurately and recall events precisely, offering reconstructions that are largely congruent. Granbois and Summers (1975) argue that where the discussion is about expensive, durable, prestige products which are of significance for all members of the private household and which require thorough deliberations before a purchase is made, then partners are more likely to agree in their recalled information than if the product involved is cheap. Krampf, Burns, and Rayman (1993) found that in around 60% of cases men and women offer statements which are congruent when recalling purchases that have involved both to a high degree; this falls to around 45% if the involvement of the partners has been small. Williams and Thomson (1995) researched a problem that has significance for many couples, the desire for children, but came to the conclusion that women and men are not able to assess the attitude of their partner accurately even when the issue is particularly relevant to both.

It seems that information provided by one partner about the behaviour of the other is generally unreliable, and that—as Park (1982) shows—even following an important decision, the attitudes of the partner cannot be reported with any greater degree of accuracy than prior to the decision. It can therefore be assumed that although men and women both participate in reaching a shared decision, they neither perceive shared experiences, nor reconstruct and report the events in the same way.

Not only do partners differ in their recall of past decision-making situations, but even a current situation may be perceived differently, and often inaccurately, by them. Where partners are asked to assess the current disposition of their partner, they are often not able to do so. Kirchler (1988a, 1989) asked 21 couples to record their feelings six or seven times a day in a time-sampling diary over the period of a month, along with the subjectively judged reasons for that feeling and their needs at that time. At the same time, they estimated the feelings, causes, and needs of their partner, with the partner present. On average, in two-thirds of cases partners were able to assess the feelings of their partner accurately: men were able to judge the causes of that state correctly in 64% of cases, and women were accurate in 69% of cases. The assessment of needs only matched those needs indicated by the partner in just over half of all cases.

Partners in close relationships describe shared events differently and are also barely able to imagine themselves in the position of their partner and give accurate information about the thoughts, interests, and even the actions of the partner. It is assumed that happy partners are more likely to be aware of the position of their partner than unhappy partners (Noller, 1984) because their ability to decode communication processes is better. This optimistic assumption has not gone unchallenged, for example, Thomas, Fletcher, and Lange (1997) found that the interpretation of video recordings of joint interactions did not become more accurate if partners were satisfied with their relationship. "Empathic accuracy", as the authors termed the congruence between one's own interpretation of behaviour and the interpretations made by another person, did not correlate with the quality of the relationship and quite often diminished as the duration of the relationship increased. Increasing relationship quality was, however, associated with increasing presumed similarity between the behaviour of the partners. Kirchler (1999) reports similar findings, as do Kirchler and Berti (1996): Happy couples describe the behaviour of the other person more accurately than do unhappy couples, because the partners behave and experience events in a similar manner. Similar ways of behaving and experiencing are the basis for high correlation between self-evaluations and evaluations of behaviour by another person, where the latter are in fact little more than a description of the respondent's own behaviour. This phenomenon is known in social psychology as the "false consensus effect", which misleads partners into thinking that their partner would also behave in a similar fashion.

One source of divergence between information collected from partners may be presumed similarities, the result of such a "false consensus effect". Another source could be different tendencies to provide socially desirable answers. If research is done on phenomena where controversial evaluations are prevalent in society, such as the exercise of power in a partnership, or dominance in decision-making situations, this could result in distorted evaluations both by oneself and by another person. Whilst social desirability and social stereotypes may lead to divergent information being provided by partners, it is also possible that they could falsely pretend that their answers agreed. If social stereotypes suggest that the man buys the car and the woman is allowed to choose the colour, for example, or she selects the pattern on the living-room furniture, then it is not surprising that a simple question as to who decides what in everyday matters results in an agreed answer from men and women. In some of these instances, there would have been no reconstruction of past complex decision-making processes, and instead what has been reported is drawn from jointly shared prejudices about gender roles.

The tendency to offer answers that conform to social norms also produces similar effects to the illusion of superiority, as reported by Buuk and Van der Eijneden (1997). In interviews about relationship quality, people often significantly overestimate their own satisfaction. The average value of judgements about satisfaction, using a 7-point scale, is often around 6, indicating a high level of satisfaction. Buunk and Van der Eijneden (1997) found in representative samples conducted in Holland that over 53% of those interviewed rated their level of satisfaction as being higher than the average level of satisfaction in the population as a whole. Around 45% believed that their relationship was as good as the average, and only 10% indicated that their relationship was worse than the average.

Divergent information may also be a result of the strong emotions often experienced in the private home. Strong emotions, as experienced in decision-making situations that involve a high level of conflict, can "blind" participants to the feelings of their partner and to details of social interactions. In fact, memories of the events of a conflict situation are recalled less accurately than events without strong emotions (Harvey, Wells, & Alvarez, 1978; Kirchler, 1988a).

A further source of divergence may lie in the relative unimportance of the everyday events being reported. Decisions in the private household are often routine actions, everyday family business, needing neither much time nor much attention, which is why they are neither perceived precisely nor adequately reconstructed in the memory. Even if past events are not remembered clearly, interviewees are required to give an answer because the question has been put. It is then not so surprising that the accounts given by partners differ and are unable to reflect what actually happened, since when memory fails the answers are more likely to be influenced by chance, or to reflect stereotypes rather than the actual events.

Finally, it is known from narrative interviews and studies of "accounts of one's own relationship" (Hinde, 1997) that partners construct different images of their shared reality and "plug the gaps" in their own memory so that the past appears consistent, meaningful and logical (Ross, 1989). People develop "accounts" of their partnership in the course of time, they reformulate and modify their memories and rework them periodically, on the basis of their emotions and discussions with their partner and with other relevant people. The randomness of subjective reconstruction was identified in a study by Holmberg and Veroff (1996): couples recounted their marriage and their honeymoon directly after the event and two years later, by which time some already had a happy relationship and some an unhappy relationship. Whereas the partners gave similar accounts immediately after the event, their accounts two years later differed to varying degrees, depending on the relationship quality.

When complex information needs to be processed with little time available, and when events have been perceived and dealt with without much attention and are therefore recalled poorly, then interviewees will often resort to stereotypes, prejudices, or schematised images in the hope that reality will correspond to this to some degree (Hastie, 1982). If complex scenarios need to be recalled, these are subjectively modified in such a way that they make sense in the current situation, regardless of the actual events in the past. For these reasons, in answer to the question as to who should be asked to give information, the reply is clear: In order to record a shared reality, it is necessary to ask all those involved in sharing it. Research methods that do not take this into account are not suitable for the analysis of everyday experiences in shared households.

If all those involved in everyday events are interviewed, then the question arises how reliably individuals can report their experiences, and what distortion of answers can be expected due to the phrasing of questions and answering options. We cannot offer an extensive treatment of errors in information processing and reporting here. Cognitive psychology has collected much information that indicates various systematic errors (e.g. Bless, 1997; Nisbett & Ross, 1980; Ross & Nisbett, 1991; Ross, 1977; Schwarz, 1996, 1998, 1999). We refer to some of these problems for the purposes of illustration.

Everyday life at home is marked by a variety of mundane, routine events that are rarely paid any attention. Because attention is directed elsewhere, the reliability of memory of those events is called into question. Memory fades if events lie a long time back in the past (Bernard, Killworth,

Kronenfeld, & Sailer, 1984). If a study of managing expenditure not only asks about expensive, durable goods, but also focuses on cheap products bought on a daily basis, then it is unlikely that those interviewed will be able to give reliable information as to how they reach decisions in general, how often they buy particular products, and how much money they would spend on things in total. Meffert and Dahlhoff (1980) believe that decisions about everyday consumer goods are recalled with much less clarity than those about expensive consumer durables. Saltfort and Roy (1981) compared data from questionnaires with diary records and found that the diaries reported the purchase of cheap, unimportant, non-fashionable products far more often than the questionnaires. It is probable that in retrospect special events are recalled more often than routine actions. Research into judgement heuristics (Tversky & Kahneman, 1974) offers an explanation for this. According to the availability heuristic, in estimating the frequency or the probability of one or more events, judgements are formed on the basis of the difficulty or ease with which individual pieces of information can be recalled or generated from memory. Since memory is dependent not only on the frequency of presentation, but also on various other factors such as the attention paid to perceived events and the depth of reflection about them, then the availability heuristic can lead to misjudgements and overestimation of the frequency of notable events. A study by Hu and Bruning (1988) showed that diaries offer more accurate (i.e. more true to life and more precise) information about the use of products than do questionnaires, at least if the product is inexpensive and rarely or habitually bought.

If attention strays and as a result difficulties occur in recalling events and in providing an account of events, then interviewees could be inclined towards answers that conform to social stereotypes, as mentioned already. This resorting to stereotypes can also be expected when those interviewed are not very involved with the events (Branscombe & Cohen, 1991), or when answers have to be given in a short space of time, for example when spontaneous answers to questions are sought (Bodenhausen & Lichtenstein, 1987; Dijker & Koomen, 1996). People are not always interested in completing lengthy questionnaires. It is not surprising that, when asked about the distribution of influence in joint decisions, partners tended to reflect traditional gender role models, whereas in diaries—where events are recorded immediately afterwards and there are fewer errors of recall or reconstruction—traditional influence patterns are much less in evidence (Kirchler, 1989).

A further fact that challenges traditional questionnaire-based studies is that experiences in the private sphere are often accompanied by intense emotions. Emotions that are brought to life in certain situations have faded again by the time the questionnaire is completed. The intensity of the situation is forgotten and the thoughts that were once wholly concentrated on the situation in hand are now given over to other things. The direct relationship between the event and the subjective experience of it cannot be properly reflected in a questionnaire. Answers to a questionnaire are guided "by the head", not the heart. Actions and reactions that took their course spontaneously at the time become rationalised after the event. In this way, past events are not so much remembered as reconstructed, not as they happened but in such a way that the course of the action appears logically coherent.

Everyday life is complex and is structured cognitively by relationship partners in their own subjective manner. The private language of the partners is an indication of the subjective organisation of shared events. In a questionnaire, the possibilities for subjective structuring of the experienced reality is severely limited. The form of the questions, their degree of differentiation and the suggested alternative answers all derive from the picture of reality held by the researcher, and little room remains for a subjective reconstruction of the reality experienced by those surveyed. Supporters of questioning techniques might counter that it would only be difficult to answer questions that did not relate to one's own picture of reality as these would therefore be incomprehensible. However, the fact that a question receives an answer is no indication that the person interviewed agrees with the way it has been put. It is easy to tick one of the alternative answers available, both to satisfy the interviewer and to escape the interview situation. Glick and Gross (1975) call for social scientific research to be less restrictive in future. They call for more open-endedness for participants in research and less intervention by the researcher. Research design and methods should allow participants to restate their subjective reality.

Although many voices have been raised against verbal reporting of past events (Nisbett & Ross, 1980; Nisbett & Wilson, 1977), market researchers rarely deviate from tried and trusted research methods. Wright and Rip (1980) argue strongly against the more recent trends in researching households, claiming that someone whose entire motivation is to recall accurately and to report what they remember will be able to restate their experiences reliably. If interviewees believe that the truthful depiction of a matter will not be used to make a fool of them, that their openness will not be used against them, that the level of accuracy in what they report can be scientifically tested and that it is also possible to reconstruct the matter without their assistance, then their responses to questionnaires prove reliable. This optimistic view is put forward despite the finding that "on average, about half of what informants report is probably incorrect in some way" (Bernard et al., 1984, p. 503). Even if the risky assumption is made that everything could be remembered exactly and would at best be reported with only conscious distortions, the use of traditional methods would still be questionable. Social scientists who rely wholly on data from questionnaires are often analysing little more than "lies".

In his criticism of the presumption of rationality in neo-classical economics, Kahneman (1994) indicates that people are barely able to indicate what their past preferences were or what their future preferences might be. People find it difficult to maximise their utility over time; they are also often completely unable to imagine, or can only imagine with great uncertainty, what their future preferences might be. In order to make rational decisions, however, they must be able to rely on their experience, in other words on their past preferences. Current alternatives are weighed up in respect of future desires on the basis of memories of past experiences. Kahneman (1994) shows that experiences are judged using the "peak and end rule", rather than taking into consideration the entire experience from beginning to end over a period of time. If an event contained negative peaks and the end was unpleasant, it is largely remembered as a negative experience. If the end was pleasant, relative to the rest of the time, then the event is still recalled as a relatively pleasant experience. An experiment to prove the peak–end rule was conducted as follows: people were asked to keep their hand in cold water for 60 seconds. The water temperature was 14°C. The experiment was then repeated, with an additional 30 seconds where the water temperature was increased to 15°C. When asked which of the two conditions would be preferred for the third experiment, the majority of participants chose the longer option. The fact that the longer experiment contained all the unpleasant features of the shorter one, but lasted for an additional 30 seconds, was not taken into account. Judgements about past experiences can be influenced entirely by the sequence of negative and neutral experiences that surround them.

The fact that memories of and reports about past events, as asked for in a questionnaire, are not free of distortions has been demonstrated by, amongst others, Bower (1981), Fiedler (1991), Forgas (1991), and Schwarz, Strack, Kommer, and Wagner (1987). Bower hypothesises that experiences that are congruent with one's feelings are remembered better than those that are incongruent. If those questioned are in a positive mood during the completion of the questionnaire, they are more likely to recall pleasant events than unpleasant ones. Accordingly, they overestimate the probability of pleasant experiences and, therefore, tend to give more positive overall evaluations. Schwarz (1987) argues that the mood at the time of responding is not the cause of errors in memory, but is instead used as a source of information in evaluating events: As an example, if employees are in a good mood when asked about their job satisfaction, then their good mood encourages them to respond that they are satisfied with their work. It also influences them to recall positive experiences rather than negative ones, overestimating the probability of pleasant experiences in the workplace and giving this undue weight in their judgement. The influence of mood on cognitive processes has been demonstrated in many simple but highly creative pieces of research. Schwarz and Clore (1983) arranged for a group of students to "find" 20 cents on a photocopier on the campus of the University of Illinois, with another group "finding" nothing. Afterwards, students were asked about their mood at that time and their satisfaction with life. Not only the mood at that time, but also satisfaction with life proved to be affected by the "found" 20 cents. Similar differences in satis-faction with life were found between groups of people who were interviewed on sunny and rainy days, or between groups of sports fans interviewed before and after a football match that their favourite team had won (Schwarz et al., 1987). Brief, Butcher, and Roberson (1995) confirm these findings, but point to differential effects: they invited colleagues in a hospital to take part in a study and greeted half of the participants with biscuits and drinks whilst the others received no hospitality. Afterwards participants were asked about job satisfaction and given a test to measure their disposi-tion towards negative feelings. Those people who were not inclined to negative affects and who had enjoyed hospitality recorded much higher satisfaction levels than those people who had had nothing to eat or drink. People who were disposed to negative feelings also tended to indicate higher levels of satisfaction if they had enjoyed hospitality beforehand; their assessment of satisfaction generally proved to be less situation-dependent than that of the people who were disposed to be in a good mood.

There is similarly evidence to suggest that the spatial architecture and the living environment can influence mood and, in consequence, judgements about satisfaction. Schwarz et al. (1987) found that the general mood is better in a pleasant room than in an unpleasant one, and that general satisfaction with life is rated more highly. If the same rooms are used to ask about satisfaction with the participant's own living conditions, then the responses obtained in the unpleasant room are more positive than those obtained from the pleasant room. It is likely that comparison processes are being applied in the pleasant room, whilst the mood experienced by participants in the unpleasant room serves as information.

Mood appears to influence judgements about frequency and evaluations in a complex way. Events that are mood-dependent are remembered with differing degrees of ease, whilst mood also serves as a source of information when judging a matter. In other situations, the atmosphere and a person's feelings are the anchors for judgements that do not correlate with either element. Bohner, Bless, Schwarz, and Strack (1988) demonstrated that people are inclined to look for the causes of negative events more intensively than after positive or emotionally neutral events. If there is an intensive search for causes, it may be assumed that events will be pursued with greater attention and information will be more thoroughly processed, with the result that negative experiences will be recalled more accurately than neutral or positive ones, unless the emotional aspects were too overpowering.

TABLE 5.1

Correlation between specific relationship satisfaction or frequency of meetings with the partner and general satisfaction with life under three test conditions

	Conditions		
	General question before specific question	Specific question directly before general question	Specific question before general question: advice about different areas
Experiment 1	$r = .16$ ($n = 60$)	$r = .55$ ($n = 60$)	$r = .26$ ($n = 60$)
Experiment 2	$r = -.12$ ($n = 60$)	$r = .66$ ($n = 60$)	$r = .15$ ($n = 60$)

Source: adapted from Strack et al., 1988; pp. 435 and 437.

Strack, Martin, and Schwarz (1988) hypothesise that people asked about satisfaction with specific areas of life will generate different answers than if asked general questions about satisfaction. Specific questions invite the recall of specific events and their evaluation, whereas general questions invite a general, largely undifferentiated act of recall. The order of specific and general questions can result in different answers, because memories and answers to one question can influence the judgement with regard to the following question. Answers were studied in response to questions about satisfaction with life in general and about satisfaction with the current loving relationship. In one instance the question about satisfaction with the relationship followed the question about satisfaction in general, and in the second instance the order was reversed: it was assumed that in assessing overall satisfaction, more specific areas would be considered here than in the first instance. In a third experimental condition, the sequence of questions again went from specific to general, but the interviewees were explicitly told before answering that satisfaction with two completely different areas of life was being researched. The response scale in each case had 11 points. Table 5.1 shows the correlation between answers to the two questions, as gathered under the three different experimental conditions. Depending on whether the general question was answered after interviewees had been reminded of specific areas or not, the correlation between the answers about satisfaction stood at different levels. As it could be objected that the correlation could have been distorted because the same scale of answers was used for both questions, Strack et al. (1988) conducted a further experiment, identical to the first but with the following change: instead of a question about the quality of the relationship, a question was asked about the frequency of meetings with the partner, and an open answer was possible. The patterns of correlation matched that of the first experiment, and are similarly shown in Table 5.1.

Questionnaire responses are ultimately also dependent on the possible alternative answers provided. This may sound banal; however, this does not

TABLE 5.2
High- and low-frequency alternative answers

| Questions: | How often do you have sex with your partner? |
| | How often do you masturbate? |

High-frequency alternative answers	Low-frequency alternative answers
( ) several times a day	( ) several times a week
( ) once a day	( ) once a week
( ) 3 to 4 times per week	( ) once a fortnight
( ) twice a week	( ) once a month
( ) once a week	( ) less than once a month
( ) less than once a week	( ) never

Source: adapted from Schwarz & Scheuring, 1988, p. 489.

simply mean that the researcher is presenting his or her picture of reality through the order of the answers and forcing those interviewed to answer within a defined framework. Schwarz and Scheuring (1988) demonstrated impressively that the differentiation contained within the scale of answers can also lead to completely different sets of results.

Schwarz and Scheuring (1988) asked about the frequency of sex with the partner and frequency of masturbation, offering in each case a 6-point scale. In one test condition, answers were differentiated using a high-frequency field, and in the other test condition a low-frequency field was covered (Table 5.2). After this a question was put about the quality of the relationship, using an 11-point scale. When high-frequency alternative answers were offered, results showed that around 77% of those interviewed had sex with their partner at least once a week, and around 69% reported a masturbation frequency of at least once a week. If the low-frequency alternative answers were used, then the corresponding figure for sex with the partner fell to around 39% and for frequency of masturbation to around 42%. Satisfaction with the relationship was, however, at the same level under both test conditions. Similar results were recorded from interviews about the frequency of television viewing (Schwarz & Hippler, 1987).

It is not only errors in memory that argue against questionnaires. In a questionnaire it is hardly possible to represent the dynamic of everyday life. The variable of "time" becomes compressed to a single "point". What is recorded is what appears in retrospect to be relatively unchanging. In doing so, it is implicitly assumed that rigid action–reaction sequences are being played out and recognised as such. However, it is precisely in everyday life that completely different topics and courses of action can be described (Pulver, 1991).

From these considerations, it would seem that neither observation procedures nor questionnaires about past events are appropriate methods of recording everyday life in the private home. The lack of ecological validity, which cannot be ignored, the problems with different recall of mundane events, errors of judgement attributable to the mood of the participants at the time of recording, and problems associated with the design of the questionnaire—all these can be reduced by using the diary procedure. Diaries, which require the recording of experiences at the time when these experiences have just been lived through, also offer the possibility of studying processes and not simply recording data from compressed experiences. It may further be hypothesised that the repeated registration of experiences in everyday life will result in a steady increase in the attentiveness of those taking part, with the result that the reports become more reliable (Rehn, 1981). Epstein (1986) reports that the accuracy of predictions also increases if aggregated data from several different recording times is available.

DIARIES

Diaries provide a means of recording everyday events, particularly private household decisions (Duck, 1991; Kirchler, 1989). A number of procedures have been developed in recent years, enabling deep insights to be gained into everyday life, with an analysis of the interaction between individual and environment. Almeida and Kessler (1998), Almeida, Wethington, and Chandler (1999), Bolger et al. (1989a, b), Csikszentmihalyi (Larson & Csikszentmihalyi, 1983), Diener (Diener & Larson, 1984), Downey, Freitas, Michaelis, and Khouri (1998), Laireiter, Baumann, Reisenzein, and Untner (1997), Larson and Almeida (1999), Pawlik (Pawlik & Buse, 1982) and Pervin (1976) among others have developed or employed interesting instruments for the study of a wide variety of problems. Hormuth (1986) and Stone, Kessler, and Haythornthwaite (1991) provide a detailed discussion of the advantages and disadvantages of various methods.

In household studies, diaries have long been used to study couples' use of time (Hornik, 1982; Robinson, Yerby, Fieweger, & Somerick, 1977; Vanek, 1974; see also the procedures of the *Österreichisches Statistisches Zentralamt*, the Austrian National Statistics Office). Larson and Bradney (1988) used diaries to record the current feelings of individuals in the presence of relatives and friends. Almeida and Kessler (1998), Almeida et al. (1999), and Bolger and associates (Bolger et al., 1989a, b) used diaries to study the experience of stress in everyday life and spillover effects of work on a couple's relationship. Laireiter et al. (1997) used diaries to analyse social networks. Diaries have also successfully been used to record interaction processes between partners (Auhagen, 1987, 1991; Brandstätter & Wagner, 1994; Duck, 1991; Feger & Auhagen, 1987; Kirchler, 1988a, c). Hinde (1997) speaks highly of diary methods for the study of close relationships, in particular of methods that require both partners to record diary entries.

However, he criticises the fact that they are far too seldom used. Recently, an increasing number of studies of everyday experiences and feelings based on diary data have been published. The following will provide a description of time-sampling diaries and events diaries, and propose a suitable method for recording everyday decisions between couples.

Time-sampling Diaries and Events Diaries

Brandstätter (1977) designed a time-sampling diary for measuring mood that took as its starting point Lersch's (1970) phenomenology of experience and Vetter's (1966) philosophical–anthropological reflections on feelings, and permitted an analysis of mood in the course of everyday life. In modified form, it also appears suited to the study of everyday life in families. Participants in the study continually record their current mood, stating the causes of their feelings and briefly noting the objective features of the situation, such as location, activity in progress, and persons present. The diary thus consists of question sheets, designed rather to help capture a fragment of memory than pre-structuring individual life. Diary entries are made several times a day, at randomly scheduled times, and over an extended period. Complete confidentiality is ensured by having the participants themselves carrying out the classificatory content analysis of the diary entries, following appropriate training. Each participant notes on a record sheet (a) the date, scheduled time, and actual time of the diary entry, (b) current feelings, (c) the quality of their current mood, (d) the source of these feelings, (e) current needs, (f) current location, (g) activity currently engaged in, and notes (h) all persons present. Instruments of personality assessment are provided in addition to the diary. This enables a differential social psychological analysis of the feelings recorded and the way they are influenced by the immediate, specific events.

A number of studies have confirmed the usefulness of the mood diary, fully justifying the considerable economic research expense. These studies required groups of 20 to 35 individuals, students (Brandstätter, 1981), housewives (Brandstätter, 1983; Rodler & Kirchler, 2000), recruits (Kirchler, 1984), unemployed people (Kirchler, 1985), and employees (Auinger, 1987; Kirchler & Schmidl, 2000) to keep diaries over a period of one to six months.

Diaries were employed primarily at the individual level. Kirchler (1988c), using a modification of the time-sampling diary designed by Brandstätter (1977), investigated relationship phenomena by having the male and female partners, at the same time, but independently of each other, record observations about their feelings in the course of everyday life. In a sample of 21 couples who had lived together in a shared home for an average of two to three years, each partner was given a diary with randomly scheduled times, identical for both partners. Six times a day over a period of four weeks, the participants each independently answered the questions from Brandstätter's mood diary, together with a few additional questions about the particular situation. If the other partner was present, the state of their feelings too was assessed, and the relative degree of dominance and current harmony of the relationship were recorded. At the end of a recording period, the contents of the completed diaries were analysed by each participant individually, following a jointly agreed scheme. Finally, the results of this content classification were transferred to a record sheet to be used for scientific analysis.

The diary provides insight into the nature, frequency, and course of development of the state of participants' feelings, into the nature and frequency of everyday events, and their influence on feelings. It also provides information about activities and social contacts. The random distribution of the six set times for recording data during the 24 hours of a day, and the extension of the recording period over four weeks, enables a typical pattern of everyday life in the couple's relationship to be constructed.

This study established that happy couples not only interact more frequently than less happy couples; they also have a more positive assessment of each other's presence, talk more frequently about personal subjects, and open up to each other even about intimate problems. Happy couples are also able to deal with conflicts in a way satisfactory to both partners. The distinction between couples is not in the frequency of conflict but in the manner of resolving it. It was found, in this study, that the reason for the dynamics of conflict taking a positive course is that happy couples are more able than less happy ones to assess their partner's current feelings and needs accurately.

If the focus of interest in the study is on specific matters, such as purchasing decisions, rather than feelings or everyday life in general, the diary needs to be completed not only at random times, but whenever the specific matter arises. The reason for this is to gather a sufficient number of relevant events. In Kirchler's study (1988c), an events diary was used alongside the couples' time-sampling diary. However, the couples did not always record the specific occurrence when the event had just taken place, although this is the recommended course in events diaries. The couples were instructed to fill in the events diary on the evening of each day. It is common, particularly in the study of everyday experiences, to ask for data to be recorded after a particular time interval, often days, but sometimes even weeks or months (Stone et al., 1991). In Kirchler's study (1988c), couples recorded the occurrence in the events diary if they had bought a product or used a service, gathered information about it, or simply mentioned a desire to purchase in the last 24 hours. The diary dealt retrospectively with the whole day just past. If in the period since the last entry decisions had been made about various products or services, the couples started by agreeing which of these they would deal with in their events diary and then answered the subsequent questions independently of each other. On the evening of each day, the couples assessed their relationship (dominance, harmony, relative contribution of resources); they answered questions about the product or service (type, cost, frequency of conversations about it, any available information about quality, importance, and benefit to the partners) and the decision-making stage (initiation, gathering of information, selection of alternatives, purchase etc.), and they described the interaction situation (location, persons present, duration, mood, the partners' style of argument, influence on the other partner, the partners' initial standpoints, strategies for solving differences of opinion, standpoints at the end of the conversation). The events diary made it possible to analyse the specific purchasing experiences within one month from the point of view of both partners.

The time-sampling diary and the (retrospective) events diary have many advantages over other methods, thus justifying the increased cost. They study relationship phenomena while they are actually taking place or can still vividly be recalled. This avoids or strongly reduces errors of recollection. Also, the diary is independently "managed" by the participants themselves, completed in their own private domain, and its contents analysed by them. Intimate situations are not distorted by the intrusion of third parties, and the pressure to create a good impression is minimal. The events recorded are studied in the context of everyday life and the flow of events, not removed from it. This method records contacts with different people, as well as activities taking place in locations outside the private sphere. It leaves partnership experiences, in this particular case purchasing decisions, within the context of social events. The fact that the partners are asked to record their entries simultaneously takes account of the partnership as a single entity. Lastly, the method provides for entries to be made several times a day over an extended period of time. The need to study processes is thus met.

Partner Decisions Diary

Experiences with time-sampling and events diaries kept by both partners confirm their adequacy for the study of economic decisions, as well as other events. However, the recording of data over a period of one month is insufficient to study decisions. The study of specific patterns of interaction between the partners, decisions being made simultaneously and other concurrent events, as well as the effect of past decisions on subsequent ones, calls for more than the design of a detailed diary. The diary entries must be gathered over a sufficiently long period to distinguish unvarying patterns from the everyday noise. The need to maintain records over a long period is often met at the expense of sample size, a point highlighted by Stone et al. (1991). Such a disadvantage is accepted when the events to be recorded are detailed ones that normally pass almost unnoticed in the routine of everyday life.

An events diary to record decision-making by couples was designed by Kirchler (1995) and tested in a pilot study (Kirchler, Skilitsi, and Radel, 1995) which involved 12 couples keeping a diary over a period of six months. In all, each participant filled in the diary on 183 days. On average, 151 conversations were recorded. These often lasted only a few minutes, but over eight hours in one case. The partners were still well able to recall these conversations in the evening, according to their own records. The commonest subjects were the children, relatives, and friends. Other frequent topics of conversation were those relating to the partnership or one partner alone. Economic questions such as expenses, methods of saving, and other money matters were topics in about 15% of cases, and professional work or housework in about one-fifth of cases. The degree of disagreement was usually slight; the greatest differences were recorded in the case of economic decisions. Economic questions also accounted for most of the conflicts recorded. Only three of the twelve couples reported a disagreement more than once a week. For these three couples, it was possible to calculate the course of influence distribution over the period of the diary. For all three, the distribution of influence was shown to have remained fairly even over this time. As in an earlier diary study (Kirchler, 1989), analysis of the daily fluctuation in influence showed a variation in degree, with the balance of influence sometimes favouring the woman, sometimes the man; it did not show repeated dominance by one partner in several consecutive decisions.

The pilot study showed that the couple diary is a suitable research instrument for recording disagreements and decisions in the partnership. Its appropriateness is indicated by the fact that the 12 couples kept the diaries for six months, and reported disagreements with the same frequency as in the literature. Downey et al. (1998) reported disagreements on 16% to 18% of the days covered by the study; Almeida, Bolger and associates (Almeida & Kessler, 1998; Almeida et al., 1999; Bolger et al., 1989a, b) reported stress-causing arguments between the partners in about 6% of cases. Within the six-month period, disagreements were not recorded sufficiently frequently to allow a detailed statistical analysis. The method therefore has to be applied over a period greater than six months. At least 50 instances must be recorded if the autoregression of influence is to be calculated separately for each couple (Box & Jenkins, 1976). Given that one disagreement a week is reported by at least a quarter of the participants, the process must be maintained for a year to achieve a total of at least 50 recorded instances. Based on the pilot study, a sample size of 40 couples would provide analysable data from 10 couples.

Following the experiences with the diary used for the pilot study (Kirchler, 1995), an improved version of the diary question sheet was developed. This is shown in Fig. 5.2a–c, together with the diary instructions. In the Vienna Diary Study, the modified decisions diary was kept by 40 couples over a period of 12 months (Kirchler et al., 1999).

The Vienna Diary Study

Working on the basis of the theoretical enquiries and experience achieved so far with the partner decisions diary in the pilot study carried out by Kirchler, Skilitsi, and Radel (1995), a study using the modified partner diary was carried out (Kirchler et al., 1999). The couples who participated in the Vienna Diary Study consisted exclusively of those living in a shared home, who had at least one child of school age. The first reason for selecting couples with one or more dependent children was to ensure a relatively homogeneous sample faced with comparable family tasks. Also, couples with children were chosen because they represent the prototypical family, and because the frequency of conflict is usually high in the stages of the family life cycle where there are dependent children (Gelles, 1995).

Procedure of the Vienna Diary Study

Various means were used to recruit couples to participate in the Vienna Diary Study: Advertisements were inserted in the local press, notices displayed at adult evening classes and kindergartens, and acquaintances of the project team were approached. They in turn told their friends about the study. In this way, 46 couples from eastern Austria were recruited. They were informed about the study and its aims, the keeping of the diary, and the questionnaires. Each couple that had expressed willingness to participate in the study was introduced to a personal assistant from among the eight members of the project team. This assistant was available to answer questions during the entire course of the study. The assistants' task was to maintain regular contact with the couples by telephone and by visiting, to collect the completed diary sheets and distribute new ones. They were also responsible for providing constant encouragement to the couples to keep their diaries conscientiously.

Keeping of the diary began after a two-day period of practice and familiarisation. Two weeks after the start of diary record-keeping, the assistants made a personal visit to the couples to discuss their experiences of the diary and to clarify any remaining questions.

Following the initial information about the planned study, each couple received the diary, consisting of a set of diary question sheets (Fig. 5.2a–c). Together with this, they received a "safe" in which to keep the completed sheets. Each partner individually was given a box with a small opening

Code:		Date:	

---

1. Did you talk to your partner today?

no	○	⟶ to Question 3
yes	○	

How long in all were
you together? ....minutes
How long in all did you
talk?..minutes

2. What issues did you talk about?

	yes	no	did you agree?	how did you feel? (, 0, +)
(a) Spending on	○	○	○ ○ ○ ○ ○ ○ ○ not at all totally	☐
(b) Savings (type)	○	○	○ ○ ○ ○ ○ ○ ○ not at all totally	☐
(c) Money matters	○	○	○ ○ ○ ○ ○ ○ ○ not at all totally	☐
(d) Work (professional)	○	○	○ ○ ○ ○ ○ ○ ○ not at all totally	☐
(e) Housework	○	○	○ ○ ○ ○ ○ ○ ○ not at all totally	☐
(f) Self / Partner	○	○	○ ○ ○ ○ ○ ○ ○ not at all totally	☐
(g) Relationship / Partnership	○	○	○ ○ ○ ○ ○ ○ ○ not at all totally	☐

Figure 5.2a (and opposite). Modified decision diary and instructions (first page; Kirchler et al., 1999).

(h) Children	○ ○	○ ○ ○ ○ ○ ○ ○ not at all totally	☐
(i) Friends / relatives / individuals	○ ○	○ ○ ○ ○ ○ ○ ○ not at all totally	☐
(j) Leisure / hobby / travel / holiday / sport (no expenditure)	○ ○	○ ○ ○ ○ ○ ○ ○ not at all totally	☐
(k) Home (no expenditure)	○ ○	○ ○ ○ ○ ○ ○ ○ not at all totally	☐
(l)	○ ○	○ ○ ○ ○ ○ ○ ○ not at all totally	☐

3. How did you feel about your partnership today?

○ ○ ○ ○ ○ ○ ○
bad   good

○ ○ ○ ○ ○ ○ ○
weak   strong

○ ○ ○ ○ ○ ○ ○
not free   free

4. Who contributed more to your relationship today (contributing money, goods, information, services, work, recognition received, etc.)?

○ ○ ○ ○ ○ ○ ○
self   partner

5. Have you made any important decisions today, without discussing them with your partner?

no   ○

yes   ○   about what? ....

(if to do with expenditure, how much money did you spend? ATS ....

If you and your partner did not talk today or did not disagree, entry ends here.

Please state what you disagreed about:

Subject:...

Where were you and your partner during the conversation?	self	☐
	partner	☐

1 = At home
2 = Semi-private location (e.g. place of work)
3 = Public place (e.g. bank, shop, restaurant, street)

Who was present (apart from your partner)?		☐
		☐
		☐

4 = Children
5 = Parents / in-laws
6 = Friends / relatives
7 = Acquaintances /relatives
8 = Experts (Sales staff, advisors)
9 = Others

What were you doing during the conversation?		☐
		☐

10 = Work (paid work)
11 = Housework
12 = Dealing with children
13 = Necessary tasks (e.g. eating, bodily care, travelling)
14 = Leisure

How long did the conversation last? ....minutes

How often have you discussed this subject before?
○ ○ ○ ○ ○ ○ ○
never   often

Who started the conversation?
○   ○   ○
self   partner   ?

Who of you has good knowledge of the subject?
self   ○ ○ ○ ○ ○ ○ ○
        no knowledge good knowledge
partner ○ ○ ○ ○ ○ ○ ○

How important is the subject to you and your partner?
for me   ○ ○ ○ ○ ○ ○ ○
          unimportant   important
partner   ○ ○ ○ ○ ○ ○ ○

If it is a money matter, how much money is at stake?
ATS........ ....

How was the atmosphere of the conversation?
○ ○ ○ ○ ○ ○ ○
unpleasant   pleasant

How objectively did each of you speak?
self   ○ ○ ○ ○ ○ ○ ○
        unobjectively   objectively
partner ○ ○ ○ ○ ○ ○ ○

Figure 5.2b (and opposite). Modified decision diary and instructions (second page; Kirchler et al., 1999).

How emotionally did each of you speak?	self	○ ○ ○ ○ ○ ○ ○
		unemotionally emotionally
	partner	○ ○ ○ ○ ○ ○ ○

Out of 100%, how much influence did each of you have?	self	_____ %	} 100 %
	partner	_____ %	

Did you make a decision?	○	○
	no (postponed)	yes

How fair do you think the decision was?	decision-making	○ ○ ○ ○ ○ ○ ○
		unfair fair
	result of decision	○ ○ ○ ○ ○ ○ ○

If you made a decision, how much do you each benefit from the result, out of 100%?	self	_____ %	} 100 %
	partner	_____ %	

How much did you and your partner each benefit in your last decision?	self	_____ %	} 100 %
	partner	_____ %	

What tactics did you each use to try to convince each other? (please indicate sequence; List 1)	self	☐ ☐ ☐ ☐ ☐
		1 2 3 4 5
	partner	☐ ☐ ☐ ☐ ☐

What type of disagreement was it?	value	○
	probability	○
	distributional	○

Are you content with the outcome of the conversation?	○ ○ ○ ○ ○ ○ ○
	not at all totally

How well do you remember the conversation?	○ ○ ○ ○ ○ ○ ○
	not at all totally

Instructions for completing the diary

Together with your partner, recall all the conversations you have had together today, and what topics were discussed in these conversations. Try to remember the conversations accurately, and recall any differences of opinion between you and your partner at the beginning, during, or at the end of the conversation. When you have decided together what it was you talked about, and which matters you disagreed about—even if the difference of opinion was only slight—please fill in the diary on your own. Begin by stating what you talked about. Then answer in detail about the conversations which represented a difference of opinion between you and your partner.

Here is some information that you will find useful in completing the diary question sheet:

In general, a box is completed by filling in a number or symbol, and a circle by putting a cross in the relevant one.

On the first page of the diary, you will find some possible topics of conversation listed, as well as some statements about feelings.

Question 1: This asks whether you and your partner have had a conversation. If you have not talked, go straight to question 3; if you did talk to each other, please answer the questions in the order that they appear.

Question 2: Here you will find a series of conversation topics. The first three relate to economic matters. The first is about expenditure on a product or service, whether expensive or inexpensive. Please specify which product or service it was. The second relates to savings, either methods of saving or actual funds. Again, please state exactly what type of savings you discussed. Your answer on the third topic is the place to mention all the money matters that do not come under the heading of the first or the second topic. Question 2 then continues with other subject areas. At the end, there is space for subject areas that do not feature in the list. These are for you to fill in yourself as required.

Record your feelings during the conversation by putting a "+" in the relevant box if you felt definitely good, and a "–" if you felt definitely bad. If, exceptionally, you cannot decide whether your feelings were good or bad, or if you were entirely indifferent, enter the symbol "0".

If you did not talk to your partner on a particular day, or did not disagree, then your entry will end at the bottom of the first page. Otherwise, turn to the next page.

All the questions on the next page relate to a single conversation with your partner. Please answer all the questions. There are lists associated with some of the questions. Wherever this is the case, please refer to the relevant list. Sometimes just one answer is required; in other cases, you can give more than one answer.

Figure 5.2c   (and opposite). Instructions for completion of the diary (Kirchler et al., 1999).

If you talked about several subjects on a given day, or if you discussed one topic several times, please complete a separate copy of the second page for each conversation.

Finally, if you happen to be on holiday or away on business at the time, please state this on your answer sheet.

On the second page, you are asked what type of disagreement you had. You need to state which category the issue mainly belongs in: probability, value, or distributional.

- Probability: It is a probability issue if you and your partner are of different opinions, but still both want the same ultimate goal. This usually arises if you have different information available, or if you see the importance of certain information differently. The discussion is therefore about the usefulness of different solutions to a problem.
- Value: It is a value issue when a difference of opinion arises from a difference in values. Based on different desires, one partner wants this, the other something fundamentally different. The sticking point of the problem is usually the difference between the desires of the partners.
- Distributional: A distributional issue is one about something that needs to be shared between two or more parties, and the wishes of everyone concerned add up to more than the total that is actually available.

List 1: Tactics

1.	Positive emotions	(flattery; being nice; behaving seductively)
2.	Negative emotions	(threats; shouting; cynicism; ridicule)
3.	Helplessness	(tears; showing weakness; pretending to be ill)
4.	Physical force	(forcing; injuring; violent or aggressive behaviour)
5.	Offering resources	(performing a service; being attentive)
6.	Withdrawing resources	(withdrawing financial contributions; punishing the other by no longer doing something)
7.	Insistence	(nagging; constantly returning to the subject; conversations designed to wear down opposition)
8.	Withdrawal	(refusing to share responsibility; changing subject; going away; leaving the scene)
9.	Open presentation of facts	(making suggestions; asking for cooperation; presenting own needs/subjective importance/own interest)
10.	Presenting false facts	(suppressing important information; distortion)
11.	Indirect coalition	(referring to other people; emphasising utility of the decision for others)
12.	Direct coalition	(discussion in the presence of others, hoping for their support)
16.	Trade-offs	(book-keeping; reminders of past favours)
17.	Integrative bargaining	(search for the best solution for all concerned)
18.	Reasoned argument	(presenting factual arguments; arguing logically)

through which to insert the completed sheets. This was to preserve the confidentiality of the diary entries, even at home. A few minutes a day were required to complete the diary sheets.

The electronic processing and monitoring of the data took place in parallel to the collection of data. This made it possible to evaluate the quality of the entries on a constant basis, and to report back to the couples in a specific manner, directing them to record their experiences accordingly.

A variety of strategies were needed to motivate the couples to maintain their diary record-keeping over the period of a year. This motivation proved to be extraordinarily time-consuming. The project team sent a number of letters to the couples, in addition to maintaining telephone and personal contact, for example to draw attention to errors in the entries. Joint meetings were also organised, at which partial results were presented, derived from the first questionnaires collected, or lectures held by experts about a topic agreed with the couples, such as aggression in schools. As an additional incentive to participate in the study—besides the personal assistant, the assurance given to the couples taking part that the results would be presented, constant telephone contact, and invitations to lectures—financial reimbursement of 726 Euro per couple was provided.

At three points during the 12-month period that the diary was being completed—at the beginning, during the recording period, and at the end—questionnaires were distributed in order to collect data on the couples' characteristics. On each occasion, these questionnaires collected socio-demographic data, assessed the harmony of the relationship following Hassebrauck (1991), and measured power relationships (Kirchler, 1988c) and sex roles orientation (Kirchler & Nowy, 1988). At the same time, a personality test (16 PA-test, Brandstätter, 1988), a questionnaire to measure the tactics used in value, probability, and distributional conflicts (Kirchler, 1993a, b), and a further questionnaire following Davis and Rigaux (1974) to measure the distribution of influence in various economic and non-economic decision situations were issued. The intention in doing this three times was to obtain stable data, and to register any changes in relationship characteristics during the period of the study. Completion of the set of questionnaires took about 60 minutes on each occasion. At the end of the one-year period over which the diary was being completed, the participants were given an additional questionnaire to record their subjective experiences with the diary. The items considered are given in Tables 5.4 and 5.5.

Couples participating in the Vienna Diary Study

A total of 46 couples commenced diary entries in the winter and spring of 1996. Of these, 40 maintained the diary over a one-year period, to the end of the study. Six couples discontinued their record-keeping early, a few days

TABLE 5.3
Couples participating in the Vienna Diary Study

	Men	*Women*
Age in years		
M (SD)	40.03 (6.26)	36.60 (5.73)
Range	29–54	26–52
Duration of living together (in years)		
M (SD)	14.28 (4.83)	13.97 (4.39)
Range	2–27	2–26
Number of children		
1	14	14
2	20	20
3	5	5
4	1	1
Age of youngest child (in years)		
M (SD)	7.74 (3.91)	7.63 (3.79)
Range	1–14	1–14
Education		
Basic	1	0
Vocational	12	16
Secondary	17	14
University	10	10
Working hours		
Full-time	38	14
Half day	1	0
Hourly	0	3
Non-working	1	15
Monthly household income in Euro		
< 1816	11	10
1817–2543	13	15
2544–3270	8	6
> 3271	8	9
Management of finances		
Separate	8	9
Joint	31	31
Missing value	1	0

Data collected at the conclusion of the diary period
(Kirchler et al., 1999).

or weeks after the start. The reasons given for this were separation of
the couple (two cases), lack of motivation or the onerousness of making the
daily diary entries (four cases). A detailed description of the couples is given
in Table 5.3.

The average participating couple had lived together in the shared home
with one or two children for more than 10 years. Their level of education

was above the national average, probably owing to the complex nature of the study, which influences readiness to participate. To obtain a more detailed impression of the participants, personality characteristics were investigated using the 16 PA-test (Brandstätter, 1988). The values for the secondary factors of the personality test were within the normal range for all 80 participants.

The relationship of the participating couples was characterised using questionnaires to measure satisfaction, dominance, and gender role orientation. The validity criteria of the questionnaires were sound: The reliability of the seven items relating to satisfaction, calculated separately for male and female partners at the three points when the measurements were made, varied between Cronbach alpha = .87 and .95; the stability of the assessments of satisfaction over the year in which diary entries were made varied around r = .72, and the correlation between the assessments of satisfaction made by the male and female partners was r = .73. The items designed to record dominance patterns also met the required criteria: reliability gave an average Cronbach alpha of .79; stability of assessment over the year was r = .81, and correlation of the assessments made by male and female partners was r = .45. Similar validity values were obtained for the scale relating to gender role orientation: Reliability was Cronbach alpha = .83; stability r = .78, and congruence of the partners' assessment r = .63. The results indicated no differences in the characteristics of the relationship, either between the sexes, or over the three points at which measurements were made. The assessments of the male and female partners over the three points were therefore averaged. On average, the couples assessed themselves as satisfied (M = 5.55; SD = 0.95; scale range 1–7); the dominance pattern appeared to be balanced (M = 4.10; SD = 0.59), and gender role orientation was categorised as modern (M = 5.89; SD = 0.64). Whereas the correlation between the assessment of satisfaction and dominance (r = −.19) and that with gender role orientation (r = −.05) were not significant, there was a significant correlation between dominance and gender role orientation (r = .41). The participating couples were therefore described only in terms of their degree of satisfaction and pattern of dominance, and in subsequent calculations, differences between satisfied and less satisfied couples, and between male/female-dominated and egalitarian couples, were calculated. Most of the couples were satisfied with their relationship, and judged the pattern of dominance in their partnership to be balanced.

Experiences with the diary

Overall, experiences with the diary were good. At the end of the diary-keeping period, participants were asked about comprehensibility of the items in the diary, ease of answering, and motivation. The comprehensibility of an instrument and the answerability of the questions are an indicator of its validity as a research instrument. The more difficult the questions are to answer, the more questionable the quality of the data, since it must then be assumed that arbitrary answers will be given.

In the first section of the post-study questions, participants had to state how difficult they found it to answer the diary question sheet. Table 5.4 gives descriptives for the items. In most cases, the mean was around or below a medium level of difficulty of 3.00. The questions on the degree of influence, on the benefit in the current instance and in the last decision appeared to be a little more difficult. The reasons for this may be that people do not like to think about questions of distribution in close relationships; nor do they like having to give the answer in terms of percentages. It is notable that the scores given by women as an assessment of difficulty were fairly consistently higher than those given by men. The mean for the 19 items was calculated as an overall difficulty score to investigate possible systematic differences. The reliability of this scale is high: the Cronbach alpha value is .87 for the scores given by the women, and .85 for the men. The correlation between the difficulty score given by the women and that given by the men is $r = .43$. Women ($M = 2.74$, SD $= 0.63$) gave higher difficulty scores than men ($M = 2.47$, SD $= 0.57$), and dissatisfied couples ($M = 2.79$, SD $= 0.42$) higher scores than satisfied ones ($M = 2.43$, SD $= 0.53$).

Four items among the post-study questions related to the participants' motives. These are of interest because a connection can be assumed to exist between motives and data quality. Systematic differences between couples are also possible: for example, dissatisfied couples might arguably be more inclined to maintain their participation for financial reasons, whereas satisfied couples would do so because their partner wished it. All the motivating factors appeared to have been involved in roughly equal share in bringing about participation: the money in prospect, the assistants' enthusiasm, their own interest, and their partner's wish to keep the diary. On average, the couples gave scores between 3 and 3.5.

The course of motivation over the year of the study was estimated. In the retrospective questions, the participants stated how high their motivation had been in each of the months of the study. The scale ranged from 0 = low motivation to 10 = high motivation.

Motivation had been high at the beginning of the study, but declined towards the end: The average motivation score in the first three months was 9; in the fourth and fifth months, 7 to 8. From then on, it declined, remaining constant between 5 and 6 until the end of the record-keeping period.

The retrospective method of the post-study enquiry is not the only means of obtaining information about motivation; it can also be concluded from the diary data themselves. Kirchler et al. (1999) examined the accuracy with

TABLE 5.4
Perceived difficulty of the diary

	Women		Men	
	M	(SD)	*M*	(SD)
1. How difficult was it to state whether you disagreed on a subject?	2.65	(1.14)	2.38	(0.90)
2. How difficult was it to state whether you felt good/ bad, weak/strong, free/not free about your partnership today?	2.48	(1.28)	2.20	(1.09)
3. How difficult was it to state who did more for your relationship and life together on a particular day?	2.25	(1.17)	2.18	(1.13)
4. How difficult was it to decide how often you had discussed a subject before?	2.68	(1.14)	2.43	(1.06)
5. How difficult was it to decide whether you were well informed about the subject?	2.18	(1.01)	2.05	(0.99)
6. How difficult was it to decide whether your partner was well informed about the subject?	2.48	(1.11)	2.13	(0.99)
7. How difficult was it to state whether you had spoken objectively with your partner?	2.45	(1.15)	2.10	(0.87)
8. How difficult was it to decide whether your partner had spoken objectively with you?	2.38	(0.95)	2.18	(0.96)
9. How difficult was it to state whether you had spoken emotionally with your partner?	2.25	(0.95)	2.00	(0.96)
10. How difficult was it to decide whether your partner had spoken emotionally with you?	2.25	(0.98)	1.90	(0.90)
11. How difficult was it to state how much influence you each had?	3.43	(1.08)	3.05	(1.13)
12. How difficult was it to state whether you found the decision-making fair?	2.70	(1.26)	2.55	(1.11)
13. How difficult was it to state whether you found the result of the decision fair?	2.68	(1.19)	2.30	(1.14)
14. How difficult was it to distinguish between the decision-making process and the result of the decision?	3.23	(1.35)	2.48	(1.36)
15. How difficult was it to state the benefit from a decision in percentages?	3.75	(1.15)	3.20	(1.24)
16. How difficult was it to state the benefit from the previous decision in percentages?	3.98	(1.17)	3.63	(1.19)
17. How difficult was it to remember the tactics you had used?	2.95	(1.20)	2.80	(1.16)
18. How difficult was it to remember the sequence of individual tactics?	2.83	(1.08)	3.03	(1.25)
19. How difficult was it to divide subjects of conversation into value, probability, and distributional issues?	2.55	(1.28)	2.40	(1.19)
Difficulty score	2.74	(0.63)	2.47	(0.57)

Note: Answer scale: 1 = very easy, 5 = very difficult; *n* = 40 couples.

Source: Kirchler et al. (1999).

which the diaries were kept for systematic trends over the record-keeping period. The items dealing with the current quality of the relationship and with contributions to the relationship, which had to be completed every day, were examined to determine the number of missing entries. First, the figures for the first and second halves of the record-keeping period were separated out. Overall the number of missing entries was slight: Out of a possible 7200 entries per half-year (180 days × 40 couples) the highest number missing per question for the entire sample was 348 (4.83%; the range being 2.42% to 4.83%). It was found that fewer entries were lacking in the second half of the year (an average of 4.32% in the first half as against 2.87% in the second); there was thus a rise in the accuracy of record-keeping. This finding contrasts with the subjective experience of the participants, which was of a decline in motivation.

A more detailed analysis of the missing entries over the 12-month period showed that for three couples, there were large gaps in which no entries were made. If these couples are discounted, then the highest number of missing entries out of a possible 1110 entries per month (30 days × 37 couples) is 56 per participant, or 5.04%. The number of missing entries was slightly higher in the fourth, fifth, eighth, and ninth month than in other months.

The final test was to find any variation in the number of conflicts recorded over the period. This was done by calculating the Spearman correlation between the number of recorded conflicts and the declared degree of motivation per month for each person. Disregarding those couples who had recorded few or no conflicts, the mean correlation for the remaining 33 couples was $r_s = .27$ for women and $r_s = .11$ for men. These values are below the critical boundary of $r_s = .591$ and thus not significant. In view of the large variance and the insignificant level of the average, we must conclude that there is no correlation between the number of recorded conflicts and motivation.

The final part of the post-study enquiry asked the participants to indicate their response to 32 statements about the study. Table 5.5 presents the items and their values. The 32 items were grouped into categories from which six indices were calculated. The items of the first group address the quality of the data obtained, especially the conscientious completion of the diary sheets. The mean of these eight items provides an index for data quality. Three items address the confidentiality of the data, especially the importance of anonymity. Nine address the critique of the method—this group contains questions about the demands of daily recording of data, or the length of the study. Four address the critique of the procedure, such as the wish for more intensive supervision by the research team. Four examine the reactive effects of the diary, i.e. changes caused by the study. A further four items look at processes of growing awareness occurring during the study.

TABLE 5.5
Participants' evaluation of the study

	Women		Men	
	M	(SD)	M	(SD)
Data quality:	4.31	(0.55)	4.40	(0.42)
	$\alpha = .85$		$\alpha = .74$	
I took the study seriously.	4.25	(0.81)	4.35	(0.62)
I believe that my partner took the study seriously.	4.20	(0.79)	4.38	(0.77)
I answered the questions on the diary sheet honestly.	4.78	(0.48)	4.78	(0.42)
I believe that my partner answered the questions on the diary sheet honestly.	4.65	(0.62)	4.75	(0.44)
I mainly made the entries at the correct time.	4.15	(0.74)	4.33	(0.73)
My partner mainly made the entries at the correct time.	4.10	(0.81)	4.40	(0.67)
In general, my entries are reliable so that they can be used in the study.	4.58	(0.64)	4.75	(0.59)
The entries provide a deep insight into my private life.	3.75	(1.19)	3.48	(1.20)
Confidentiality:	2.83	(1.00)	2.70	(0.92)
	$\alpha = .60$		$\alpha = .41$	
It is extremely important to me that all data remain anonymous.	3.68	(1.46)	3.85	(1.35)
I was sometimes concerned that other people would read my entries.	2.08	(1.21)	1.78	(1.27)
I kept my entries secret from my partner.	2.73	(1.30)	2.48	(1.47)
Critique of method:	2.71	(0.81)	2.83	(0.87)
	$\alpha = .85$		$\alpha = .87$	
I often thought of discontinuing the entries.	2.55	(1.28)	2.70	(1.34)
I found it burdensome to make the entries every day.	3.28	(1.28)	3.50	(1.30)
I found it increasingly difficult to make the entries every day.	3.28	(1.24)	3.50	(1.38)
The record-keeping period was too long.	3.23	(1.44)	3.45	(1.41)
I felt the demands of the study to be too much for me.	1.68	(0.89)	1.65	(0.89)
I would be prepared to participate again in a similar study. (−)	2.48	(1.41)	2.55	(1.47)
The method used is suitable for recording everyday decisions. (−)	2.50	(1.01)	2.70	(1.04)
The method used is suitable for recording differences of opinion. (−)	2.65	(1.12)	2.53	(0.93)
This is a good method for research into relationships. (−)	2.80	(1.22)	2.85	(1.12)

(continued opposite)

The six indices were examined for systematic differences between men and women, satisfied and dissatisfied couples, and male- or female-dominated couples and egalitarian ones. No differences were found, leading to the conclusion that the data quality relating to all the participating individuals and groups is very good, that the participants took the study

TABLE 5.5
(continued)

	Women		Men	
	M	(SD)	M	(SD)
Critique of procedure:	2.07	(0.68)	2.13	(0.68)
	$\alpha = .47$		$\alpha = .36$	
There ought to have been more meetings with the entire research team.	2.33	(1.15)	2.60	(1.35)
I would have liked more intensive supervision by the research team.	2.03	(1.00)	2.10	(1.08)
The purpose of the study is clear to me. (−)	1.70	(0.99)	1.93	(1.10)
I am sure that all the diary entries and answers to the questionnaire will remain anonymous. (−)	2.23	(1.25)	1.90	(1.06)
Reactive effects:	1.88	(0.97)	1.67	(0.71)
	$\alpha = .84$		$\alpha = .68$	
The study has changed our partnership.	1.90	(1.30)	1.53	(1.01)
The study unsettled me.	1.58	(1.03)	1.53	(1.01)
The study has had an effect on my feelings.	2.18	(1.34)	1.85	(1.05)
The study has changed our daily routine.	1.85	(1.05)	1.78	(0.86)
Growth in awareness:	2.96	(0.87)	2.71	(0.76)
	$\alpha = .72$		$\alpha = .46$	
I learnt a great deal from the study.	2.90	(1.30)	2.70	(1.32)
The study made me view our daily life with greater awareness.	3.38	(1.25)	3.15	(1.39)
We often discussed the study at home.	3.23	(1.03)	2.80	(1.04)
I often discussed the study with other people (friends, acquaintances, . . .).	2.35	(1.17)	2.20	(1.16)

Note: Agreement with items (answer scale: 1 = not true, 5 = true). Values were reversed for items marked (−); the figures given represent the mean after reversal. α indicates Cronbach alpha.

Source: Kirchler et al. (1999).

seriously and were confident that entries would remain anonymous, that any criticisms of method and procedure were slight, and that the diary had caused hardly any reactive effects.

The quality of the diary

The validity of the diary can to some degree be concluded from the subjective experiences described. Values for reliability and validity were calculated in addition to analysing these experiences.

Only variables for which data are available for each and every day can reasonably be used to measure the reliability of a diary method. The reliability of the decisions diary was assessed using the four questions on the current quality of the relationship ("feeling bad versus good, weak versus strong, not free versus free with regard to the relationship") and contribution of resources.

The average value for these four items on days of odd and even number was calculated for each person. Systematic differences between assessments of a relationship on odd and even days cannot be assumed to exist; therefore a high correlation indicates that the characteristic concerned has been reliably recorded. The reliability for even and uneven weeks and months was then determined. The odd–even reliability figures for the four items, separately calculated for 40 men and women, produce an average between .95 and .99 both for the odd and even days and for the odd and even weeks and months.

The mean of the answers on the three relationship items in the first half of the year (days 1–180) and the second half (days 181–360) was calculated for each person. The correlation of these mean values was then analysed. These correlations also were consistently above $r = .85$, indicating great stability in the entries.

To arrive at a more detailed assessment of data stability, the entries were grouped into monthly intervals of 30 days each. The entries for each 30-day period were averaged for each person, to yield 12 indices per person on well-being, strength, and freedom in the relationship and for contribution of resources. The intercorrelation of these indices was examined. For the items on quality of relationship, the correlation figures lay between $r = .40$ and $r = .96$. Particularly high correlations were found between consecutive months ($r = .79$ to .92); the correlations decreased as the time lapse increased. The stability was slightly lower for the question relating to contributions to the relationship. For women, it lay between $r = .19$ and $r = .87$; for men, between $r = .25$ and $r = .80$. Here, too, there was a high correlation between the average data for consecutive months ($r = .57$ to .87).

The final investigation into the stability of the data was made on a consecutive day basis. The consistency of current feelings and those on the previous day, two days before, three days, etc. up to seven days was determined. Correlations between data on well-being, strength, freedom, and contributions to the relationship on consecutive days ranged from $r = .27$ to .41. However, the correlation between the current assessment and that obtained two, three, and up to seven days before declined to $r = .26, .19, .16, .16, .15,$ and .15.

It can be concluded that, for the four criteria examined, the diary exhibits extremely satisfactory characteristics, with high odd–even reliability figures and a high level of stability. Correlations between the entries for the current day and those for previous days at greater distance were considerably lower than for consecutive days. This indicates stability, and also an adequate degree of variability in the data entries.

Validity aspects were also examined. For the Vienna Diary Study, validity was operationalised as agreement between the entries in the questionnaire and in the diary study. Since the men and women had not always answered all the questions, analysis of the validity of the instrument was limited to those entries for which figures were available from both partners on a given day. The fields of dominance and satisfaction were examined first. Next, entries on the degree of influence in subject areas from the questionnaire (Davis & Rigaux, 1974) were compared with the diary, and finally, entries on the use of tactics (Kirchler, 1993a).

Dominance was studied by first examining the difference between the general strength in the relationship, derived from the diary, and the dominance index from the questionnaire. The analysis related to the entries on current relationship quality under the diary item "weak–strong". Keeping the personal parameters constant (the couples were considered as dummy variables in partial correlations) the correlation found between the aggregated diary entries of the male and the female partner was $r = .33$ ($p < .01$). In the same way as the dominance index had been derived from the difference between the questionnaire entries of the male and female partner, the diary entries describing the current "difference in strength" were used to produce an index. This index was calculated for each couple and compared with the dominance index from the questionnaire. The correlation of these two values was $r = .31$ ($n = 40$; $p = .05$).

Next to be examined was the connection between the strength in the relationship on conflict days and the dominance index from the questionnaire. Only the diary entries made on days when both partners had registered a conflict were analysed. The difference in strength on these days was calculated per couple. Three couples who had not registered any conflicts were excluded from this analysis. Four couples who had reported fewer than five conflicts were also excluded. The correlation between the difference in strength and the dominance index was $r = .27$ ($p = .13$).

Lastly, the connection between the partners' entries on the distribution of influence in conflicts and the dominance index was examined. Keeping the personal parameters constant, agreement between the entries made by the male and the female partner about the woman's degree of influence was $r = .53$ ($p < .01$). The partners' diary entries for the year were averaged; the entries of the male and the female partner were then combined. The correlation between the dominance value for the couple based on the questionnaire and the degree of influence was $r = .45$ ($p < .01$).

With respect to dominance, it can be concluded that that there is only an inadequate correlation between the diary question on current strength in the relationship and the dominance index from the questionnaires. The correlation of the entries on distribution of influence and the data from the questionnaires is on the other hand adequate.

Satisfaction was studied by first examining the connection between well-being in the relationship shown by the diary and the satisfaction index from the relevant questionnaire. The correlation between the entries of the male and female partner about the current quality of the relationship was $r = .48$ ($p < .01$). The diary entries of men and women were averaged as for the satisfaction index from the questionnaire. The correlation between the aggregated values for the year and the satisfaction index from the questionnaire was $r = .60$ ($p < .01$).

In the next step, the analysis was limited to days of conflict. Couples who had reported fewer than five conflicts were again excluded. The correlation between the aggregated values for the conflict days and the satisfaction index was $r = .58$ ($p < .01$).

The third step was to examine satisfaction with the outcome of the conflict. Keeping the personal parameters constant, the correlation between the partners' entries was $r = .44$ ($p < .01$). They were averaged to produce an index. The correlation between the aggregated values for the diary question relating to relationship quality recorded for conflict days and the satisfaction index was $r = .44$ ($p = .01$).

Lastly, the correlation between the frequency of conflicts and the satisfaction index was computed. The number of days on which both partners had reported a conflict was determined for each couple. The Spearman correlation between this value and the satisfaction index was $r = .14$ ($p = .43$) for the 33 couples considered. There is no significant relationship between frequency of conflict and the quality of the partnership. The validity findings for satisfaction are very sound: correlations exist between the diary entries and those in the questionnaire. There is, however, no relationship between satisfaction and the number of conflicts. This is consistent with the literature.

Further investigations concerned whether there is a correlation between the use of various influence tactics as presented in the questionnaire (Kirchler, 1993a) and the frequency with which they are reported in the diary. Assent to 15 tactics (the following tactics: tactic 13: "fait accompli", tactic 14: "deciding according to roles", tactic 15: "yielding according to roles" were not considered, because no data on these were collected in the diary: see Table 7.5) was compared with the relative frequencies of the tactics used, related to the number of conflicts recorded per couple. The correlation between the values for use of tactic 1 (positive emotions) by the 33 couples who reported conflicts in the questionnaire and the frequency with which its use is reported in the diary was calculated. This value, $r = .29$, indicates a slight but positive correlation. Correlations were similarly calculated for all the other 14 tactics. The average correlation was $r = .52$ ($p < .05$) for the sample of women, and $r = .60$ ($p < .05$) for the men.

Finally, the correlations were computed between the relative influence recorded in the diary in economic decisions, in decisions about professional work and housework, child-related problems, relationship problems, and leisure matters on the one hand and the estimate of influence in these decision-making areas from the questionnaire, following Davis and Rigaux (1974). No significant relationships were found between these.

In conclusion we can state that the diary used in the Vienna Diary Study does appear to be suitable for recording the complex events of couples' everyday life: the participants' subjective experiences of the diary were positive, the results of data analyses relating to missing values, recording of conflicts, etc. are good, and the reliability and validity of the diary appear sufficiently high.

Disadvantages of the Vienna Diary and diaries in general lie in the enormous effort in convincing people to participate for a long period of time, in organising large and representative samples, in data handling procedures and statistical analyses of diary entries. Change of participants' behaviour due to diary keeping and increased attention has frequently been a critical argument against diaries but has not been observed in the present study.

The Vienna Diary Study provided a large quantity of data giving insight into decision-making processes in private households (see Kirchler et al., 1999). Where close relationships and decisions are discussed in the following chapters, the findings quoted are frequently those of this study.

CHAPTER SIX

Close Relationships and Influence in Decisions

INTERACTION AND DISAGREEMENTS OVER EVERYDAY MATTERS

Everyday life usually leaves partners in close relationships hardly any time for shared activities. Paid professional work, by one or both partners, is very time-consuming: Apart from a few minutes before setting off for work in the early morning, and a few hours in the evening after work, but with housework still to be done, only the weekends give them time for each other. In the Vienna Diary Study, 40 couples reported seeing each other roughly every day (87% of days in the year), but spending only about three to four hours of daytime in each other's company. Satisfied couples spent approximately 14 minutes less together than dissatisfied ones, and egalitarian couples were together less for approximately 20 minutes than male- or female-dominated couples. During their time together, partners talked for about one hour a day on average. Dissatisfied couples, despite spending 14 minutes longer together, spoke to each other less on average (approximately 15 minutes) than satisfied ones. This difference between satisfied and dissatisfied couples may be seen as indicating not only a quantitative difference but also a qualitative difference in their use of shared time. The estimates of time spent together and of interaction time in the Vienna Diary Study are higher than in other studies (see Kirchler, 1989). The fact that estimates were to be made on the evening of the day when diary entries were written up, rather than immediately following the interaction, may account for this.

The conversations related to subjects such as (a) economic matters (spending, savings options, money matters in general), (b) work (professional work, housework, jobs in the home), (c) the relationship (self, partner, the relationship itself), (d) matters relating to children, (e) leisure (friends, relatives and other people, leisure activities such as travel, holidays, and sport), and (f) other, miscellaneous topics. The frequency with which the subjects were discussed varied, as did the degree of disagreement. This is shown below and in Table 6.1.

With regard to economic matters, the couples discussed expenditure on average on 40% of days when they talked to each other during the year. The partners' opinions usually differed little; well-being was relatively good during the conversations. Dissatisfied couples reported less agreement than satisfied ones. This difference between happy and unhappy couples was observed in nearly all conversation subjects. In considering expenditure, autonomous and joint decisions must be analysed separately. Autonomous decisions were seldom registered. The taking of an autonomous decision by one partner was reported on average on 4% of the days covered by the year-long study. Women reported taking autonomous decisions more often than men. The couples discussed savings on about 5% of days during the year of the study. Other money matters were discussed on 14% of days by satisfied couples, and on 17% of days by dissatisfied ones.

Professional work was discussed quite frequently, on 41% of days. Housework was the topic discussed in 26% of conversations. Jobs to do with the home were the subject of 17% of conversations. In happy partnerships, the degree of agreement was again higher than in unhappy ones.

The couples talked about themselves or concerns to do with their partner 38% of the days on which they had a conversation. Again, the disagreements in unhappy relationships, especially according to the female partner, were more serious than in happy ones. Happy couples discussed their relationship more frequently than unhappy ones.

Conversations relating to the children accounted for the greatest proportion, occurring on 80% of the days on which the couples had talked. This is unsurprising, given that a criterion of selection when couples were chosen to participate in the study was to have a child of school age living in the household.

Topics relating to friends, relatives, and acquaintances and leisure time were discussed on one in two days. There was again a marked difference between the degree of agreement by happy and unhappy couples.

In some cases, the conversations involved disagreements between the partners. The women's diaries recorded 49,520 conversations; the men recorded 46,880 conversations. On average, three to four conversations were reported per day on the first page of the diary sheets. Women reported that conversations led to 1211 disagreements, and men 1169. In 1096 cases, both partners' entries related to the same disagreement.

When the conversation topics (Table 6.1) were counted, it was found that economic subjects occurred less often than those relating to the children, friends and leisure matters, work and housework, and relationship problems. However, economic subjects more often led to conflicts which were further described in the diaries (diary page 2). As already reported, the

TABLE 6.1
Summary of frequency of interaction and conversations by couples over one year

		Women		Men	
		M	(SD)	M	(SD)
Conversation days in the year (median)		320		320	
Time together per day (minutes)		221.25	87.89	220.50	87.04
Conversation time per day (minutes)		54.63	37.83	57.44	35.83
Conversation:					
(a)	Economic matters				
	Spending (frequency of conversation)	0.40	0.21	0.41	0.21
	Level of agreement	6.29	0.60	6.34	0.53
	Well-being	2.68	0.30	2.72	0.27
	Savings (frequency of conversation)	0.05	0.04	0.05	0.05
	Level of agreement	6.22	1.21	6.39	0.68
	Well-being	2.56	0.59	2.64	0.46
	Money matters (frequency of conversation)	0.15	0.11	0.15	0.11
	Level of agreement	6.21	0.78	6.28	0.70
	Well-being	2.54	0.40	2.56	0.37
(b)	Work				
	Professional work (frequency of conversation)	0.41	0.22	0.40	0.20
	Level of agreement	6.29	0.81	6.35	0.65
	Well-being	2.56	0.42	2.58	0.37
	Housework (frequency of conversation)	0.27	0.16	0.25	0.16
	Level of agreement	6.06	0.75	6.13	0.67
	Well-being	2.49	0.39	2.55	0.35
	Jobs in the home (frequency of conversation)	0.17	0.21	0.17	0.12
	Level of agreement	6.28	0.68	6.31	0.62
	Well-being	2.64	0.36	2.68	0.35
(c)	Relationship matters				
	Self/partner (frequency of conversation)	0.39	0.23	0.36	0.24
	Level of agreement	6.10	0.90	6.22	0.70
	Well-being	2.53	0.39	2.56	0.37
	Relationship (frequency of conversation)	0.23	0.18	0.23	0.18
	Level of agreement	5.73	1.04	6.08	0.83
	Well-being	2.50	0.42	2.62	0.33
(d)	Children (frequency of conversation)	0.82	0.17	0.79	0.17
	Level of agreement	6.45	0.60	6.51	0.47
	Well-being	2.75	0.26	2.77	0.24

(continued overleaf)

TABLE 6.1
(continued)

		Women		Men	
		M	(SD)	*M*	(SD)
(e)	Friends and leisure				
	Friends/other people (frequency of conversation)	0.52	0.17	0.48	0.17
	Level of agreement	6.43	0.38	6.47	0.50
	Well-being	2.67	0.38	2.70	0.30
	Leisure (frequency of conversation)	0.43	0.18	0.42	0.18
	Level of agreement	6.36	0.56	6.44	0.49
	Well-being	2.77	0.21	2.83	0.15
(f)	Other topics (frequency of conversation)	0.04	0.06	0.04	0.05
	Level of agreement	5.04	2.62	5.64	2.12
	Well-being	1.86	1.06	2.29	0.88

Note: The diary was kept for an average of 359 days. The average values for the time in minutes, frequency of conversation as the relative frequency of conversations on days when there was interaction (multiple references), the mean of the level of agreement (scale range: 1 = complete difference of opinion, 7 = complete convergence of opinion) and of well-being (scale range: 1 = bad, 3 = good) were calculated as follows: first, the average values for the variable in question in the diary were calculated for each person. The mean of the individual average values for 40 women and 40 men was then computed.

Source: Kirchler et al., 1999.

women's diaries recorded 49,520 conversations; 7760 of these concerned economic matters, of which 3.56% led to conflict, which was then described in more detail in the diary. The men recorded 46,880 conversations, 7480 discussions of economic matters, of which 3.63% were conflicts. Discussions about work-related matters, topics regarding the children, discussions about the relationship and leisure time, respectively, led to conflict in 2.3%, 1.9%, 3.1%, and 2.0% of the cases. Figure 6.1 shows the distribution of conflicts by topics. Considering the total number of conflicts, about 23% concerned economic matters; 21%, 20%, 20%, and 16% concerned work, leisure, children, and relationship matters. Conversations about expenditure and other economic issues seem to be particularly relevant and liable to cause conflict in relationships.

In the following, conflict situations are described in more detail. A total of 255 instances of conflict recorded by both men and women related to economic matters. Of the 40 couples, 33 women and 34 men reported mainly value and probability conflicts about buying clothes, health expenditure, restaurant meals, about the purchase of picture frames, a camera, a guitar, and household gadgets, holiday, food, a car, the payment of bills, securities, and housekeeping money among other things. Detailed analysis of the economic conflicts shows the most frequent cause to be spending on leisure,

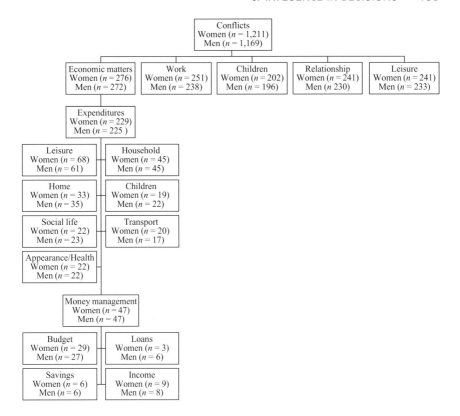

Figure 6.1 Frequency of conflict in the diaries of the 40 couples (Kirchler et al., 1999).

at over 23%. Another 16% of conflicts concerned household expenses. Different attitudes to expenditure on the home accounted for about 12% of disagreements. Expenditure for the children (games, school fees, clothing, etc.), in connection with social life (gifts, parties, etc.) and transport (car, public transport, etc.) were each the subject of 7% to 8% of discussions. Six per cent of discussions concerned appearance (cosmetics, clothes). Expenditure on health was reported by men and women to be the topic in about 2% of cases. The amounts being spent ranged from under 10 Euro to over 70,000 Euro. The median figure for the amounts reported by the women was just over 700 Euro; the men put the expenditure figure considerably higher at over 3000 Euro. In the savings and money management category, the main topics of conflict were the bank and the individual's salary account, in about 10% of cases; in 2%, partners quarrelled about savings, in 1% to 2% about loans, and in about 3% about individual or joint income.

Conflicts about economic matters occurred mainly at home and some-times in shops, the bank, or the street. Children were present in half the cases. Most conversations occurred during leisure time or while doing nothing, but about a quarter of disputes about money occurred while carrying out necessary tasks at home. The conversations were usually initiated by the female partner. Average duration was about 15 minutes, in some cases, barely 1 minute; in others, up to 50 minutes. The men judged their knowledge of economic matters to be higher than that of their partner. Women judged theirs higher than that of the men. The atmosphere of the discussion on economic matters was in general fairly good. However, women in unsatisfactory relationships frequently complained that it was unpleasant. Although in general the women's manner of discussion was described as more emotional than the men's, dissatisfied women claimed to speak more objectively than their partners. In disagreements about economic matters, men had on average more influence on the outcome (approximately 54%) than women (approximately 46%). Both men and women overestimated their own influence, compared with their partner's assessment. Their estimates of the distribution of benefit also differ, women claiming 46% of benefit as against their partner's 54%, and men estimating roughly equal benefit for their partners at 49% to their own 51%. The couples reached a decision in about two-thirds of the disagreements. In the remaining third, discussion was broken off and often resumed later.

The topic of "work" covered mainly disagreements over housework, paid professional work, and jobs connected with the home, since repairs were often the subject of discussions about the home. Conflicts concerned the positioning of a lamp, preparation of lunch, timing of home repairs, repair-ing picture frames, faulty lamps, or a water tap, watering the garden, the conduct of housekeeping and childcare, the return to a career, conflicts at work, etc. The discussion was more often begun by the women than by the men. Independently of the level of satisfaction or power relations in the partnership, women claimed better knowledge of this subject than their male partners and to consider it more important than the men. The men con-firmed the women's statements: They considered work, especially house-work, less important to them than to their female partner. Women judged their own influence in work matters to be 52%, and men's 48%. Men judged similarly (52% for the women; nearly 50% for themselves). However, women in male-dominated relationships saw themselves as having much less influ-ence (44%) than did women in egalitarian (56%) or female-dominated rela-tionships (55%).

Disagreements regarding children concerned a wide variety of subjects, from the children's use of leisure time to school matters, and from children's untidy rooms to problems and questions of parenting. In over 80% of cases, the partners were at home during the argument and the children were frequently present. Dissatisfied men and women found the atmosphere of discussions about children's matters to be particularly unpleasant. Women in unsatisfactory relationships considered their partner's manner of discussion to be less objective than did women in satisfactory partnerships or men, whether in happy or unhappy relationships. In conflicts about matters concerning children, women claimed to have had a 48% share of influence, the men having had 52%. The men claimed 49%, their wives having had 51%. In satisfactory relationships, both men and women thought that they and their partner had equal influence.

Conflicts about the person, their partner, or the relationship included lack of time for each other, insufficient acknowledgement within the relationship, one partner having little understanding of the other, or not showing sufficient consideration for that partner's needs; wishes of a sexual nature, long-standing hassles, and opportunities for self-fulfilment. A typical situation of disagreement between partners about their relationship may be described as follows: Discussions on average last 12–13 minutes. The shortest time given for a conversation was 4 minutes, the longest, 40 minutes. During the discussion, in over 80% of cases, the couples are at home; in 58% of cases, the children are present. In 50% of cases, they are engaged in leisure activities or doing nothing, and in 20% of cases, they are engaged in housework. Women not only took the initiative in starting discussions more frequently than men, but also indicated that the subject was more important to them than to their partners. The atmosphere of the discussion was judged more negatively by the women than by the men, especially in unsatisfactory relationships. In about half the conflict situations it was indicated that a decision had been postponed. This is hardly surprising when the discussion centres on the self, the partner, or the relationship. Looking at relative influence, it was found that women rated their partners' influence as greater than their own (53% versus 48%). Men believed influence was equally distributed.

Disagreements on leisure topics included joint sporting activities, invitations from friends, relatives and acquaintances, holiday and travel plans, cinema, theatre, concerts, and museum visits. In general, disputes on leisure matters were initiated equally often by men and women. However, in male-dominated relationships, the man took the initiative more often; in egalitarian relationships, the woman took the lead. Regarding their level of influence in disputes about leisure, women indicated they had 49% as compared to their partners' 51% influence; men said the exact opposite. A decision was reached in two-thirds of cases, and no agreement in one third.

The brief description of conversations and disagreements reported in the diary shows the variety of everyday life situations within close relationships. It also shows some typical patterns of who starts a dispute, where the partners are and who else is present, what simultaneous activities are performed while arguing with each other, how often a disagreement is settled or postponed, and how influential women and men are. In general it was found that conversations about economic matters, work, the relationship, children, and leisure activities occur almost every day. Conflicts are, however, reported rather rarely. While economic matters are among the less frequent with regard to conversation, they present the most often mentioned conflicts.

In the following chapter, a closer look is taken at partners' influence within everyday conflicts, especially economic decisions. Emphasis is given to determinants of spouses' relative influence. Results of numerous studies on consumer behaviour, the social psychology of close relationships, and family sociology as well as the Vienna Diary Study are summarised. Chapter 7 is dedicated to the dynamics of decision-making: links between past and present decisions and compliance-gaining tactics. Most of the results discussed in Chapter 7 were obtained from the Vienna Diary Study and refer to decision-making situations described earlier.

THE INFLUENCE OF PARTNERS IN CONFLICTS AND DECISION-MAKING

Decision-making processes in private households are complex. In market and consumer research, interest centres on economic decisions, above all purchasing decisions. In most consumer studies, decision-making is often looked at purely in terms of the balance of influence between the partners. They ask whether the male, the female, or both partners have the final say, which partner has greater power, and who takes which decisions when. Information from interviews normally covers the incidence of autonomous decisions by one partner, the number of joint decisions, and the relative distribution of influence between partners in making joint decisions. Economic studies traditionally focus on decisions rather than the differences of opinion that sometimes precede a decision; these disagreements may be broken off to deal with "everyday business" and then forgotten or shelved. In the present chapter, we mainly review studies of economic decisions in private households. We refer in some instances to findings from the Vienna Diary Study relating to discussions and decision-making on economic and other matters.

Influence Distribution in Relation to Gender

Kirchler (1989) summarised the results of a series of studies undertaken between 1956 and 1988, mainly in Anglo-Saxon contexts, on the relative influence of men and women in decision-making. In particular these studies examined relative influence in purchasing decisions. Following his review, Kirchler (1989, p. 169) reaches this conclusion: "On average—regardless of the time, place, sample size, gender of the interviewees, and product focus of the research—men and women indicate that slightly more than half (53%) of decisions are reached jointly. The remaining 47% of decisions are slightly more often taken by men on their own (52%) than by women alone (48%). Therefore both partners have roughly the same say." To avoid misunderstanding we should point out that the category of joint decisions encompasses not only those instances where both partners are involved in joint discussions from start to finish, but also those instances where sometimes the man and sometimes the woman makes the decision.

Men and women participating in the Vienna Diary Study reported that over the range of topics involving discussion and decision-making, the woman had about 49% of the influence and the man 51%. Of the 1180 conflicts described by the women, in 44% of cases the balance of influence between the partners was evenly spread; the men reported 1137 conflicts, and estimated that in 46% of cases the balance of influence was equal between the partners. In around 55% of conflict situations the balance of influence swung in favour of the woman or the man. Extreme relationships where one partner alone had complete say were rare, occurring in roughly 1% to 2% of cases. Women reported having had no influence over 1.5% of cases, but having decided alone in 2.3%. The figures for men were 1.5% and 1.2% respectively.

Where discussions were about economic matters, the average influence exerted by women fell to 46%, whereas the men's rose to 54%. In discussions about matters relating to children, relationship issues, and leisure matters, the balance of influence was 49% for women and 51% for men. The only area where women exerted slightly more influence than men was over career and housework issues, women having 52% and men 48% of the say. Large differences in influence between men and women were only found in a few isolated instances. In these relationships, one side (male or female) indicated they had only a third of the say whilst their partner had two-thirds, regardless of the issue.

Overall, the various studies of purchasing decisions in the family and the Vienna Diary Study show the distribution of influence between partners to be fairly equally balanced, whether in economic decisions or in disputes on other matters.

Influence Distribution in Relation to Product Type and Characteristics

Statements about the distribution of influence generally relate to average values. A differentiated approach should be taken to interpreting these. The partners' influence varies in relation to the content of the discussion. In discussions on expenditure, the partners exert differing degrees of influence according to the commodity being considered. A review of several studies showed that, in the past, the product areas in which the husband or wife had control corresponded to the traditional division of roles (Kirchler, 1989): Technical items fell within the man's responsibility, kitchen items within the wife's. Figure 6.2 indicates the average distribution of influence between the partners in decisions on various issues. It shows the man deciding "if the purchase of a car, a camera, TV, or stereo is being considered, but also about a refrigerator or dishwasher. . . . The woman decides on furnishings for the home (furniture, carpets, etc.); she is—as might be expected—responsible for the kitchen (cooking utensils, kitchen equipment, cooker) and for providing and preparing meals (food items, coffee), care of the home (cleaning materials, vacuum cleaner) and bodycare items (toothpaste, deodorant, cosmetics). The woman calls the doctor when needed, and buys the medicines." (Kirchler, 1989, p. 174).

Even when differences in influence between the partners correspond not only to the type of product under consideration, but also to its characteristics, the picture still reflects traditional expectations: it is more often the man than the woman who decides what price is acceptable and what method of payment to use. In the past at least, he was more likely to dominate the decision as to where to shop and when to buy. The woman's say more often related to the choice of colour, style, or model (Kirchler, 1989). Despite an apparent overall balance in the distribution of influence, men and women dominated decisions in different areas, at least in the past: he being responsible for technical matters, she for aesthetic ones.

In this discussion, reference is made to past studies of relative male–female influence and its dependence on product type and characteristics; the style of writing itself underlines this by observing the past tense. This might strengthen the impression that today, there are no gender and product-based patterns of influence to detect. This is not the case: when partners are asked the same simple question as in the past, as to who has how much influence, their answers indicate the traditional pattern of roles, even today. For example, Mayerhofer (1994) and Duda (1994) report with regard to an Austrian study in which 251 men and women participated that the woman decides on the design of the refrigerator, washing machine, microwave, vacuum cleaner, and coffee machine, and the man still decides on technical equipment, price, make, and retail outlet for TV and video equipment, video cameras, CD players, hi-fi equipment, and cameras. However, the question must be asked whether the interviewees were remembering and reporting their share of influence, or whether they were "escaping" their interviewers in a difficult situation by "taking flight" into stereotypical responses.

Influence Distribution in Relation to Decision Stage

The attempt to subdivide decision-making processes into different stages was based on the assumption that the course of a decision has a definable

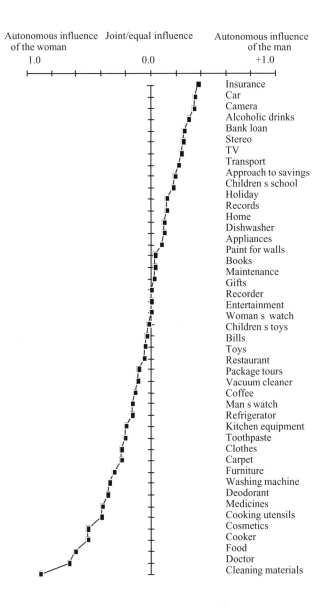

Autonomous influence of the woman	Joint/equal influence	Autonomous influence of the man
1.0	0.0	+1.0

Insurance
Car
Camera
Alcoholic drinks
Bank loan
Stereo
TV
Transport
Approach to savings
Children s school
Holiday
Records
Home
Dishwasher
Appliances
Paint for walls
Books
Maintenance
Gifts
Recorder
Entertainment
Woman s watch
Children s toys
Bills
Toys
Restaurant
Package tours
Vacuum cleaner
Coffee
Man s watch
Refrigerator
Kitchen equipment
Toothpaste
Clothes
Carpet
Furniture
Washing machine
Deodorant
Medicines
Cooking utensils
Cosmetics
Cooker
Food
Doctor
Cleaning materials

Figure 6.2   Influence distribution in relation to the type of goods under consideration (following Kirchler, 1989, p. 174).

145

beginning and proceeds to a precise end. It is assumed that when a desire arises, the partners proceed via the collection of information and choice to action. In the case of spending, this means a purchase. Decision processes are not conclusively ended, even after action has been taken. Partners often seek information retrospectively, in order to justify their action. The intention here is not to argue against the linearity of decision-making processes, even though plenty of studies call it into doubt (e.g. Braybrooke & Lindblom, 1963; Park, 1982). The issue is the development of influence patterns from the stage when the desire arises, through the information stage to the purchase of a commodity. Davis and Rigaux (1974) is a classic work on the distribution of influence in purchasing decisions which also provides information about the changes in patterns of influence during the process.

Wolfe (1959), Davis and Rigaux (1974) and others carried out their studies of influence distribution in household decisions using questionnaires asking who makes particular decisions. The response options ranged from "the man decides alone" via "both decide jointly" to "the woman decides alone". Four categories of control can be set up on the basis of the data obtained: decisions controlled (a) by the man or (b) by the woman; (c) made jointly; and (d) made sometimes by the man, sometimes by the woman. Davis and Rigaux asked couples which partner had most influence in the purchase of 25 items: the man (score points = 1), the woman (3), or both together (2). They also distinguished between the initiation stage, the information-gathering stage, and the purchasing stage. As suggested by Wolfe (1959), they then calculated the arithmetical mean of the answers obtained from every participant completing a questionnaire. This represents the relative influence of the partners. The percentage of joint decisions was calculated (i.e. the proportion of answers indicating that joint decisions had been taken, in relation to the total number of answers). The first of these values indicates the distribution of influence between man and woman; the second reflects the extent to which the decision-making is a joint matter. These two values provide the basis for constructing a schematic representation—the roles triangle—subdivisible into four categories of control: (a) decisions for which 50% of couples questioned report equal influence by both partners in the purchase of a particular product is termed syncratic. Where this value lies below 50%, the decision is termed autonomous. Where the balance of influence clearly favours either the man or the woman, the decision is called (b) male- or (c) female-dominated. If the man and woman decide on their own a roughly equal number of times, and that area of decision-making is not primarily under the control of one partner, these decisions are called (d) balanced decisions. Davis and Rigaux (1974) found that the proportion of syncratic decisions declines between the initiation stage and the information-seeking stage, rising again around the point of purchase. Similar results were

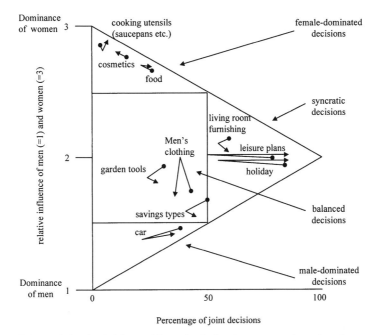

Figure 6.3   Variation in decision-making roles during three stages of purchase in ten selected product categories (Kirchler, 1988d; Kirchler & Kirchler, 1990). The arrows indicate the changes in decision-making roles from the desire (represented by a circle) through the information-gathering stage (change of direction) to the purchasing stage (arrowhead).

obtained when the study was repeated in Austria. Figure 6.3 presents part of these findings. A total of 99 families participated, consisting of husband, wife, and one child in the late teenage years. Autonomous purchases were made more often in the Austrian sample than Davis and Rigaux' results indicate. Above all, the information-gathering stage (as opposed to the initiation of the desire) was performed autonomously (Kirchler, 1988d; Kirchler & Kirchler, 1990). The finding that, in particular, information is gathered individually, with the purchase often being made jointly, was confirmed in the Vienna Diary Study, in which the 40 couples completed the Davis and Rigaux questionnaire three times, in addition to the diary.

Influence Distribution in Relation to the Relative Resource Contributions of the Partners

In his equity theory, Adams (1965) describes how people in social interaction situations seek an equitable distribution of resources, which may be either costs or gratification, of a material or non-material kind. People compare their own contributions to a budget and the recompense they receive with other people's, and regard the distribution of resources as just if they find them to be roughly equivalent. Justice is seen as a desirable goal. When related to influence in decision-making situations, this would mean that partners' dominance varies according to their contributions to the joint household budget. The partner who does more within the household, who can provide more financial resources, or can make a greater contribution to the couple's standing, thereby earns the right to greater influence in decisions.

Blood and Wolfe (1960) pointed to the importance of current social norms and the partners' relative contribution of resources, especially in purchasing decisions. In accordance with the relative resource theory, influence in household decisions lies almost entirely with the partner who is educated to a higher level, has a better paid job, has trained for a more prestigious profession, and in general commands more of the material and non-material goods the other needs.

The relative resource theory has been repeatedly confirmed in the past. If the dominant partner is the one who brings in more money, it follows that men would dominate in purchasing decisions as long as women did not undertake paid work, or while they followed careers with lower social esteem or lower income. Working women would logically have greater independence and greater influence at home than those not in paid work. Ruhfus (1976) looked at a number of studies, reaching the conclusion that the man must abdicate some authority and thus influence if his wife works. Scanzoni and Szinovacz (1980) believe that women who are in paid work and have a progressive attitude become tougher negotiating partners, fighting for their share in the decision-making and achieving it.

Life-cycle research provides further confirmation of the relative resource theory. It states that both partners have approximately equal say at the beginning of a relationship. Decisions are often taken jointly. Later, the partners share out tasks and become responsible for specific areas; increasingly, decisions are made autonomously. On the arrival of the first child, the woman's dependence on the man increases, and her influence declines. When the youngest child reaches school age, she becomes progressively less dependent, can resume paid work, and gains in influence. Once the children are working and able to leave home, the woman regains the degree of influence she had at the outset. The loss of influence by women with small children was often attributed to the reduction in the woman's contribution of resources. A woman whose time is mainly taken up with childcare is far less able to contribute material resources to the joint cause than a woman without children. Robertson (1990) argues that working women have more influence on important decisions than other women, probably because they bring more resources into the home than those not in paid work. Housewives meanwhile tend to have the say in less significant decisions about minor, everyday matters.

Studies in present-day industrialised countries of the present rarely confirm the relative resource theory. Webster (1995) finds that resource contributions are significant in particularly demanding purchasing decisions, but that a number of other factors help determine influence distribution. A study by Kirchler (1989) found that the partner who contributes more resources has no greater influence than the other. In the Vienna Diary Study (Kirchler et al., 1999), the partners' relative contribution of resources was likewise shown to be without significance. In the diary, participants daily recorded the level of their own contribution to the relationship on the day in question. The diary asked for their subjective opinion on material and non-material contributions. The relationship between the subjective contribution of resources and influence in current disagreements was calculated using partial correlations, keeping the relationship characteristics constant by using couple-specific dummy variables. In the 1171 entries by the women a correlation of $r = .007$ ($p = .82$) was found; in the 1128 entries made by the men, the correlation was $r = -.011$ ($p = .71$).

In contrast to Pahl (1989), Pross (1979, p. 149) believes that the significance of relative resource contributions has changed with time. "The fact that the man earns the money no longer means that he is master in the house."

Influence Distribution over Time and in Relation to Cultural Environment

According to Blood and Wolfe's (1960) theory of relative contribution of resources, the distribution of influence between partners is determined not only by their contributions, but also by social norms. A gender-specific variation in the distribution of influence is to be expected, governed by the values of society. These may favour either the traditional division of roles in the home (the man being responsible for matters outside the home, and for technical and important financial decisions; the wife for cooking, home-making and the children) or the modern, liberal view that the partners each allow the other equal competence and influence in various spheres of life. Social norms are all the more likely to explain influence distribution between partners, the more those partners have internalised society's values (Qualls, 1987).

Social norms and subjective values are not stable. There has been much discussion in recent decades about a change in values in industrialised countries, and a consequent change in roles in the home. The eclipse of traditional roles has brought an increasing equality of rights for partners in formerly distinct spheres of responsibility. Partners seek a greater share in decision-making instead of deciding autonomously. They either make more joint decisions or establish a balance of influence in various areas, including those that used previously to be male or female-dominated. This last appears more likely according to a review of various data from different studies (Kirchler, 1989). The interest of the "new" working wife no longer focuses primarily on food, cooking utensils, and items of home decoration; she is increasingly interested in tools and equipment that used to lie almost exclusively in the husband's domain. For example, Snyder and Serafin (1985) report that women are involved in 81% of new car purchases—cars were formerly an overwhelmingly male concern. The man for his part increasingly takes decisions about home furnishings and cooking utensils himself, rather than leaving them to his partner.

Social norms constitute binding guidelines for behaviour within the family. Society's ideas as to what is appropriate change over time. They also vary in relation to social class and cultural background. Joint decisions are more common in middle-income households of middle status than in upper- or lower-class households (e.g. Dahlhoff, 1980; Mayer & Boor, 1988). The reason is probably that modern attitudes have replaced traditional ones in middle-class homes. Partners may decide autonomously in lower-class homes because they still adhere more strongly to traditional norms, and observe a strict division of roles on that basis. They are each deciding within their own sphere of autonomy. In upper-class families, on the other hand, autonomous decisions may be the consequence of spending freedom: Money is not scarce, so everyone can buy what they wish, frequently without the need to discuss spending plans with a partner.

Values vary not only in society and over time, but between different cultures. In traditional societies, autonomous decision-making—differentiated according to product—is found mainly in lower-class families with a patriarchal power structure. Webster (1994) reports, for example, that in South American families men decide about important purchases such as TV sets, cars, and insurance if they adhere to the traditional values of their group. Women have more power where the men have given up traditional concepts. In societies in transition from traditional values to modern, liberal ones, the inherited norms cease to be binding, and matters are decided by the relative contribution of resources. The relative resource theory has frequently been confirmed in societies in the throes of a change in values. In liberal societies, a balanced distribution of power between the man and the woman is seen as fair. Partners usually decide autonomously or jointly, independently of gender or of the category of the commodity. Taken overall, both partners have equal influence. Rodman (1967) believes that the relative resource theory is valid in societies where social norms are changing and thus become ineffective. Where clear value concepts exist, whether traditional or liberal, the contribution of resources loses its significance because social norms are more powerful in determining the dynamics of interaction.

Influence Distribution in Relation to Relative Subject Knowledge and Relative Interest

Studies of group psychology point not only to the normative pressure that can be exerted by one partner on the basis of the role stereotypes or concepts of justice held by society, but also to pressure based on information. In a discussion situation, the opposing party finds information hard to resist (Burnstein, 1982). Armstrong and Anderson (undated) investigated the importance of factual information in discussions. They asked a couple, at home, to discuss the discipline to be imposed on a boy who had behaved unfairly in an argument with a friend. One partner received more factual information than the other. The partner with greater information was inclined to rely more on the knowledge they themselves possessed, rather than on their partner's, and the person with less factual knowledge showed a greater willingness to accept their partner's opinion. The authors conclude that women do not yield the argument more than men because society requires them to be more yielding, nor because their contribution of resources is less than men's; they do so if the man has greater knowledge of the subject than they do. If they have a well-founded argument, they insist. It is the degree of competence and information that counts. In purchasing decisions too, the partner who dominates appears to be the one who is better informed about the goods under consideration (Burns, 1976; Corfman, 1987; Corfman & Lehmann, 1987; Qualls, 1987; Webster, 1995; Davis, 1972).

A diary study by Kirchler (1989) confirmed that, in purchasing decisions, it is not only the partners' competence that is influential in deciding the outcome of a decision; so is relative interest. Seymour and Lessne (1984) also stress the significance of subjective interest and involvement. The greater a partner's interest in a commodity, the more information that partner will gather, and the more purchasing alternatives are considered, the greater that partner's knowledge, competence, and, ultimately, influence will be.

The Vienna Diary Study undertook an extensive analysis of the significance of these factors, subject knowledge and importance or interest, in disagreements. A total of 40 couples reported daily whether a disagreement had been resolved, who had begun the discussion, how much knowledge each had of the topic, and how important the discussion was to the man or the woman. They were asked to assess the climate of the discussion, and to record how objectively and emotionally they had each spoken. Finally they recorded the degree of influence enjoyed by each partner. The data were used to calculate, firstly, the correlations between the determinants of influence investigated in the study and the actual influence exerted by the partners, and, secondly, regressions, with the most important determinants of influence as predictors and relative influence as the criterion. Since the

TABLE 6.2
Determinants of influence in the Vienna Diary Study

Determinant of influence	Couples' entries	M	SD	Partial correlation with relative influence
Relative influence (self)	Woman	48.45	18.79	
	Man	51.04	17.70	
Interest and importance				
Who began discussion	Woman	.54	.50	.16**
(0 = partner, 1 = informant)	Man	.40	.49	.18**
Importance for self (1 = Topic	Woman	5.61	1.65	.19**
is unimportant, 7 = important)	Man	5.35	1.57	.16**
Assessment of importance for	Woman	5.21	1.64	−.16**
partner	Man	5.57	1.52	−.16**
Knowledge				
Own knowledge of subject	Woman	5.27	1.57	.13**
(1 = slight, 7 = good)	Man	5.43	1.34	.15**
Assessment of partner's	Woman	4.99	1.59	−.15**
knowledge	Man	5.20	1.45	−.17**
Mood of conversation	Woman	4.18	1.86	.08*
(1 = unpleasant, 7 = pleasant)	Man	4.36	1.75	−.04
Manner of speaking				
Own objectivity	Woman	4.85	1.72	.03
(1 = unobjective, 7 = objective)	Man	5.27	1.46	−.03
Assessment of partner's	Woman	4.77	1.69	.10**
objectivity	Man	4.73	1.65	−.05
Own emotionality	Woman	4.73	1.66	.06
(1 = unemotional, 7 = emotional)	Man	4.26	1.63	.16**
Assessment of partner's	Woman	4.44	1.61	−.12**
emotionality	Man	4.64	1.64	−.02

Note: The 33 women and 33 men who had registered more than five conflicts during the one-year period of the study recorded in total 1127 and 1083 conflicts respectively. The degrees of freedom of the conflict correlations are 1093 (women) and 1049 for the sample of men. The effect of the personal parameters was removed from the partial correlations. Levels of significance: ** $p < .01$; * $p < .05$.

Source: Kirchler et al. (1999).

participants had recorded differing numbers of conflicts, the couples were held constant in the correlation calculations by use of dummy variables. Table 6.2 records the results, demonstrating the significance of subjective importance and knowledge. The manner of speaking also proves to be significant.

The determinants of influence were further examined in a multiple regression analysis. First, the personal parameters were considered as dummy variables in the list of predictors; then, the relative subjective importance to self and to the partner, the relative knowledge, and the perceived degree of emotionality in the individual's manner of speaking. The differences between the entries for self and for the partner were calculated. Personal parameters and the influence determinants both proved to be relevant. It was possible to explain 21% of the variance in the female sample, and 16% among the men. In the first regression model, considering personal parameters, an R^2-adjusted figure of .12 ($p < .01$) is obtained for the women, and .05 ($p < .01$) for the sample of men. In a further model, considering the relative subjective importance, relative knowledge and relative emotionality, the R^2-adjusted figure rises by .08 ($p < .01$) and .11 ($p < .01$) respectively, to .21 for the women and .16 for the men. It may be interesting to note that the personal parameters explain considerably more variance in the sample of women than men. It appears that particular relationship characteristics, as perceived by the women, are more significant predictors of relative influence than as perceived by the men. This result appears again in all the subsequent regression analyses, and could indicate that women largely experience the distribution of influence at home as set role segmentation, whereas men's experience of relative influence fluctuates in response to the current determinants. A distribution of influence that is entrenched in their favour does not accord with the spirit of the times, so might be suppressed by the men. Women meanwhile might continue to see themselves in the weaker position. The statistical results are clear: Out of a total of 33 women, 8 stated that they generally had significantly less influence than their partners; 2 that they had significantly more. Average influence, independently of conversation topic and calculated over the entire year of the study, was below 34% for 8 women; 2 women assessed their influence at about two-thirds. In the sample of men, only 2 recorded an unbalanced distribution of influence of below 45% or over 55%. The men in couples 33 and 37 assessed their general influence at 63%.

In the aforementioned regression analysis with all diary entries relating to disagreements in general, the partners report that relative knowledge, subjective importance, and manner of speaking all have a marked effect on relative influence. For the sample of women, relative importance, relative knowledge, and emotionality were significant determinants of influence, with weights beta = .17 ($p < .01$), beta = .16 ($p < .01$), and beta = .09 ($p < .01$) respectively. For the men, beta values of .13 ($p < .01$), .23 ($p < .01$) and .13 ($p < .01$) respectively were obtained.

In the Vienna Diary Study, we were able to analyse five different topics of disagreement. Multiple regressions were also computed separately for these five topics with the relative knowledge, relative importance, and relative emotionality as predictors of influence. Table 6.3 lists the significance of the predictors for economic issues, work issues, relationship issues, matters

TABLE 6.3
Results of regression analyses in respect of various determinants of influence by conflict issue

	Economic issues	Work issues	Children's issues	Relationship issues	Leisure issues
The variance explained by personal parameters (regression model 1: couples as dummy variables) and explained variance due to relative importance, relative knowledge, and relative emotionality (regression model 2)					
Regression model 1					
R^2-adjusted					
Women	.07*	.12**	.21**	.27**	.01
Men	.00	.02	.14**	.05	.06
Regression model 2					
R^2-adjusted					
Women	.23**	.22**	.25**	.31**	.07*
Men	.16**	.15**	.21**	.18**	.10**
Regression weights (beta values) of determinants of influence from regression model 2					
Relative importance					
Women	.15*	.17*	.24**	.10	.16
Men	.18*	−.04	.27**	.15	.05
Relative knowledge					
Women	.32**	.20**	.01	.04	.01
Men	.35**	.30**	.08	.22**	.05
Relative emotionality					
Women	.08	.14	−.01	.18*	.17*
Men	.08	.20*	.03	.23**	.21*

Note: In regression model 1, personal parameters only were considered, i.e. couple-specific dummy variables were included in the regression. Model 2 also considers relative importance, knowledge, and emotionality. For economic conflicts, the additional consideration of relative importance, knowledge, and emotionality in the analyses of the data from women and men explained 16% of the variance. Level of significance: ** $p < .01$; * $p < .05$.

Source: Kirchler et al. (1999).

relating to children, and leisure issues. In the analysis of the female sample, there was a significant relationship between the personal parameters and the relative influence of the partners for four of the five types of issue. For the male sample, only matters relating to children showed any significant relationship to the personal parameters. This means that from the women's point of view, the distribution of influence is significantly dependent on the characteristics of the couple. The men see the distribution of influence as far more clearly determined by other parameters. In conflicts on economic issues, relative knowledge and relative importance mainly count. The manner of speaking has no significance. In conflicts about the relationship on the other hand, an emotional style appears decisive. This also applies in conflicts about leisure and friends. In conflicts about paid professional work and housework, the partner who is better informed is likely to enjoy greater influence; subjective importance also counts according to the women. In disagreements relating to the children, the partner with more say is the one for whom the subject is more important.

Influence Distribution in Relation to Emotions and the Quality of the Relationship

The partner with greater love is more likely to yield in conflict situations. Relative love and satisfaction, among other variables, should determine the balance of influence between spouses (Seymour & Lessne, 1984). Loving couples in a harmonious relationship are known to interact differently from those who are unsatisfied with their relationship. The quality of the relationship and emotions have so far seldom been investigated as determinants of influence.

Park and colleagues in particular (Park, Tansuhaj, & Kolbe, 1991; Park, Tansuhaj, Spangenberg, & McCullough, 1995) point to the importance of not ignoring the role of emotions, given that decision-making between intimate partners takes place in a context where feelings are particularly crucial. "The relationships between family members which create notions of hearth and home are centered on the deepseated affection members have for one another. The implications of such interpersonal affection pervades all family decisions" (Park et al., 1991, p. 651). The role of emotions in decision-making manifests itself in a variety of ways. The authors sum it up in the form of six propositions:

P1: Affectional bonds may inhibit hard-line, uncompromising, self-interest positions as members are cognizant and have a desire to maintain their long-term affective relationship. A willingness to acquiesce to members' desires follows.

P2: The greater an individual member's requirements/need for intimate relationships with family members the greater will be the use of conflict avoidance strategies.

P3: The intimacy of family members affects the means for solving conflict. Highly intimate members may resolve conflict in more cooperative manners such as bargaining, trading, logical persuasion, and problem-solving (Sheth and Cosmas, 1975). Conversely, low intimacy families may make greater use of coercion, authority, formal authority and the like.

P4: Greater intimacy of families may result in greater incidence of joint decision-making as opposed to single member decision-making dominance.

P5:   The impact of the affection component in family decision-making may differ by product class and type. Products that involve the entire family by means of joint usage, involvement, or interest will likely reflect more affectional elements than those which are used exclusively by only one member of the family.

P6:   Similarity of goals and values among members may reduce family decision conflict levels (Park et al., 1991, p. 654).

According to Park et al. (1995), shared love and empathy, as opposed to feelings of guilt and shame, lead above all to a consonance between the partners' preferences, and reduced intensity of conflict. An empirical study by Qualls and Jaffe (1992) confirmed that there is a negative correlation between conflict intensity and similarity between the partners in the matters of sex roles, influence structures, and the importance of a decision. Positive emotions suppress conflict resolution tactics such as punishment, threats, autonomous decisions, forcing, egocentric and avoidance tactics. In harmonious relationships, where the partners love each other and are amicably disposed to each other in decision-making, cooperation and a willingness to make sacrifices in the interests of deepening the relationship can be expected (Van Lange et al., 1997).

Little account has been taken of the quality of the relationship and the emotions existing between the partners in purchasing decisions. In those rare cases where it has been done, it was seldom possible to demonstrate a connection (Kirchler, 1989). Whereas Schaninger and Buss (1986) found that women in stable relationships have more influence than those in unstable ones, other studies deny the assumption of any correlation between the stability of a relationship or satisfaction with it and the woman's influence. What is not disputed is that behaviour in interactions is seen to vary according to satisfaction, and also that differences are observed in the couples' conduct of their expenditure. Schaninger and Buss (1986) demonstrate that in happy relationships, more money is invested in shared objects than in the sort of objects that can easily be apportioned if the couple separates. A series of further studies confirmed that happy and unhappy partners use different tactics of influence and persuasion (Kirchler, 1993a; Kirchler & Berti, 1996; Kirchler et al., 1999).

The Vienna Diary Study points to differences in influence distribution in happy and unhappy relationships. Independently of the substance of the disagreement, entries by both men and women showed that satisfied partners, men or women, enjoy slightly greater influence than dissatisfied ones when the topic is important to them. Separate analyses for economic issues, conflicts about work, children, the relationship, and leisure showed that relative importance is of greatest significance in happy relationships when the subject of the dispute between happy partners is their relationship, themselves, or the other partner.

Influence Distribution in Relation to Past Decisions

Pollay (1968) was one of the first authors to point to the significance of past decisions on the dynamics of current decision-making. According to his concept of benefit debts, which he calls "utility debts", the partner whose wishes were realised or whose argument held sway in the past has a benefit debt to settle, and must restore the balance of a notional utility account by yielding in another decision.

Corfman and Lehmann (1987; see also Corfman, 1985, 1987) demonstrated in purchase decision studies that partners' influence depends importantly on decision-making history, especially the distribution of influence in past decision situations. They also demonstrated a positive correlation with the relative interest in a particular commodity and the partner's expert knowledge. The value of the relationship was another relevant determinant of influence. Partners were increasingly willing to yield according to the importance they placed on improving the quality of the relationship or avoiding conflict. Partners' relative contributions of resources were without significance. As regards the importance of past influence, Corfman and Lehmann (1987) assume an unwritten law of equality, according to which the partners try to equalise their relative influence over several decisions, with first one, then the other partner having the say. Corfman and Lehmann (1987) believe that it is the fact rather than the degree of influence that matters. Partners appear to forget the absolute amount of influence, but not who had the say; the partner who determines the outcome of one conflict must yield in the next.

The significance of decision-making history will be examined later when the interconnectedness of decisions is discussed. That will investigate the influence of benefit debt on current decisions, and the significance of differences in influence between men and women in the past.

Influence Distribution Between Parents and Children

Studies of decisions in private households mainly consider the man and woman. Children, third parties in the decision with a nonetheless important influence, are not considered. Lackman and Lanasa (1993), for example, report that children in the US between the ages of 4 and 11 personally spend five billion dollars a year, and help decide on expenditure of 130 billion dollars. Children between the ages of 12 and 19 spend an annual 55 billion dollars, controlling jointly with their parents another 249 billion dollars. The influence of children and young people in decision processes is disputed. Some authors speak of a process of democratisation within the family, with children's influence increasing; others see children's influence as negligible.

In an Austrian replication of the study by Davis and Rigaux (1974; Kirchler & Kirchler, 1990), the young people questioned had hardly any influence over the decisions in Figure 6.2, according to their own statements and those of their parents. Children and young people decide autonomously about a commodity in 2.6% of cases; in 0.1% they decide in conjunction with their father, in 6.2% in conjunction with their mother, and in 9.7% with both parents. Children mainly had influence in decisions about toys or clothes; they shared in discussions about leisure and holidays, or the type of school they should attend. They also shared in decision-making by their mother about the purchase of cooking utensils, food, and cosmetics.

Children share in purchasing decisions about items that involve them. They also have considerable right to express their views when the parents disagree and can intervene actively in the decision as coalition partners. In the Vienna Diary Study (Kirchler et al., 1999) men and women mainly reported using coalition tactics to persuade their partner when children were present. Children were present in 80% of the cases in which women reported using coalition tactics, and in 90% of those reported by men. Ward and Wackman (1973) sent out questionnaires in which the mothers of 5- to 12-year-old children stated how often their children successfully influence a decision. Whether children's wishes are met depends essentially on the category of the product. Mothers often allowed their wishes over the purchase of cereals, snacks, sweets, and juice. Children's wishes were less often influential in decisions about other foods such as bread and coffee. An Italian study reported similar findings. Mauri (1996) asked about the influence of children in various product categories and the mothers' readiness to fulfil the children's wishes. This revealed that children mainly want to have their opinions heard over toys, ice cream, trainers, books, sweets, and fizzy drinks. They are less often interested in helping to decide about coffee, pet food, records, food, radios, cassette recorders, and cameras. Figure 6.4 shows the average frequency of requests to be heard and the mothers' willingness to listen to children's wishes. Children are shown to want a share in decisions over products that particularly affect them, and mothers often accede to their wishes when these are expressed. A study by Winter and Mayerhofer (1983a, b) similarly showed that children between 4 and 9 years often express their wishes about toys, ice cream, and sweets, and that such wishes are often fulfilled. Food, clothes, and shoes seem to have little importance for children in this age group. They express their wishes about them less frequently, and any such wishes are seldom fulfilled.

The age of the children is of significance, as well as the product type: Older children are accorded far greater rights to express their wishes than younger ones, and are increasingly being given more say in matters outside children's concerns (Caron & Ward, 1975; Jenkins, 1979; Mehrotra & Torges, 1977). Beatty and Talpade (1994) investigated the influence of

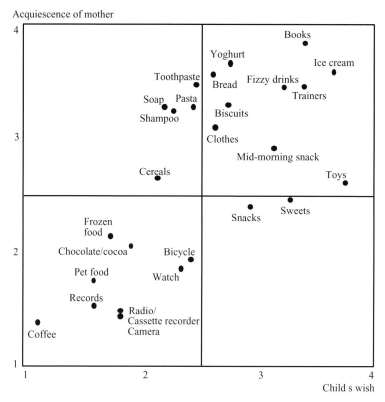

Figure 6.4 Frequency of children's requests for their wishes to be heard in the purchase of various products and mothers' willingness to accede (Mauri, 1996).

teenagers (average age 18 years) in decisions about TV sets, stereo and telephone equipment, and furniture for use by themselves and the whole family. This showed that children are allowed to express their views particularly when they are motivated to share the decision. They are listened to if they are going to use the product. Young people's product knowledge and personal income were of little importance.

The views of children and young people are not always heard. Their influence in discussions about buying a car, furniture, household equipment, life insurance, etc. is slight (Filiatrault & Ritchie, 1980; Kirchler, 1989). Children in one-parent families have in principle greater influence than children in families with both parents (Ahuja & Stinson, 1993). Older children have more influence than younger, and firstborn children are more likely than others to be involved in purchasing decisions (Moschis, 1987; Shim, Snyder, & Gehrt, 1995). Even where the children's direct influence is not great, their influence as coalition partners for their parents is still considerable. If parents cannot agree, disputes are often settled through the children's intervention, or when one partner points out the importance of the decision for the children.

In conclusion, it may be said of partners' influence in decision-making—especially in purchasing decisions—that studies from the 1960s onwards indicate a fairly even distribution of influence. One or the other partner will have greater influence, depending on the issue to be decided, product type for example, and on which aspects of the various alternatives are discussed. Further determinants of influence are cultural values, and, linked with these, sex role orientation. Depending on the culture, there will also be the partners' relative contribution of resources, their relative subject knowledge and interest in the decision, and the distribution of benefit debt from past decisions. Regarding the influence of children, it seems that their direct influence is often overestimated, but that they do influence decisions indirectly as coalition partners.

CHAPTER SEVEN

Close Relationships and Decision Dynamics

> *If we simply live immersed in the (stream of consciousness),*
> *we encounter only undifferentiated experiences that melt into one*
> *another in a flowing continuum.*
> —Schultz (1973, p. 17); quoted in Duck (1994, p. 39)

THE INTERCONNECTEDNESS OF DECISIONS

The Conceptual Background to the Interconnectedness of "Business" in Close Relationships

The development of biology and zoology into scientific disciplines can be traced to the appearance of the theory of evolution, which provided a tool for the establishment of a taxonomy of forms and species. This laid the necessary foundation for further progress. Plants and animals are clearly defined natural entities that can be grouped into logical categories. In psychology, where the object of research is human experience and behaviour, which change constantly with the course of time, the task of isolating these objects of study into units of experience and behaviour is difficult indeed. If a taxonomy of such units could be set up, this would mark just one further step towards establishing a common basis for the study of psychological matters.

Speaking of everyday experience, Pulver (1991) writes that psychology has to date ignored the elements of which everyday experience is built up. He feels that it may in consequence have failed to create a taxonomy of psychological research phenomena, leaving it today with a blind spot in its view of everyday human life. There is a need for naturalistic, empirical research to learn about the world in which we live and which we seek to study. Dörner (1983, p. 24; quoted in Pulver, 1991, p. 28) says: "Psychology has bypassed certain stages of development as a science which may in fact be essential. Consider the painstaking efforts made in biology . . . starting with the precise description of the subject matter to be studied. We search in vain for an equivalent stage of 'collecting beetles and butterflies' in psychology. There are hardly even rudimentary moves towards creating a general morphology of human behaviour and experience."

The description of complex everyday incidents, experience, and behaviour, constantly changing and developing in the course of human life, has been largely neglected. If one author offers a detailed definition, a prototypical description, or a systematic analysis of some field of psychological research, it seldom happens that others share the same conceptual framework. Psychology is far from having commonly accepted definitions of the objects it sets out to investigate, let alone a commonly accepted taxonomy of ways of experiencing and behaving. Psychology, along with other disciplines that investigate close relationships, has rashly bypassed the (necessary) step of undertaking a systematic analysis of its field of enquiry. These disciplines are now engaged in the meticulous scientific investigation of one feature after another, only to make the repeated discovery that a slight change in the focus of attention, in the circumstances of the situation, or some other variable, brings down the edifice of the theory that had been constructed to explain such matters as interaction processes, planning, and action. This in turn requires new or more complex theories to be devised, whose value is once more limited. It becomes even more impossible to see the wood of human experience for the trees being placed in it, which are far in excess of the woodland being explored and described. The problems of investigating a constant flux of changing phenomena are enormous.

Decisions in close relationships are also continually shifting. It is hard to isolate them from each other and from other activities. It is nevertheless entirely possible to speak about decisions in an unreflecting way, as if decisions had a clear-cut beginning and end, and so represented clearly identifiable, separate events. If partners are asked to describe their everyday experience, they recount a host of activities: shopping, preparing meals, sending the children to school and collecting them, supervising homework, cleaning the house, doing the washing, going to work and quickly looking in on their parents on the way home, getting dripping taps repaired, planning leisure time, maintaining contact with friends, arranging invitations, and arguing about the TV programme. These activities may become a priority to be carried out or something to be shelved according to the needs of the moment, and the attitudes and intentions that happen to prevail. Partners experience everyday life as structured events, and are able to talk about them. People are not only able to provide information about their experiences, but group similar events into categories that they find meaningful; they generalise, and recount how they normally organise and experience a particular situation; they explain how they normally reach a decision, and say how their partner always behaves when talk turns to a particular subject. They do so despite the wisdom of millennia; it was Heraclitus who said that it is impossible to sail up the same river twice (Duck, 1994).

How are specific occurrences distinguished from the events simultaneously occupying the background or foreground of our experience? How can particular occurrences be lifted out of the flow of time and experience and set apart from others? The study of decision-making in close relationships poses the question as to when a decision begins or ends, and how to define the boundaries that separate it from other activities happening at the time. The current literature about economic decisions does not offer an answer. The approach adopted assumes decisions to be given, isolated entities that can at best be seen as beginning with one partner expressing the desire for a commodity, continuing with the gathering of information, and ending with the choice of one of the possible alternatives and the purchase itself. Hinde (1997, p. 40) writes fittingly: "Most relationships involve interactions of diverse types, and those interactions affect each other. Any marital therapist would agree not only that what goes on in bed affects what goes on at the breakfast table, but also that the atmosphere at the breakfast table affects that in bed." Specific experiences at home affect other areas of private experience. A series of studies of the spillover effects of problems at work on stress at home and vice versa provide convincing proof that the analysis of one area of experience in isolation, whilst ignoring others, is inadequate (e.g. Almeida & Kessler, 1998; Almeida & Wethington, 1996; Bolger et al., 1989a, b).

Applied to decision-making, this means that decision processes cannot be analysed adequately without at the same time considering the context in which they are set, past and concurrent events, as well as consequences and goals projected into the future.

The expression used by Billig (1987) to describe life as a whole, "unfinished business", well describes everyday life and decisions in close relationships. Decisions follow closely on from experiences in past decision-making processes and their outcomes, and determine future processes. A decision often leads to further decisions or dialogue between the partners, opening up disagreements in other areas. When partners make promises about their future behaviour in order to gain advantage in a current decision, they sometimes decide the outcome of future decisions.

Partners' behaviour, decision-making in particular, is orientated towards the future. However, the present does not erase the past. Partners retain at least some memory of their interaction processes, and refer to the outcomes of past decisions during current ones. Duck (1994, p. 52) writes that experiences in permanent flux and constant change prompt the conclusion that relationships are not psychologically immutable facts, but a collective whole of "unfinished businesses", open to constant re-interpretation and reformulation in the light of unfolding events. "Living in a relationship is thus also living with continual and sequential explanation or interpretation in a world of changing possibilities, not living with finalities and unchanging certainties that some people would prefer to find." Everything seems geared to the future, yet the past remains alive: "the past is not sacred. Examining the past includes the possibility of rethinking it in some way." (Duck, 1994, p. 54). It is therefore essential to view couples' behaviour in the context of time.

As the partners constantly interpret and discuss shared experiences, common conceptions are formed, a shared "knowledge" of their common "reality", and "accounts", which in their turn enable the prediction of future events, based on the argument that the past can predict the future. Such common "accounts" of the past make it possible to anticipate the future and to justify particular behaviour.

The events occurring amid the stream of everyday life are sometimes planned and deliberately brought about; sometimes they are simply interpreted as such. They may be reformulated to appear reasonable, and so that overall behaviour is felt to be justified. Besides using goals and past events to justify certain action, there can be a process of retrospective rationalisation. For this, the flow of events must be broken down into segments. These segments must have an internal unity, and stand in a subjectively defined, coherent relationship to each other. Everyday life, in short, and its multiple complex of events, are subjectively (re)organised as an individual and as a couple, and so made comprehensible (Duck, 1994).

Events such as decision-making processes inevitably lack sharply defined boundaries separating them from other events in the flow of time. If decision-making processes are to be analysed, then those who make them must first recognise, then observe and describe them. Decisions as observable units are hard for non-participants to recognise, but must be identifiable by the decision-makers themselves, even if they are difficult to define. Faßnacht (1995, p. 112), in the context of a systematic analysis of behaviour, calls this type of process, arguments and the like, a *Zeitwert* (time-related value). He says:

> Though they can in principle be enumerated, observable units . . . are by no means as easily defined as may appear at first sight. If, while the event is in progress, one tries to identify the beginning and end of arguments in time, one soon encounters difficulties. The beginning and end of the behaviour are always fairly diffuse transition zones to our perception. What appears conceptually and in terms of content to be a unity, becomes problematic when

we try to define it in time. For from the point of view of perception, the unity in time of any particular unit of behaviour is by no means as clear-cut as common speech might suggest with its well-defined vocabulary. There may well be a close connection here with the fact that units in terms of content are often abstract units. Such units—concepts—cannot be enumerated. The practical problem of defining time boundaries in concrete terms cannot therefore be solved, even by highly differentiated theoretical analysis. Practice will no doubt bring improvement in placing the division. At the final count, it will only be possible to achieve a high degree of objectivity in placing the division if we alter the degree of resolution: in the interests of greater objectivity, we shall dispense with precision, and coarsely tune our observation. We see once more the importance of correct resolution in the discovery process.

Everything that applies to the scientific observer applies also to the study participants involved as interview partners or in replying to questionnaires, who must observe their experience and behaviour introspectively in the process.

In the analysis of everyday experiences such as decisions in close relationships, certain occurrences need to be "extracted" from the course of events without losing sight of the whole. Individual experiences depend on other, concurrent and subsequent events. However, Pauleikhoff (1965, p. 75; quoted in Pulver 1991, p. 39) emphasises: "In order to see the whole, it is not so much the external course of the day's events that is important, but much more its inner form. The inner essence is the main thing. We need to discover details and to understand the whole from the point of view of the person living and experiencing that day."

How can individuals and couples be instructed to observe and then describe their experiences during decision-making processes in such a way that both they and other couples can provide comparable accounts of their experiences, set in the course of the day's events? How can this be done so that the results can then be summarised, without running too great a risk of reducing various phenomena, each specific to the relationship and the particular situation, to a mere average, and consequently of making invalid statements, because the details have become lost in the process? It must in addition be possible to instruct couples successfully how to identify and describe decision-making processes in a comparable way according to defined criteria, so that we can generalise the findings.

Pulver (1991) demonstrated a suitable procedure in his description of his everyday experience over a period of several years. His careful procedure can be taken as a model for recording decision-making within a relationship. Pulver (1991, p. 80f) summarises his method for recording everyday working life in the following points. It should not be difficult to take and reapply the essential aspects to the purpose of research into decisions in close relationships:

1. The day's events are not observed from outside but reported as seen from within . . .
2. However, they are not . . . recounted in retrospect by the person involved, but recorded directly as they occur.
3. The course of the day's events is not recorded in the form of a continuous process (though even narrative is only able to approximate to this), but as a sequence of more or less self-contained units . . .
4. The units into which the day is subdivided are not defined by set limits imposed from outside . . ., nor are they arbitrary or "born of chance" . . ., but determined by the subject themselves in accordance with their own experience.
5. The day's events to be recorded cover only the "working day" [making it a specific area of experience and behaviour: authors' note] though this is understood in a broad sense.
6. The individual activities are not simply . . . evaluated according to general categories, but captured and processed according to their (thematically) individual character.
7. It is not the "typical" or "average" day that is of interest . . ., nor are sample days selected . . .; rather, the investigation extends over a long, continuous series of days. The sequence of working days is recorded in an unbroken chain, and not just the work of one day.
8. The focus is not just the events in the series themselves, but also the longer or shorter-term linkage between them, done by recording the causative moments behind changes of activity, and the business of planning and determining.
9. In contrast to all other . . . studies of the course of everyday life, the collection of data is limited to one person.

Applying this to the study of decision-making in close relationships, the individuals making the decisions should also be the ones to observe and record them. Since it is difficult to record the information during the decision process itself, the partners should be instructed to observe what is happening and record it shortly afterwards. It is the couples who define what is a decision, working on the instruction to interpret this as communication and action concerning an issue addressed in common, which involves the motive of realising a goal, and choosing one alternative out of several possibilities (e.g. the purchase of a commodity). The subject matter to be recorded includes all economic and non-economic decision-making processes arising from a difference of opinion between the partners, set in the context of everyday life. It is usually the case that the generalisation of the findings is of interest—as in the Vienna Diary Study quoted above. This being so, it seems appropriate to investigate more than one couple, and to carry out some analyses using the entire sample, some using sub-groups, and some in relation to individual couples.

Decisions can be defined as thematic topics (see below), characterised by the wish of one partner for one of various possible alternatives, communication of that wish to the other partner, and discussion of it through to its realisation or abandonment. That discussion is experienced by the partners as a decision-making process in which both make known their views, try to settle differences of opinion, and finally take action to realise the wish, shared or otherwise. The unity of a decision topic is held together by the actions, discussions, and emotions of which it consists. This applies even if the decision is interrupted by other everyday activities and resumed later. When a decision topic becomes the focus of the couple's attention, other topics of everyday life are forced into the background. The subject matter of a decision must be pursued as a topic for a while at least before other topics can be discussed and the decision once more consigned to the diffuse general course of events. There it swims in the stream with other topics until "landed" and brought to a conclusion or forgotten and allowed to swim away undealt with.

Thematic topics are, according to Pulver (1991, p. 132), "thematically self-contained sequences of activity or discontinuous series of such, which despite interruption belong together in terms of content". Decisions so seen are thematically coherent communication objects and sequences of activity with the desire and aim of planning some matter, gathering information about it, and realising one of the possible alternatives on the basis of the partners' wishes. Within everyday life, the partners' aims and wishes are imprecisely differentiated, while still being distinguishable, governing the partners' behaviour for a time. The other thematic topics currently in the background can suddenly intrude and alter the interaction between the partners. March and Simon (1958, p. 99) write with respect to decisions in organisations that there is always one current topic in the negotiation, with a number of other latent topics constantly "lurking" and awaiting their hour. Topics often coincide with other, concurrent ones. "The thematic principle that binds them together . . . maintains their integrity in the melée of activities and beyond" (Pulver, 1991, p. 133).

Disagreements and decisions are thematic topics. Pulver (1991, p. 154) defines thematic topics as "a matter (a task or object of attention) which occupies me once or repeatedly, in passing or exclusively for a time, or one with which I intend to occupy myself; which I perceive as a coherent unity separate from other tasks or objects of attention or which I place of my own accord in a united relationship". Seen in this light, conflicts and decisions are coherent bodies of subject matter, the object of communication and activity, that have significance for individuals and couples. Partners actively turn their attention to decision topics, make certain plans of action, and commit themselves to deal with them, at least for a time. Decisions, a special type of topic, can like other types occupy the "arena of activity" (Pulver,

1991, p. 153) and dominate the course of behaviour during that time. The structure of an individual's or a couple's course of behaviour is mainly governed by the alternation between concerns of different thematic content.

Having clarified what a thematic topic is, and that decision-making processes can also be viewed as thematic topics, we must ask how individual decisions and other topics are interconnected to create the sum of everyday events. Analyses to date have shown that decision processes relating to a particular topic are interconnected in the dimension of time with past and future—anticipated—decisions. We must also assume a structural connection between decisions and simultaneously existing topics in the current situation in which the dynamics of decisions and other activities affect each other, even if the focus of attention is on the decision topic. Certain cases from the Vienna Diary Study illustrate the extent to which various topics of everyday life in close relationships are interwoven. These involve the purchase of a present for the couple's son and the decision to buy a guitar, as described earlier.

Decisions such as purchasing decisions are not finished and forgotten once the purchase has taken place. Instead, along with other experiences, they form the basis of future joint decisions; they constitute the partners' knowledge of behaviour in those decisions, such as the nature of the influence tactics employed. The manner of interaction is a determinant of influence in future decisions. So too are explicit promises and implicit demands and commitments made by a partner in a particular decision situation to obtain his or her wish. Just as consecutive decision processes can be seen as interconnected, so interconnections can be found between topics dealt with simultaneously. For example, a husband may agree to his wife's plans for leisure pursuits if she agrees to his wish to buy certain goods.

In addition to the interdependence of topics in terms of time and subject matter, topics of varying degrees of importance emerge. Chattoe and Gilbert (1997) distinguish five levels of importance: the first of these contains life events such as marriage, children, decisions about profession and career, house purchase, etc. Next come insurance, pension plans, savings decisions, and the like. On the third level are decisions about holidays, part-time work, and so on. The next level below contains lesser savings decisions such as a weekly sum put aside for extra expenses. The authors place daily purchases as a group on the fifth and final level. Decision topics on the same level may be dealt with in succession or simultaneously; different levels in the hierarchy are often dealt with simultaneously.

Should we conclude from this pattern of interconnectedness in everyday matters that all activity in a partnership is mutually determined, and that everyday events in their entirety serve the one end of establishing the harmony of the relationship, or indeed other overarching individual goals? Seen from one point of view, the answer is yes, because all the various elements swim along in the same stream. Everyday life is not divisible into objectively determinable, isolated thematic units. From another point of view, we must recall that partners in close relationships, like any other individuals, do identify episodes of experience that they distinguish from other events, at least in retrospect. They do group events into categories that they experience as homogeneous. We can therefore speak of episodes and categories of experience, and group these into still larger classes. Purchasing decisions are one such category. They can be subdivided into decisions to buy everyday requirements or goods for the longer term, and these in turn into decisions about the coffee for everyday consumption or home furnishings, to select an example. Decisions on plans for joint leisure time concern friends and acquaintances, sporting and cultural activities, travel, and much more.

We know from studies of mental book-keeping processes (Brendl, Markman, & Higgins, 1998; Heath & Soll, 1996; Kahneman & Tversky, 1984; Thaler, 1980, 1985, 1994) that people construct categories of experience that they build up and evaluate quite independently. In the case of purchasing decisions, they create categories of goods and allocate budgets which as consumers they want to spend but not to exceed. They must therefore keep mental accounts of expenses and of the remaining possibilities. Thus people carry on mental book-keeping of their leisure expenditure, such as a theatre visit. An example of this is that most people would decide to buy a theatre ticket costing US$10 even if they discovered on reaching the box office that they had just lost US$10. However, if the same people had previously bought a ticket costing US$10 and then discovered that they had lost it, they would hesitate to buy a replacement (Thaler, 1992).

People allocate budgets for other sorts of expenditure too, and keep mental account of planned expenses that have to be met from available resources. It can happen that if no more money is earmarked for a particular area of expenditure after certain purchases have been made, then no more money is spent in that area, even if it is needed and further expenditure would be wise. On the other hand, if there are "savings" in other "accounts", this money may be spent even if further purchases are not wise (Heath & Soll, 1996). The question here is how people define the categories or accounts or manage to maintain even approximate accounts.

Mental book-keeping can also be applied to non-material values such as influence in conflicts and decision-making situations, or the benefit to one partner from the outcome of a decision. When one partner has exercised enough influence within a joint decisions account, the other partner has the say in the decisions following. How the influence is distributed will depend whether they strive to achieve an equal balance of influence immediately or accept an unbalanced distribution for some time. That balance, however, must be achieved eventually. When one partner resists the other's opinion and tries to win the argument, this may have less to do with interest in the commodity than with the desire to bring the non-material resources of influence and benefit into a balance perceived as fair.

This suggests that partners group their decisions into categories, and keep track of the influence they each exercise in each category. In egalitarian relationships at least, the amount of influence felt to be exercised in the various decision categories would be evenly distributed over time. Another reasonable assumption is that mental account is kept of influence in general, and that it must be distributed over topics in accordance with accepted rules.

Account may be kept in a similar way of perceived benefit in decisions. For example, one partner may influence a decision that benefits the other, such as when an item of clothing is bought for that partner to wear. In that case preference may be given in the next decision (or a concurrent one) to the option that benefits the other. Pollay (1968) described book-keeping and benefit debt. Corfman and Lehmann (1987; see also Corfman, 1985, 1987) also examined the issue, and demonstrated empirically that there is a negative correlation between influence and benefit to one partner in the past and their benefit and influence in the present.

Studies addressing the dynamics of decision-making in close relationships have so far paid little attention to the interdependence of decision-making situations. Indeed, this comment applies to decisions research in general, which has concentrated on isolated incidents, leaving emotions and connections in time out of account (see Barry & Oliver, 1996). The time has therefore come to analyse decisions set in the context of concurrent activities, and of other experiences, both past and anticipated, under the umbrella of a psychology of everyday life in close relationships. We need to examine how far benefit and influence debts are effective in a current situation and to what extent we can assume the existence of separate mental accounts that keep independent track of benefit and influence relationships in different subject areas, and seek to equalise them over time.

The intention is not to imply that individuals in general and partners in close relationships in particular are to be viewed as "calculating machines with an enormous capacity to collect, categorise, store, and elaborate information". Any mental book-keeping can only be approximate. Such a variety of decisions and other activities exists that precise book-keeping would demand differentiated accounts of the balance of benefit and decision, and of variables that are hardly measurable and can carry different weight in different situations. We should not so much assume precise, differentiated accounts as an approximate recollection of the past, which may vary considerably from one partner to the other.

We have seen that partners can pursue different goals in joint decisions. They may need not only to realise the personal goal represented by the decision, such as a desire to purchase, but to clarify the starting situation, that is, settle demands and commitments arising from the past, or to fulfil an overarching aim such as the maintenance or improvement of harmony in the relationship. We should always assume that partners who value their relationship will try to take decisions and settle disagreements in a way that preserves the relationship.

When the desire to maintain or improve the relationship dictates a route or represents a goal, then the current desires that define a particular decision may assume differing importance, depending on the interaction principle that underlies the relationship. Less track (if any) is likely to be kept of demands and commitments in harmonious relationships, dominated by the love principle, than in relationships characterised by the egoism principle or equity principle. Decisions may in the one case be viewed in isolation from other decisions and topics, because it is seen as intrusive or unnecessary to monitor the distribution of resources. In economic relationships, rigid monitoring may be necessary to avoid further damage to the relationship, or out of fear of losing if the other partner egoistically maximises his or her benefit.

The Vienna Diary Study by Kirchler et al. (1999) investigated the interconnectedness of disagreements and decisions in the everyday life of 40 couples. Each participant's diary entries were analysed to see if the subjectively perceived influence reported for one conflict with their partner was determined by the influence in reported past conflicts. The analysis also looked at the benefit derived by partners in past decisions, to see if it determined the distribution of benefit in current decisions.

The Influence of Decision-making History on Current Decisions

In the Vienna Diary Study, the influence of history on current disagreements and decisions was examined. The partners recorded day by day whether they had disagreed that day. If a conflict had occurred, they noted the topic and the degree of influence exerted by each partner (0 to 100%). If a decision had been reached, they also noted who had derived how much benefit (0 to 100%) and how much benefit had been enjoyed in the last decision they remembered. The diary provided the following information from each partner:

(a) Had the couple had a disagreement?
(b) If so, was a decision reached?
(c) The subject of the disagreement (economic matter, work, issue relating to the children, relationship issue, leisure matter).

(d)   The distribution of influence between the male and the female partner (0 to 100% of the influence for the one partner and 100 to 0% for the other) in current and past conflicts and decisions.

(e)   The distribution of benefit between the male and female partner (0 to 100% and 100 to 0%).

(f)   The distribution of benefit between the male and female partner in the last decision they remembered (0 to 100% and 100 to 0%).

Two variables are available by which to investigate the significance of the couple's history: "relative influence" and "relative benefit". Analysis of influence distribution looked at disagreements in general, without reference to whether a decision had been reached; relative benefit was only calculated for disagreements that ended in a decision.

Both relative influence and relative benefit were reported using a scale from 0 to 100%. Analysis of the precise values recorded is appropriate if the partners keep account of benefit and influence, and maintain an accurate memory of distribution. If on the other hand we assume that, whilst keeping account, they only remember whether they had more, less, or equal benefit or influence in comparison with their partner, it is better to examine "contrasts". In this case the values to be used in the statistical analysis are adapted: the scale of past benefit (or influence) is reduced to three categories, reflecting whether it was less (−1), equal to (0) or higher (+1) than the other partner's. We shall refer to these two types of memory as "exact" and "contrasted" values.

In the theoretical discussion of the interconnectedness of activities in close relationships, we considered the idea that experiences in one area of decision-making affect those in another. These considerations would imply that the equalisation of influence or perceived benefit occurs across a range of topics or disagreements. Unresolved influence or benefit debt affects the dynamics of the disagreement irrespective of current topic. We also considered separate, topic-specific book-keeping. If couples distinguish between conflicts about economic matters, work, leisure, etc., we must assume that the imbalance of influence and benefit which arose in a particular decision-making area is resolved in the same area. In order to investigate the significance of past influence and benefit on current conflicts, we need to consider, on the one hand, a general budgeting model (which aims to achieve a balance across the whole range of conflict areas), and on the other, a specific budgeting model (which calculates the balance separately for different subject areas).

We considered finally whether partners in close relationships accept imbalance in the distribution of benefit and influence temporarily, but aim to redress it at the first available opportunity, or whether they grant each other "credit", and seek to equalise the balance over the span of several

TABLE 7.1
Operationalisation model for decision-making history

Time-frame	Memory	Budgeting of relative influence and benefit	
		General	Topic-specific
Short (last decision)	Exact (distribution of influence and benefit: 0–100%)	Last incident model	Specific last incident model
	Contrasted (distribution of influence and benefit: −1 = less than partner, 0 = equal, +1 = higher than partner)	Last incident contrasted model	Specific last incident contrasted model
Long (last three decisions)	Exact	Moving average model	Specific moving average model
	Contrasted	Moving average contrasted model	Specific moving average contrasted model

Source: Kirchler et al. (1999).

conflict and decision situations. In terms of the analysis of the decision-making history, this means examining, first, the relevance of the distribution of influence and benefit in the last conflict (last incident models), and secondly, the distributions in the last two, three, or more conflicts. We investigated general and specific "moving average models" of budgeting.

To conclude, the Vienna Diary Study examined the decision-making history for relative influence in disagreements and relative benefit in decisions using a number of regression models. These are summarised in Table 7.1. For each of these models, the analysis was first carried out without taking account of satisfaction/dominance. The moderating influence of the relationship characteristics was investigated in a further step of the analysis. In the following section we report the results for the interpretation of past influence, and thereafter the results for benefit debt.

Equalising the Partners' Relative Influence

It is generally assumed that processes of equalisation take place over time, leading to the establishment of an equal balance of influence between the partners in the long run. These processes may occur by chance, or may follow some particular system. Some form of book-keeping is required to deal with systematic processes. The models in Table 7.1 present various modes of book-keeping. The most fundamental difference between these models lies in the "budgeting": The equalisation processes occur either in a general, comprehensive way across all subject areas, or in a subject-specific way. The second form of differentiation between models is the "time-frame": Equalisation may take place immediately, in the very next conflict, or longer term, by granting credit. The third distinction relates to the "memory" of past differences in influence: What the couples remember may not be the exact level of influence, but simply whether one partner had more, less, or equal influence compared to the other.

(a)   The "last incident" model describes a method of book-keeping that relies on the last conflict, irrespective of the issue discussed. According to this model, the influence history means the level of influence in the last conflict alone. The "last incident contrasted" model follows the same logic, but looks only at whether the partner in question had more, less, or equal influence. The values were either -1, 0, or $+1$ instead of varying from 0 to 100% as reported in the diaries.

(b)   The "moving average" model describes book-keeping with the granting of credit. This means that differences in influence do not have to be resolved in the very next conflict; it can be done in a later one. No theoretical estimate of the length of credit can be made, but the present investigation looks at the average influence in the last three conflicts. According to this model, influence history means the average influence in the last three conflicts, irrespective of issue. The "moving average contrasted" model is a variation of this model: the influence in each of the last three conflicts is first categorised as more, less, or equal, and the average of these categories is then calculated.

(c)   The "specific last incident" model describes a method of book-keeping with separate accounts. The mental book-keeping is issue-specific, so that differences in influence are equalised within separate subject areas. No equalisation is attempted as between subject areas: an influence deficit in economic matters would not be resolved by greater influence in the next conflict about leisure. Influence history according to this model means influence in the last conflict in this specific subject area. Five subject areas have been defined: (1) economic matters, (2) work, (3) children, (4) relationship issues, and (5) leisure. The "specific last incident contrasted" model is identical to the specific last incident model except for the fact that it uses contrasted values: It only distinguishes between more, less, or equal influence.

(d)   Finally, the "specific moving average" model describes a method of book-keeping with credit in separate accounts. It assumes that equalisation processes occur within specific subject areas, but do not have to be resolved in the very next conflict. In the Vienna Diary Study, the investigation took a span of three conflicts.

According to this model, influence history means average influence over the last three conflicts in that specific subject area. A variation of this is the "specific moving average contrasted" model, which investigates the same process using contrasted values.

As stated above, processes of equalisation over time are assumed. This requires a process termed "equity effect" by Corfman (1987), i.e. a negative correlation between influence history and current influence. The Vienna Diary study in this context uses the term "equalisation process". The opposite case, a positive correlation, would lead to an entrenchment of existing influence differences over time. This effect would indicate role segmentation in the distribution of influence.

The way in which influence history and current influence are connected constitutes a rule governing the interaction between the partners. According to the love model (Kirchler, 1989), it can be assumed that the rules of interaction differ in line with the quality of the relationship, and that happy couples in particular seek equalisation of relative influence over a longer time period than unhappy ones, the latter striving for an early restoration of balance.

Hierarchical regression models were used to analyse the relevance of influence history for the influence in the current disagreement. (1) In the first step of the regression analysis, personal parameters were included to account for individual characteristics. These personal parameters were dummy variables for each except one person. This first step allows consideration of the importance of individual differences in the level of influence. (2) In the second step of the regression analyses, the conflict-specific determinants of influence were included. These determinants, already discussed in Chapter 6, are (a) relative importance of the topic discussed, (b) relative knowledge about the topic, and (c) relative emotionality of discussion style. This step accounts for those variables originating in the current situation of disagreement. (3) In the third step of the regression analyses, influence history was included. For each of the history models described above (last incident, last incident contrasted, moving average, etc.), these regression analyses were run separately for men and women. Numerous data controls were conducted to exclude problems caused by multicollinearity; neither tolerance values, condition indices nor the respective Durbin–Watson statistics indicated such problems.

Table 7.2 summarises the results of four models of influence history: the last incident model, last incident contrasted model, moving average model, and the specific moving average model. Results of the other analyses are not given because they do not add to the information obtained.

Analysing the data of women using the last incident model, the first step of the regression explains 15% of variance ($R^2 = .15$). The personal

TABLE 7.2
Results of the regression analyses with influence as the dependent variable

Model	Women				Men			
	R^2	R^2 adjusted	Difference R^2	Beta	R^2	R^2 adjusted	Difference R^2	Beta
Last incident model:								
1 (Personal parameters)	.15	.13	.15**		.07	.05	.07**	
2 (Influence variables)	.23	.20	.08**		.18	.15	.10**	
Importance				.17**				.12**
Knowledge				.13**				.22**
Emotionality				.09**				.13**
3 (Influence history)	.23	.21	.00		.18	.15	.00	
Influence history				.04				−.05*
Overall model	.23	.21**			.18	.15**		
Last incident contrasted model:								
1 Personal parameters	.15	.13	.15**		.07	.05	.07**	
2 (Influence variables)	.23	.20	.08**		.18	.15	.10**	
Importance				.17**				.13**
Knowledge				.13**				.22**
Emotionality				.09**				.13**
3 (Influence history)	.23	.21	.00		.18	.15	.00	
Influence history				.05				−.05*
Overall model	.23	.21**			.18	.15**		
Moving average model:								
1 (Personal parameters)	.15	.13	.15*		.07	.04	.07**	
2 (Influence variables)	.23	.20	.07**		.16	.14	.10**	
Importance				.17**				.13**
Knowledge				.13**				.21**
Emotionality				.09**				.12**

3 (Influence history)	.23	.20			.16	.13		
Influence history			.00				.00	
Overall model	.23	.20**		.05	.16	.13**		-.01
Specific moving average models:								
Economic matters:								
1 (Personal parameters)	.17	.09	.17*		.03	.00	.03	
2 (Influence variables)	.31	.23	.14**		.19	.09	.16**	
Importance				.14				.07
Knowledge				.30**				.33**
Emotionality				.05				.09
3 (Influence history)	.32	.23			.26	.17		
Influence history			.01				.07**	
Overall model	.32	.23**		-.13	.26	.17**		-.30**
Work:								
1 (Personal parameters)	.20	.13	.20**		.15	.06	.15	
2 (Influence variables)	.34	.26	.14**		.31	.22	.16**	
Importance				.29**				-.01
Knowledge				.09				.40**
Emotionality				.15				.06
3 (Influence history)	.34	.26			.37	.27		
Influence history			.00				.06**	
Overall model	.34	.26**		-.06	.37	.27**		-.30**
Children:								
1 (Personal parameters)	.34	.27	.34**		.30	.21	.30**	
2 (Influence variables)	.37	.28	.03		.31	.20	.01	
Importance				.20				.08
Knowledge				.01				.03
Emotionality				.03				.02

(continued overleaf)

TABLE 7.2
(continued)

Model	Women				Men			
	R^2	R^2 adjusted	Difference R^2	Beta	R^2	R^2 adjusted	Difference R^2	Beta
3 (Influence history)	.38	.28	.00		.39	.28	.08**	
Influence history				−.08				−.40**
Overall model	.38	.28**			.39	.28**		
Relationship issues:								
1 (Personal parameters)	.34	.28	.34**		.12	.05	.12	
2 (Influence variables)	.39	.32	.05*		.25	.17	.13**	
Importance				.12				.26**
Knowledge				.08				.12
Emotionality				.10				.18
3 (Influence history)	.40	.33	.01		.25	.16	.00	
Influence history				−.18				.03
Overall model	.40	.33**			.25	.16**		
Leisure:								
1 (Personal parameters)	.08	.00	.08		.12	.04	.12	
2 (Influence variables)	.15	.06	.07*		.16	.06	.04	
Importance				.13				−.03
Knowledge				.00				−.06
Emotionality				.22*				.21
3 (Influence history)	.15	.05	.00		.19	.09	.03*	
Influence history				.00				−.21*
Overall model	.15	.05			.19	.09*		

Note: 1 (Personal parameters) The model only includes person-specific dummy variables. 2 (Influence variables) Relative importance, relative knowledge, and relative emotionality in speaking are used as determinants of influence in the second step of the regression. 3 (Influence history) Analysis of effect of influence distribution in the last decision and in the last three decisions respectively on current influence distribution. Significant results are indicated by ** ($p < .01$) and * ($p < .05$).

Source: Kirchler et al. (1999).

parameters included in this step contribute significantly to the explanation of influence, reflecting differences in influence level between individuals. The second step, where the influence variables importance, knowledge, and emotionality were included, explains an additional 8% of variance (difference $R^2 = .08$). These variables have a significant relation to the influence gained in the current discussion. Relative importance of the topic (beta = .17), relative knowledge on the topic (beta = .13), and the relative emotionality of the discussion style (beta = .09) increase the influence women have in a disagreement situation. If she is more competent than her partner, if the topic is more important to her than to him, and if she discusses more emotionally than he does, then she has more influence. The third step of the regression includes the influence history, which in this model is the influence in the last conflict, regardless of topic. In this step of analysis, no increase in explained variance can be observed (difference $R^2 = .00$), and the relation of influence history to current influence is insignificant (beta = .04). The model overall explains 23% of variance. In the male sample, the explained variance is 17%.

In the last incident contrasted model, influence history was considered as whether the person has had more, equal, or less influence than the other partner in the last disagreement, regardless of topic. Table 7.2 shows that the results are virtually identical to those of the last incident model.

In the moving average model, influence history was considered as the average influence in the last three disagreements, regardless of topic. Here also the results are very similar to those described above.

The results of the specific moving average model are particularly interesting. Here the five topics (economic matters, work, children, relationship issues, and leisure) are analysed separately, and influence history is considered as the average influence in the last three discussions of the same topic area. For economic matters, the data of men show a significant effect of influence history (beta = $-.30$), indicating an equalisation process over time. For the data of women on economic matters, the effect of decision history was approaching significance (beta = $-.13$, $p = .12$). For men, significant effects of influence history were also found for discussions about work (beta = $-.30$), children (beta = $-.40$) and leisure (beta = $-.21$).

It was expected that past distribution of influence between the partners would exert an equalising effect on current decisions; the partner with less influence in the past would enjoy greater influence in the present conflict and vice versa. No convincing results were obtained from those regression models that did not distinguish between the different subject areas of the decisions. On the other hand, significant results were obtained for regression analyses calculated separately for conflicts on economic matters, work, children, relationship issues, and leisure. The specific last incident model, which analyses the significance of influence distribution in the last conflict, showed a trend towards influence history in economic conflicts in the sample of men. This effect of history became more pronounced and statistically significant in the model that considered the last three conflict situations. Equivalent results were obtained from calculating the exact percentage distribution of influence between the partners and from simply considering whether the influence exerted by one partner over the other was greater, less, or equal.

The specific moving average model produced results suggesting that women as well as men have greater influence in conflicts about economic matters when they are better informed about the subject in question, and also when they had less influence in the previous conflicts. The fact that relative knowledge is significant ought to ensure the wisdom of the decision made about an economic problem. The fact that influence is being equalised between the partners may act to preserve the relationship over time.

An equalisation effect over time was also found for discussions about work, children, and leisure issues. However, this only applied to the male sample. In the female sample, influence history was irrelevant. A surprising result, which appeared consistently across all the analyses, was that the personal parameters were given noticeably greater weight by the sample of women than by the men. This result was also found in the analyses of the significance of relative knowledge and interest. It could indicate that equalisation effects are more important for men than for women, and that women's influence is more inclined to depend on the specific characteristics of the relationship. Equalisation effects play no part when relationship issues are discussed.

In addition to the analyses described, the impact of satisfaction and dominance patterns on the relation between influence history and current influence was investigated. Interaction terms between satisfaction and the influence variables, as well as between satisfaction and influence history, were included in additional steps of the regression analyses. Likewise, this was done for dominance. Although theory suggests a moderating effect of satisfaction and dominance on the relation between influence history and current influence, only a few significant results were found. Because of the very small explanation of variance, these analyses are not reported in detail. The importance of decision history for current influence seems to be equal for satisfied and dissatisfied couples, as well as for male-dominated, female-dominated, and egalitarian couples.

The results of the Vienna Diary Study support the hypothesis that book-keeping and equalisation effects occur, particularly over economic matters. Partners appear to differentiate between the various areas of decision-making, and to seek a balance in influence distribution over time. The distribution of influence probably plays no significant part in other subject areas, when the person, their partner, or the relationship is under discussion.

Where one partner is dissatisfied with the behaviour of the other and both are discussing their points of view, it does not matter who is right; the important task is to prevent undesirable consequences.

The Influence of Benefit Debt on Current Decisions

In the Vienna Diary Study, 40 couples participated. Of these, 31 women and 29 men reported over the year of the study at least five disagreements in which a decision was reached. An average of 63% of disagreements ended in a decision. There were in all 767 decisions reported by women and 743 reported by men available for analysis. The benefit to the individual partners was frequently equally distributed (54% of cases). The women estimated their own benefit from the decisions at 45.27%; the men put the figure for themselves slightly higher at 49.50%.

The question that arises here is whether benefit debt affects decision-making. Pollay (1968) assumes that the benefit derived by one partner from a particular decision has to be redeemed at a later date, so that the other partner acquires increased influence and benefit in future decisions. The Vienna Diary Study investigated what determines current benefit. Regression analyses were carried out with current benefit as the dependent variable and (apart from personal parameters, as already discussed) past benefit and current relative influence as predictors. The regression models considered, on the one hand, decisions in general, on the other, particular subject areas. They looked either at the last decision (last incident model) or at the last three such incidents (moving average models). Table 7.3 gives the results of the analyses of the last three incidents. These are statistically slightly more significant than the analyses using the last incident alone.

All the analyses show clearly that the partner who has the say also derives greater benefit. Current relative influence was a significant predictor of relative benefit in all the analyses. The findings concerning benefit debt are inconclusive: all the subject-specific analyses produced negative beta values, indicating that benefit debt was being equalised. However, significant weights were produced in only about half the cases. As in the analyses of the equalisation of relative influence over time (Table 7.2; Table 7.4), the regression analyses that took benefit as the dependent variable (Table 13) found that the weights for past influence and past benefit were not significant in the models that did not differentiate between subject areas. The models that did differentiate subjects showed at least a trend towards an effect of past influence and also of past benefit on the current distribution of influence and benefit in the expected direction. Since the global model represents the sum of the subject-specific results, it might have been expected to produce a significant value, simply because the results of the individual subject areas all point in the same direction. The result obtained,

TABLE 7.3
Results of the regression analyses with benefit as the dependent variable

Model	Women				Men			
	R^2	R^2 adjusted	Difference R^2	Beta	R^2	R^2 adjusted	Difference R^2	Beta
Moving average model:								
1 (Personal parameters)	.14	.10	.14**		.08	.04	.08**	
2 (Influence variable)	.27	.24	.13**		.25	.22	.17**	
Current influence				.41**				.43**
3 (Benefit history)	.27	.24	.00		.26	.22	.00	
past benefit				-.01				-.06
Overall model	.27	.24**			.26	.22**		
Specific moving average models:								
Economic matters:								
1 (Personal parameters)	.25	.14	.25*		.18	.04	.18	
2 (Influence variable)	.35	.24	.10**		.41	.31	.24**	
current influence				.36**				.49**
3 (Benefit history)	.38	.26	.02		.42	.30	.01	
past benefit				-.23*				-.09
Overall model	.38	.26**			.42	.30**		
Work:								
1 (Personal parameters)	.19	.09	.19		.17	.03	.17	
2 (Influence variable)	.28	.17	.08**		.31	.18	.15**	
current influence				.33**				.35**
3 (Benefit history)	.28	.16	.00		.36	.23	.05*	
Past benefit				-.05				-.31*
Overall model	.28	.16*			.36	.23**		

Children:

	(1)	(2)	(3)	(4)	(5)	(6)	(7)	(8)
1 (Personal parameters)	.18	.05	.18		.12	.00	.12	
2 (Influence variable)	.51	.42	.33**		.19	.06	.07	
current influence			.00	.67**			.10*	.35*
3 (Benefit history)	.51	.41			.29	.16		
past benefit				−.03				−.42*
Overall model	.51	.41**			.29	.16		

Relationship issues:

	(1)	(2)	(3)	(4)	(5)	(6)	(7)	(8)
1 (Personal parameters)	.19	.06	.19		.18	.06	.18	
2 (Influence variable)	.36	.24	.17**		.35	.24	.18**	
current influence			.01	.59**			.05	.49**
3 (Benefit history)	.37	.23			.40	.28		
past benefit				.14				−.24*
Overall model	.37	.23*			.40	.28**		

Leisure:

	(1)	(2)	(3)	(4)	(5)	(6)	(7)	(8)
1 (Personal parameters)	.11	.00	.11		.07	.00	.07	
2 (Influence variable)	.29	.18	.18**		.29	.18	.23**	
current influence			.02	.48**			.00	.51**
3 (Benefit history)	.31	.19			.30	.16		
past benefit				−.21				−.02
Overall model	.31	.19**			.30	.16*		

Note: 1 (Personal parameters) The model only includes couple-specific dummy variables. 2 (Influence variable) Current relative influence is considered in the second step of the regression. 3 (Benefit history) Analysis of the effect of benefit distribution in the last three decisions on current benefit. Significant results are indicated by ** ($p < .01$) and * ($p < .05$).

Source: Kirchler et al. (1999).

though at first sight implausible, is explained from the statistical point of view by the fact that the value used for the non-subject-specific analyses is that from the last decision. The values for past benefit and past influence may therefore relate to decisions on a mixture of subjects. For the subject-specific analyses, the values used were those for the last decision about the same subject. There is therefore a difference between the data used. The absence of significant values in the global model and the finding that the aggregated values weakened each other indicate that the couples observe separate book-keeping accounts for each subject: equalisation of benefit and influence are occurring within segregated subject areas. Significant results might have been obtained with data from a larger sample of couples or decisions. Also, if finer distinctions had been made in the grouping of topics, this would have made it possible to test the theoretical assumptions of separate book-keeping more clearly.

A further step in the analysis took the current relative influence as the criterion instead of relative benefit. The regression models described above were again used. The analyses with relative influence as the dependent variable produced similar results to those with relative benefit as dependent variable. Table 7.4 presents the results of the non-subject-specific moving average model and the subject-specific moving average model. The weights for past benefit in the subject-specific analyses again showed at least a trend towards an effect for this. The values in the global model were not significant. These results once more seem to indicate separate book-keeping, and to show that partners' influence in decisions does partly depend on the degree of influence and the degree of benefit enjoyed in past decisions.

INFLUENCE TACTICS

The move from divergence to convergence of opinion

The description of decisions by partners in the home has taken as its starting point the needs and wishes of one or both partners. It is assumed that one partner can either decide spontaneously, habitually or take autonomously an extended decision, depending on the substance of the decision and the structure of the relationship. The active partner may also involve the other in the decision, and inform him or her of their wish or their preferred alternative. If the other agrees, and both partners seek to arrive at a joint decision on the alternative to be realised, problem-solving and decision-making mechanisms are activated. The partners' preferences may be more or less well considered; the couple now enquire into them, compare and adapt them to suit. If the other refuses, dissent exists, and attempts at explanation, persuasion, and negotiation follow. With the intention of avoiding a heated conflict

TABLE 7.4
Results of the regression analyses with influence as the dependent variable

Model	Women				Men			
	R^2	R^2 adjusted	Difference R^2	Beta	R^2	R^2 adjusted	Difference R^2	Beta
Moving average model:								
1 (Personal parameters)	.19	.15	.19**		.08	.04	.08**	
2 (Influence variables)	.27	.23	.08**		.20	.16	.12**	
Importance				.20**				.18**
Knowledge				.12**				.22**
Emotionality				.07				.11**
3 (Benefit history)	.27	.23	.00		.20	.16	.00	
past benefit				.03				-.01
Overall model	.27	.23**			.20	.16**		
Specific moving average models:								
Economic matters:								
1 (Personal parameters)	.30	.19	.30**		.09	.00	.09	
2 (Influence variables)	.48	.38	.18**		.54	.44	.45**	
Importance				.27*				.33**
Knowledge				.27*				.47**
Emotionality				.03				.03
3 (Benefit history)	.48	.37	.00		.55	.44	.01	
past benefit				-.04				-.10
Overall model	.48	.37**			.55	.44**		
Work:								
1 (Personal parameters)	.27	.17	.27**		.10	.00	.10	
2 (Influence variables)	.47	.37	.20**		.27	.10	.17**	
Importance				.17				.11
Knowledge				.24*				.30*
Emotionality				.35**				.22
3 (Benefit history)	.47	.36	.00		.30	.12	.03	
past benefit				.06				-.23
Overall model	.47	.36**			.30	.12**		

(continued overleaf)

TABLE 7.3
(continued)

Model	Women				Men			
	R^2	R^2 adjusted	Difference R^2	Beta	R^2	R^2 adjusted	Difference R^2	Beta
Children:								
1 (Personal parameters)	.26	.15	.26*		.23	.16	.23*	
2 (Influence variables)	.31	.16	.05		.29	.15	.06	
Importance				.25				.19
Knowledge				−.04				−.19
Emotionality				.05				.05
3 (Benefit history)	.33	.16	.02		.30	.14	.01	
past benefit				−.19				.11
Overall model	.33	.16*			.30	.14*		
Relationship issues:								
1 (Personal parameters)	.48	.39	.48**		.22	.10	.22	
2 (Influence variables)	.57	.47	.10*		.46	.33	.24**	
Importance				.13				.42**
Knowledge				.23				.23
Emotionality				−.03				.16
3 (Benefit history)	.58	.46	.00		.46	.33	.00	
past benefit				−.13				.04
Overall model	.58	.46**			.46	.33**		
Leisure:								
1 (Personal parameters)	.17	.05	.17		.14	.00	.14	
2 (Influence variables)	.29	.16	.12**		.23	.07	.09	
Importance				.06				.02
Knowledge				−.04				−.06
Emotionality				.35**				.32*
3 (Benefit history)	.31	.17	.02		.29	.13	.06*	
past benefit				.20				−.35*
Overall model	.31	.17*			.29	.13*		

Note: 1 (Personal parameters) The model only includes couple-specific dummy variables. 2 (Influence variables) Relative importance, relative knowledge, and emotionality in speaking are considered in the second step of the regression. 3 (Benefit history) Analysis of the effect of benefit distribution in the last three decisions on current relative influence. Significant results are indicated by ** ($p < .01$) and * ($p < .05$).

Source: Kirchler et al. (1999).

and realising their own wishes, the partners progress through various decision-making stages. They move to and fro between the desire stage and information-gathering, try by factual argument, manipulation, flattery, or threats to persuade the other to yield, or offer an exchange deal.

The aim in conflict situations is to adapt the partners' respective points of view to each other, and to make the other partner modify his or her position (Scanzoni & Polonko, 1980; Szinovacz, 1987). Processes of communication serve to "move" the standpoints. A step-by-step transformation of standpoints is achieved through conversation to reduce the divergence until the partners can agree on a common course of action, such as the purchase of a commodity. This step-by-step transformation is achieved not only by the exchange of factual information, but by the use of "tactics". It often promises to be more effective to communicate that factual information in a particular way, for example, not to play all one's cards at once, or to display emotion.

In works of social psychology dealing with influence in group discussions, models were developed to illustrate the transformation of divergent points of view (e.g. Brandstätter, Stocker-Kreichgauer, & Firchau, 1980). Brandstätter and colleagues use the so-called "balance model" to illustrate the steps in this transformation. The balance model is based on the assumption that the attitude of the partners at any given stage is the result of the weighted average of processed, past, and newly received information. Their initial attitude is the result of experience or information. Newly received arguments for and against have the effect of reinforcing the initial attitude, bringing about acquiescence, or increasing opposition. The fewer the arguments that the partners know or have processed, the greater the weight accorded to newly received information. As the conversation progresses and most of the arguments have been presented, newly arriving arguments have little effect. If all arguments are of equal value, the weight accorded to new arguments decreases progressively, so that in a borderline case when a large amount of information has already been exchanged, further arguments produce no further change. Formally expressed, the balance model states that attitudes are changed in proportion to the distance between the position of the receiving person's attitude and the position of an argument perceived by them. The willingness to alter an attitude depends on the initial position and the current position. The evolving attitude of a discussion partner $(E_t - E_{t+1})$ is given by the sum of the w_1-weighted argument–recipient distance $w_1 (E_t - S_{t+1})$ and the weighted distance from the initial position $w_2 (E_t - E_0)$. Formally expressed this is:

$$E_t - E_{t+1} = w_1 (E_t - S_{t+1}) + w_2 (E_t - E_0).$$

In disagreements, discussion between the partners serves to modify the differing standpoints until they converge. A partner's willingness to modify a standpoint and yield to the other partner's point of view depends in the first instance on the quality of the factual arguments, but emotions also play a part (Barry & Oliver, 1996). Other factors too, besides those subsumed under the heading "informational pressure", influence the processes of transformation. Partners use a variety of tactics to persuade each other. A research project at the University of Vienna, spanning several years, investigated the tactics employed by partners in purchasing decisions (Hölzl & Kirchler, 1998; Kirchler, 1993a, b; Kirchler & Berti, 1996; Kirchler et al., 1999; Zani & Kirchler, 1993). The results of this research project are summarised below.

A Taxonomy of Tactics

In the literature, a myriad of more or less theoretical approaches to compliance-gaining messages can be found as well as descriptions of numerous different tactics and strategies. Kellermann and Cole (1994), in fact, claim a taxonomic disorder and strategic confusion in the field. The present approach to derive a list of tactics used in decisions within the household was, first, to collect tactics–taxonomies in the literature, second, to gain information about tactics by interviews of couples, and third, to classify the various tactics according to their similarity. An analysis of various social psychology studies on influence tactics (Falbo & Peplau, 1980; Howard, Blumstein, & Schwartz, 1986; Nelson, 1988; Sillars & Kalbflesch, 1989; Sillars & Wilmot, 1994; Spiro, 1983) and an interview study in which 35 married couples stated what they would do to persuade their partner of the advantages of their point of view (Kirchler, 1990) produced 18 different tactics that may be employed by partners in conflicts (Table 7.5):

Conflict Avoidance Tactics (Tactics 13, 14, 15 in Table 7.5). Davis (1976) speaks of a "role structure" tactic in joint purchasing decisions. This is a type of conflict management designed to avoid future conflicts. Role competence is assigned to a particular partner, and this decides who will take on which tasks in future, including the responsibility and the control over decision-making. Social stereotypes and expert knowledge usually form the basis of role segmentation. Once the task areas have been assigned, each partner largely accepts that the "specialist" will make any necessary decisions autonomously, bearing in mind the other's wishes, and so maximising joint utility.

A second strategy is the one that Davis (1976) calls "budget strategy". This involves rules not associated with a particular person, such as the dictates of the wallet. These too are set rules that operate automatically to direct decision or, still better, action, with no need for discussion.

TABLE 7.5
Classification of tactics

Tactic content		Tactic label	Examples
Emotion	1.	Positive emotions	Manipulation, flattery, smiling, humour, seductive behaviour
	2.	Negative emotions	Threats, cynicism, ridicule, shouting
Physical force	3.	Helplessness	Crying, showing weaknesses, acting ill
	4.	Physical force	Forcing, injuring, violence, aggression
Resources	5.	Offering resources	Performing services, being attentive
	6.	Withdrawing resources	Withdrawing financial contributions, punishing
Presence	7.	Insisting	Nagging, constantly returning to the subject, conversations designed to wear down opposition
	8.	Withdrawal	Refusing to share responsibility, changing the subject, going away, leaving the scene
Information	9.	Open presentation of facts	Asking for cooperation, presenting own needs, talking openly about importance/interest to self
	10.	Presenting false facts	Suppressing relevant information, distorting information
Persons	11.	Indirect coalition	Referring to other people, emphasising utility of purchase to children
	12.	Direct coalition	Discussing in the presence of others
Fact	13.	Fait accompli	Buying autonomously, deciding without consulting partner
Role segmentation	14.	Deciding according to roles	Deciding autonomously according to established role segmentation
	15.	Yielding according to roles	Autonomous decision by partner according to role
Bargaining	16.	Trade-offs	Offers of "trade-offs", book-keeping, reminders of past favours
	17.	Integrative bargaining	Search for the best solution to satisfy all concerned
Reasoned argument	18.	Reasoned argument	Presenting factual arguments; logical argument

Note: Some studies of tactics take account of all 18 tactics. Occasionally 15 tactics are discussed. In these cases, tactics 13, 14, and 15 have been omitted. A few other studies examined 17 tactics. There, tactic 15 was omitted.

Source: Kirchler (1989).

"Role structure" and "budgets" are arrangements that have developed over time and are accepted. They govern the outcome of disagreements by making one partner assume immediate responsibility for the issue. Joint decision-making is thus avoided and the possibility of conflict reduced. Tactics 14 and 15 are conflict avoidance tactics. Tactic 13, which faces one partner with a fait accompli, also avoids decision-making conflicts.

Problem-solving Tactics (Tactic 18 in Table 7.5). Problem-solving tactics are reasoned arguments and discussions mainly based on factual information. They serve to clarify the situation, and are mainly used when partners agree on the basic aims and are trying to realise them jointly. For example, if the partners agree that they need to buy a new car and also on the essential characteristics it should have (e.g. cheap, comfortable, safe), their task is to evaluate the various alternatives and select the car most likely to fulfil the requirements. They need to collect product information and clear up areas of doubt. The task is the same as that facing an individual making a purchasing decision. The difference that distinguishes a group or couple's decision is that it is a joint effort by two or more people to make the best choice for them.

Reasoned argument can mainly be expected to occur in situations where partners hold differing opinions about the likelihood of various consequences of the decision: i.e. where there is an objective or probability conflict. If one partner believes that a certain type of car best fulfils their requirements, and the other partner opts for another model, further discussion is needed to establish who is right. Both partners are pursuing the same interests, so it is not a matter of "winning" or of avoiding defeat; the aim is to minimise costs and maximise utility. Reasoned argument is tactic 18.

Persuasion Tactics (Tactics 1 to 12 in Table 7.5). If the partners are not in agreement over the underlying values, so that reasoned argument cannot convincingly show one point of view in the discussion to be the best, persuasion tactics are often applied. Davis (1972, 1976) quotes coercion and coalition pressure, threats to accept no responsibility, and ongoing criticism or nagging as persuasion tactics. The "joint shopping trip" is another tactic. If the uninterested partner can be persuaded to come to the store and is there shown the "advantages" of, for example, an item of clothing, then the interested partner has a "foot in the door" and the goal is nearly achieved. "Feminine intuition" is another persuasion strategy: A woman knows when and how to make sure that her husband cannot say no. The man too knows how to persuade his wife to agree to his wishes. The right amount of attentiveness at the right moment is highly effective. Deutsch (1973), Rubin and Brown (1975), Scanzoni and Polonko (1980), Straus (1979), Szinovacz (1987), and Tedeschi and Lindskold (1976) speak of verbal and non-verbal tactics that hurt the other person, or represent recommendations, warnings, promises and threats. Sternberg and Dobson (1987) add to this list the threat to withdraw financial resources, forming coalitions with third parties, manipulation, exploitation of the other's weaknesses, attacks on their self-esteem, and separation. Various persuasion tactics were discovered in studies. These are summarised in Table 7.5 under tactics 1 to 12 (Falbo & Peplau, 1980; Howard et al., 1986; Nelson, 1988; Spiro, 1983).

Bargaining Tactics (Tactics 16, 17 in Table 7.5).   In probability conflicts and value conflicts, the aim is to find the best solution or to arrive at a consensus between the partners' differing points of view. In distribution conflicts, it is to persuade the other partner to make "advantageous" con-cessions. From an economic point of view, the greater the other's concessions and the less is offered in recompense, the more advantageous the bargaining. The term "bargaining" refers to processes in which two or more people decide how to apportion the resources available, and what share of the costs each must bear. Distribution problems can arise when limited financial resources have to cover the needs of the individual or group, or when settling benefit debt. Conflicts of interest exist, and the parties try to resolve them by demands and offers from the one side and counter-offers from the other (Crott, Kutschker, & Lamm, 1977; Rubin & Brown, 1975; Scanzoni, 1979b; Smith, 1987; Strauss, 1978).

Rubin and Brown (1975) state that the first steps in bargaining situations are directed towards clarifying the positions of the partners. The manner of the opening statements does more than set out the demands; it often also determines the emotional climate of the whole negotiation. Partners in close relationships already share a great range of common experience before the negotiation begins; the course of that negotiation will vary accordingly. It depends on whether there is a climate of trust or mistrust, whether the partners are inclined to cooperation or competition, and whether they seek to maximise joint utility or their own only. According to the quality of their common experience and their interest in the decision, the partners will make high initial demands and move towards agreement step by step, or make known their demands at the outset and insist on them.

Cooperation and readiness to make concessions are often described as successful bargaining tactics. That involves making compromises. Yet com-promises are usually a second-best solution for both partners, because agreeing involves giving up their preferred alternative. If negotiation is seen as something more ambitious, an opportunity to broaden the range of decision options, then integrative solutions will often be possible, represent-ing an ideal solution for both partners. "Integrative bargaining" (Pruitt & Lewis, 1977), as opposed to bargaining in which the couple achieve agree-ment by compromise and mutual rapprochement, but sacrifice the true fulfilment of their needs, is a method of creative problem-solving. It opens up the possibility of finding new options that fully meet the needs and wishes of both partners. Integrative agreements are often difficult to achieve. They demand considerable problem-solving skills, the willingness to work constructively at the matter, and a readiness to strike out in new directions. Success in finding an integrative solution brings greater gain for the partners than bargaining that ends in compromise. Integrative bargaining solutions result in greater satisfaction with the relationship (Canary & Cupach, 1988; Pruitt & Lewis, 1977).

Decisions in private households frequently present the opportunity for integrative bargaining. Integrative solutions are possible precisely because the couple have a shared past and future, and decisions do not exist in isolation. Various negotiating tactics can be used to arrive at an integrative proposal to solve a problem:

(a)   Pruitt (1986) speaks of increasing the size of the "distributional cake". This involves increasing the resources beyond those originally planned. For example, if a couple wish to spend their holiday together, but the husband would like to stay by the sea and his wife in a mountain resort, an integrative solution might be for them to boost the time and money they put into the holiday, and go together to both places.

(b)   A second method, "non-specific compensation", allows for one partner to support the other's wish, and be permitted in return to realise a wish of their own in a subsequent decision. An example of this is for the wife to go along with her husband's holiday plans, and for him to buy her some clothes that she wants.

(c)   The third method Pruitt calls "log-rolling". Both yield in the aspect of the decision that means most to the other partner. The couple in the above example might decide to go to the seaside, but to book into a high-quality hotel, on the grounds that to the husband, the location matters more than the lodgings, while to his wife, the quality of the accommodation is more important than the place.

(d)   The fourth method, the reduction of inconvenience, allows for one partner to have their wish, but to minimise the cost to the other. In our example, the wife might accompany her husband to the seaside, on condition that he rents a quiet house with a garden, where she can escape the noise and bustle of holidaymakers.

(e)   The final method Pruitt calls "bridging". Neither partner's wish is realised. They seek a third option, very like a compromise. If the husband wanted to stay by the sea in order to swim, and his wife wanted the peace, tranquillity, and relaxation of a mountain resort, the couple might choose a lakeside holiday.

There must be trust between partners seeking an integrative solution, particularly when the decisions are widely separated in time. Tactics 16 and 17 present negotiating tactics. These include mutual rapprochement and integrative solutions.

Profile of the Application of Tactics

Which tactics do partners use in conflict and decision situations? A questionnaire was devised (Kirchler, 1993a) to investigate the frequency with which the 18 tactics are used in various situations. A conflict situation (a value conflict, probability conflict, or distributional conflict) was described to the participants, who were asked to imagine it and to say whether they would use certain given tactics. The questionnaire was answered by about 500 couples in Austria (Kirchler, 1993b) and Italy (Zani & Kirchler, 1993). Table 7.6 presents the average values for agreement that they would apply the 18 tactics for men and women in the Austrian and Italian samples. The Italian men and women agree more often than the Austrians to showing weakness, less often to offering resources, and more often to the open presentation of facts or the presentation of false facts. They agree less often that they would try to gain influence by means of indirect coalition. The cultural differences between the two groups are slight, taken overall.

The average agreement by the Austrian sample to using the tactics was analysed in detail. Correspondence analysis was applied to the average agreement scores on the one hand and relationship satisfaction (happy versus unhappy couples), dominance pattern (egalitarian versus male or female-dominated couples), length of relationship (above or below 14 years), gender, and type of conflict (value, probability, or distributional) on the other. Fig. 7.1 presents the bidimensional results of the correspondence analysis with agreement scores as dependent variable and 18 tactics as row variables, split by relationship satisfaction, dominance, length of relationship, gender, and conflict type as column variables. The two dimensions explain 79% of inertia. The results show that the quality and length of the relationship are particularly important with regard to choice of tactics. Satisfaction and length of partnership are placed on the opposite poles of the first dimension. Integrative bargaining tactics, positive emotions, and the open presentation of facts are mainly chosen in harmonious relationships as opposed to disharmonious ones. Older couples frequently stated that they decided according to role segmentation. These couples seem to have defined their respective roles and developed conflict avoidance tactics with increasing age, awareness of each other's wishes and behaviour, and experience in conflict situations. The choice of tactics also depends to some extend on gender and on the type of conflict. Especially in distributional and

TABLE 7.6

Influence tactics of 223 Italian and 252 Austrian women and men

Tactics	Women's answers		Men's answers	
	Italy	Austria	Italy	Austria
1. Positive emotions	3.30 (1.27)	3.46 (1.49)	3.19 (1.21)	3.40 (1.33)
2. Negative emotions	2.29 (0.99)	2.17 (1.04)	2.30 (1.14)	2.19 (1.09)
3. Helplessness*	2.35 (1.20)	2.09 (1.20)	2.15 (1.08)	1.84 (0.98)
4. Physical pressure	2.93 (1.36)	2.78 (1.29)	2.72 (1.45)	2.62 (1.32)
5. Offering resources*	2.34 (1.06)	2.87 (1.32)	2.36 (1.14)	3.09 (1.31)
6. Withdrawing resources	1.86 (0.90)	1.72 (0.84)	1.87 (0.94)	1.74 (0.94)
7. Insisting	2.93 (1.37)	3.06 (1.44)	2.87 (1.34)	2.98 (1.37)
8. Withdrawal	4.04 (1.44)	3.88 (1.38)	3.82 (1.30)	3.60 (1.31)
9. Open presentation of facts*	5.52 (1.07)	4.99 (1.20)	5.17 (1.07)	4.84 (1.28)
10. Presenting false facts*	3.57 (1.26)	3.10 (1.19)	3.49 (1.38)	3.10 (1.30)
11. Indirect coalition*	3.68 (1.38)	4.25 (1.34)	3.63 (1.34)	4.26 (1.31)
12. Direct coalition	3.20 (1.69)	3.27 (1.67)	2.88 (1.58)	3.08 (1.68)
13. Fait accompli	1.96 (1.02)	1.92 (1.17)	2.19 (1.35)	2.36 (1.34)
14. Deciding according to roles	1.94 (1.03)	1.94 (1.15)	2.18 (1.34)	2.42 (1.44)
15. Yielding according to roles	2.18 (1.24)	2.32 (1.41)	2.12 (1.20)	2.16 (1.18)
16. Trade-offs	3.03 (1.44)	3.10 (1.46)	2.70 (1.31)	2.86 (1.33)
17. Integrative bargaining	5.90 (0.96)	5.71 (1.07)	5.60 (1.08)	5.46 (1.07)
18. Reasoned argument	5.37 (1.04)	5.33 (1.13)	5.33 (1.12)	5.50 (1.05)

Note: The means (and standard deviation in brackets) relate to answers on a seven-point scale of 1 = tactic would certainly not be used to 7 = tactic would definitely be used. An asterisk next to the tactic means that differences between the Austrian and Italian samples in the use of that tactic were found. In those cases, differences were shown between the answers given by both men and women in both cultural groups.

Sources: Kirchler (1993a); Zani and Kirchler (1993).

probability conflicts different tactics are used. With regard to gender, the results did not demonstrate that women use emotionally loaded tactics more than men, or that men use factual and rational tactics more than women. Earlier studies had often supported the assumption that women use softer tactics, and that men are more rational. Current studies are also investigating this (see Carli, 1999; Schwarzwald & Koslowsky, 1999). Important differences in the use of tactics depending on dominance between the male and female partner were not found in the Vienna Diary Study and neither in a former investigation by Kirchler (1993b).

In the Vienna Diary Study (Kirchler et al., 1999), 37 couples described around 1200 conflicts over the course of a year. Men and women reported using on average two to three tactics per conflict to obtain their way. The 37 women reported 2329 tactics and the 37 men 2195. The frequency of tactic use was analysed. The number of tactics relative to the conflicts recorded was calculated separately for each individual, the reasoning being that the

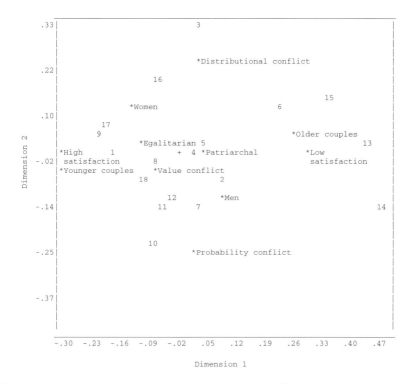

Figure 7.1   Agreement to use of 18 tactics in relation to quality of relationship, dominance pattern, gender, type of conflict, and length of relationship (following Kirchler, 1993b). Explained variance: dimension 1 = .67; dimension 2 = .12. Numbers represent the 18 tactics (Table 7.5).

number of tactics registered depends on the number of conflicts. The couples had all recorded different numbers of conflicts (out of a total of 40 couples, three had recorded no conflicts, one couple had recorded just one conflict, and one couple at the other extreme 109 conflicts. The average number was 30 to 32). The averages of the individual relative frequencies were calculated for the couples who had recorded more than five conflicts over the year. These averages represent an estimate of the frequency with which the tactics are used. Table 7.7 presents the relative frequencies of the tactics used by 31 women and men, and the tactics they perceived their partners to be using.

Agreement to use various tactics in the questionnaire studies by Kirchler (1993a) and Zani and Kirchler (1993) and the use of tactics reported in the diary (Kirchler et al., 1999) are highly correlated. The correlation of the women's entries in Tables 7.6 and 7.7 is $r(15) = .56$ ($p = .01$); and $r(15) = .73$ ($p < .01$) for the men's entries. Both in the study carried out by Kirchler

TABLE 7.7
Relative frequency of the use of tactics in the Vienna Diary Study and partner's
perception of tactics

Tactic	Entries by women		Entries by men	
	Description of self	Description of partner	Description of self	Description of partner
1. Positive emotions	.08	.09	.11	.11
2. Negative emotions	.19	.16	.12	.21
3. Helplessness	.07	.02	.03	.09
4. Physical force	.02	.03	.02	.01
5. Offering resources	.03	.03	.04	.03
6. Withdrawing resources	.05	.03	.02	.02
7. Insisting	.19	.16	.20	.20
8. Withdrawal	.16	.23	.16	.18
9. Open presentation of facts	.41	.26	.42	.32
10. Presenting false facts	.03	.10	.03	.04
11. Indirect coalition	.12	.07	.07	.07
12. Direct coalition	.04	.05	.06	.03
16. Trade-offs	.04	.04	.03	.04
17. Integrative bargaining	.29	.25	.30	.29
18. Reasoned argument	.30	.29	.37	.25
Total	2.03	1.79	1.98	1.91

Note: Number of couples = 31 (couples who had reported fewer than five conflicts during the year were excluded from the analysis). The Diary Study did not collect data on tactics 13, 14, and 15 (confronting the other partner with a fait accompli, deciding autonomously according to roles, and yielding according to roles).

Source: Kirchler et al. (1999).

(1993a) and in the Vienna Diary Study, the most frequently used tactics were reasoned argument, open presentation of facts, and integrative bargaining. However, the reporting of current behaviour in the diary differed from the answers in the questionnaire in showing that women use tactic 2 (negative emotions), and tactic 3 (helplessness) more frequently than men, and tactic 18 (reasoned argument) less frequently. Gender differences in the use of reasoned argument were found in the diary, but not in the Italian and Austrian questionnaire studies and nor in the questionnaires that were completed by the participants of the Vienna Diary Study themselves. Negative emotions is the only tactic to emerge from both the diary and questionnaires as being more likely to be used by the female sample than the male sample. Interestingly, the two techniques—diary and questionnaire—led to different results: Whereas questionnaires show socially agreed similarity between men and women in the use of tactics, the diary, which continuously collects current self-reported behaviour, reveals traditional gender differences.

Women in happy relationships used tactics 6 (withdrawing resources) and 11 (indirect coalition) less than those in unhappy ones. Happy men tried to persuade their partners by offering resources (tactic 5) more often than unhappy ones. As in the study by Kirchler (1993a), relationship satisfaction proved to be a significant moderating variable in the use of tactics: insisting, withdrawal from a discussion, and open presentation of facts occurred less often among happy couples than unhappy ones. Hardly any connection was found between the dominance pattern in the relationship and choice of tactics, though partners in male-dominated relationships appeared more likely to use positive emotions and the offer of resources, and less likely to use rational argument than partners in other types of relationship. Partners in egalitarian relationships presented false facts to each other less often than those in male or female-dominated ones.

Regarding perception of the other partner's tactics, high correspondence was found between self- and partner description on an aggregated level: The correlation between the women's average statements about their tactics and those of the men about the women's tactics is $r(15) = .93$; $p < .01$; the correlation between the men's statements about their own tactics and the women's account of them is $r(15) = .90$; $p < .01$ (see Table 7.7). Besides the high correlation between the profiles of self and partner tactic use, Table 7.7 shows that the women more often felt that the men were withdrawing from the discussion and presenting false facts. They felt less often that they were presenting the facts openly or arguing in an integrative or factual way. Men, on the other hand, reported less often that women would use open presentation of facts, indirect coalitions and reasoned arguments than women did themselves.

Those studies that used questionnaires to obtain information on the use of tactics enquired into the usual tactics as used in economic decisions. In the Vienna Diary Study, participants recorded their use of tactics in both economic and non-economic matters. Table 7.8 summarises the relative frequency of tactic use in different conflicts. This was again calculated separately for each person individually in relation to the number of conflicts. The total relative frequency for all 15 tactics is greater than 1.00 because more than one tactic was applied per incident. The averages of the individual relative frequencies were calculated for the sample as a whole. Table 7.8 presents the mean relative frequencies of tactic use by women and men in different conflicts. The totals of the relative frequencies show how many tactics were used on average per individual conflict. Thus women and men in economic conflicts applied an average of 2.14 tactics; in discussions about relationship issues they used 2.30 tactics. Table 7.8 also gives the number of couples who had provided information on each type of disagreement. This is because not all the 40 couples who participated in the Vienna Diary Study recorded the same selection of conflicts.

TABLE 7.8
Relative frequency of the use of tactics in the Vienna Diary Study in relation to subject of conflict

Tactic	Economic matters	Work	Children	Relationship issues	Leisure
1. Positive emotions	.10	.08	.10	.08	.08
2. Negative emotions	.12	.14	.27	.25	.13
3. Helplessness	.03	.04	.05	.10	.04
4. Physical force	.01	.01	.04	.02	.00
5. Offering resources	.02	.06	.01	.02	.02
6. Withdrawing resources	.05	.05	.02	.07	.01
7. Insisting	.19	.19	.16	.23	.18
8. Withdrawal	.16	.15	.19	.30	.17
9. Open presentation of facts	.53	.48	.40	.48	.43
10. Presenting false facts	.02	.03	.03	.02	.04
11. Indirect coalition	.09	.10	.11	.07	.11
12. Direct coalition	.06	.03	.05	.04	.06
16. Trade-offs	.04	.03	.01	.04	.05
17. Integrative bargaining	.29	.29	.31	.24	.31
18. Reasoned argument	.43	.42	.34	.34	.40
Total	2.14	2.10	2.09	2.30	2.03
Number of couples	(n = 19)	(n = 18)	(n = 15)	(n = 12)	(n = 14)

Source: Kirchler et al. (1999).

Reasoned or factual argument and open presentation of facts were quite frequently used in economic conflicts. Factual argument also features in an above-average number of conflicts about work. This is not surprising since work-related topics often were probability conflicts. When the partners discussed issues to do with the children or their relationship, they quite frequently employed emotionally loaded tactics such as negative emotions. Factual argument was rarer. Tactics such as helplessness, insisting, and withdrawal were particularly used in disagreements on relationship issues.

Differential analysis showed that the choice of tactics in economic conflicts was independent of gender. The finding that men more frequently use factual argument, quoted above, does not apply to economic matters. The only important difference in the choice of tactics was between happy and unhappy couples: happy couples more often tried to solve economic conflicts using trade-offs. Partners in female-dominated relationships tended more than others to use rational and factual argument in discussions about economic matters, work, and children. The choice of tactics indicated that women are more emotional than men when children or the relationship are at issue. They used negative emotions and helplessness, or left the scene, more often than men.

Action–Reaction Sequences in the Application of Tactics

Research has also been undertaken into which tactics are used in reaction to a particular tactic used by the other partner. Dörfler-Schweighofer (1996) interviewed 200 couples, who on average had lived in a shared home for over 12 years, about the tactics they themselves used and about the tactics they used to react to an attempt by their partner to influence them. Of the 18 tactics listed in Table 7.5, all except the conflict avoidance tactics 13, 14, and 15 were studied.

Couples recalled a conflict situation where a joint purchasing decision was being made. If both partners could not remember such a situation, then three imaginary conflict situations were described to them. These related to disagreements over the distribution of a joint lottery win, the choice of a holiday destination and the choice of an item of furniture (see Kirchler, 1993a). Once both partners had remembered the conflict situation or had imagined the chosen imaginary situation as vividly as possible, they separately filled out questionnaires about the choice of tactics and about the character of the relationship (the dominance structure and satisfaction with the relationship).

Using the questionnaire that has already been described to record tactics, the interviewees had to indicate how likely it would be that they would use each of the 15 tactics indicated in order to assert their purchasing desire in the chosen conflict, as currently recalled. These data represent the base probabilities for the use of different tactics. To investigate reaction probabilities, the interviewees were asked to imagine that their partner was using one of the 15 tactics in the chosen conflict situation. They then had to indicate how likely they would react using each of the 15 tactics indicated. This resulted in a 15×15 matrix of conditional probabilities, covering all possible action–reaction combinations.

Hölzl and Kirchler (1998) undertook a detailed analysis of the data gathered by Dörfler-Schweighofer (1996). Firstly, they investigated whether the application of individual tactics could be explained by reference to the factors of gender, relationship satisfaction (harmonious versus non-harmonious relationships) or dominance structure (egalitarian, female- or male-dominated). As in earlier studies (Kirchler 1993a, b; Zani & Kirchler, 1993) and in the Vienna Diary Study, the tactics most likely to be used were open presentation of facts (9), integrative bargaining (17), and reasoned argument (18). By contrast, the tactics least likely to be used were negative emotions (2), physical force (4), withdrawing resources (6), and helplessness (3). Physical force (4) was indicated as being more likely to be used by men in male-dominated relationships and by women in female-dominated relationships than by men or women in partnerships with different power structures. The same finding was made in respect of the tactic of insisting (7), with the dominant partner in a relationship indicating a greater probability of using that tactic. Interactions using the tactic of withdrawal (8) showed a different pattern: whereas men used this tactic similarly whatever the dominance structure, women in male-dominated relationships indicated a significantly higher probability of use than those in female-dominated relationships.

Irrespective of the dominance structure, gender differences between the partners were apparent in respect of the tactics of open presentation of facts (9), forming indirect coalitions (11), trade-offs (16), and integrative bargaining (17). All these tactics were more likely to be used by women than by men.

Regardless of gender, the greatest differences were again found between satisfied and dissatisfied couples. There was a higher probability of using integrative bargaining (17) and reasoned argument (18) in satisfactory partnerships than in unsatisfactory ones. Dissatisfied partners indicated greater use of the tactics of negative emotions (2), physical force (4), withdrawing resources (6), insisting (7), presenting false facts (10), forming indirect coalitions (11) or direct coalitions (12), and trade-offs (16).

The study also analysed the influence of the actions of one partner on the reactions of the other partner. In complex statistical analyses, reaction probabilities were calculated relative to the different tactics. In addition, the pattern of reactions was also analysed with respect to gender and relationship structure. A detailed presentation of the results can be found in Hölzl and Kirchler (1998). All the analyses confirmed that the use of a tactic is dependent on the tactic used previously by the other partner. Each of the 15 tactics studied influenced the reactions that followed; however, the degree of influence varied. The actions of negative emotions (2), physical force (4), and withdrawing resources (6) produced significant changes in the reactions (the strength of the effect being respectively $\eta^2 = .35$, $\eta^2 = .34$ and $\eta^2 = .28$) by comparison with the other tactics ($\eta^2 \leq .10$). What follows is a summary of the changes brought about by the action of a partner, looking at each action separately. Figure 7.2 shows the relationship between the different action–reaction sequences in diagrammatic form.

(a) If one partner used positive emotions (1), the other reacted by offering resources (5) with a higher probability than the given base probability for that tactic. Regardless of gender, relationship satisfaction or power distribution, partners reacted more strongly than usual to an attempt to put them in a good mood (1) by offering small rewards (5) and tried to convince the other in that way. An increased probability, if only slightly greater than the base probability, was indicated for the tactics of helplessness (3),

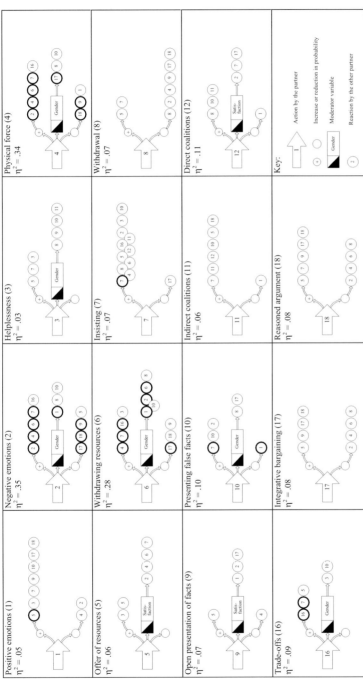

Notes: For every action by a partner the changes in the tactics of the other partner are shown. The magnitude of these changes can be seen from the effect size given. Moderator variables are included in the diagram of reactions to a tactic employed by one partner, where these reactions showed significant variation depending on the gender of the reacting partner or on relationship satisfaction. Apart from the moderator variables, in each case those reactions are shown that were used significantly more or less often than the given base probability values. The tactics listed alongside the "+" symbol are those whose reaction probabilities are significantly above the base probability values, and below those values following the "–" symbol. Heavily printed circles around tactics indicate that the absolute value of this deviation is greater than .10 (the range of the reaction probabilities extends from –1 to +1).

Figure 7.2 The effect of the tactics of one partner on the reaction probability of the other partner (Hölzl & Kirchler, 1998).

insisting (7), open presentation of the facts (9), presenting false facts (10), integrative bargaining (17), and reasoned argument (18). Only the tactics of negative emotions (2) and physical force (4) were shown to be less likely to be used.

(b)   Using negative emotions (2) to achieve a goal dramatically altered the usual behaviour of the other partner ($\eta^2 = .35$), with men and women reacting differently: the interaction between reaction and gender was statistically significant. Gender differences were, however, found in only three tactics: Women were even less likely than men to react with positive emotions (1). Men reacted more than usual by withdrawing (8), and women presented false facts (10) more than usual. Both partners are less likely to react with "friendly" tactics: the use of the tactics of positive emotions (1), offering resources (5), open presentation of facts (9), integrative bargaining (17), and reasoned argument (18) fell markedly. By contrast, "unfriendly" tactics were used more frequently: negative emotions (2), physical force (4), withdrawing resources (6), insisting (7), and trade-offs (16).

(c)   If one partner used helplessness (3) to achieve a goal, then men and women again reacted differently. Men reacted with increased likelihood of withdrawal (8), open presentation (9), and forming indirect coalitions (11), whereas women were less likely to show these reactions. Women were more likely, and men less likely, to present false facts (10). Both sexes showed an increased tendency to react to helplessness with their own helplessness (3), the offer of resources (5), or by insisting on their own viewpoint (7).

(d)   The tactic of using physical force (4) also revealed gender-specific differences in reactions. Men were more likely than women to react by withdrawing (8). Women were more likely than usual to present false facts (10). Both men and women indicated they were less prepared to react with integrative bargaining (17), although this diminished response was more significant amongst women. In other respects, the pattern was similar to that found in reaction to negative emotions (2): "Unfriendly" reactions (2, 4, 6, 7, 16) were more likely, and "friendly" reactions (1, 9, 17, 18) were less likely.

(e)   If one partner used the offer of resources (5) to reach a goal, the reaction depended on the level of satisfaction with the relationship. People in unsatisfactory relationships indicated probability levels for unfriendly tactics (2, 4, and 6) below their base levels, whereas satisfied partners showed no change from the base level. By contrast, satisfied partners showed increased probability of insisting (7), whereas dissatisfied partners did not show this. In both satisfactory and unsatisfactory relationships, the offer of resources (5) significantly increased the probability of a return offer of resources (5). In this situation, reciprocity norms may be coming into play. There was a similar, slight increase in the probability of helplessness (3) being used as a tactic.

(f)   There were gender-specific reactions to withdrawing resources (6). Women were even less likely than men to react by using positive emotions (1), although they were still more likely to react using this than negative emotions (2) or by withdrawing resources (6). In reacting to this tactic, men again indicated they were more likely than women to react by withdrawal (8), whereas women were more likely than usual to react by presenting false facts (10). Generally, the likelihood of reacting with "unfriendly" tactics (2, 4, 6, 7) and trade-offs (16) or helplessness (3) increased, whereas the probability of "friendly" reactions (1, 9, 17, 18) diminished.

(g)   Insistence by one partner (7) led to no change in "friendly" tactics (1, 9, 18) and caused a reduction in the likelihood of integrative bargaining (17), irrespective of other factors. All other reactions tended to show an increased level of probability. One possible interpretation of this could be the appearance of reactance phenomena: Insistence by one partner causes the other partner to become defiant, and the persuasion tactics they employ are thus strengthened.

(h)   If one partner tried to achieve a goal by withdrawing (8), the probability of reacting by offering resources (5) and by insisting (7) was increased. The probability of the other partner also withdrawing (8) was diminished. Interestingly, the probability of use fell in respect of both clearly unfriendly and clearly friendly tactics (2, 4, and 9, 17, and 18).

(i)   If one partner openly presented facts (9), the reaction depended on relationship satisfaction. In satisfactory relationships, the probability of reacting with positive emotions fell (1). In both satisfactory and unsatisfactory relationships, negative emotions (2) were less likely to be used—although this effect was more marked in unsatisfactory relationships than in satisfactory ones. Regardless of relationship satisfaction, it was more likely that withdrawing resources (5) would be used, and less likely that physical force (4) would be used.

(j)   If a partner did not openly present the facts, but instead presented false facts (10), then it was gender rather than relationship quality that determined the reaction. Men reacted by withdrawing (8) with a greater degree of probability than usual, whereas women were less likely than usual to use integrative bargaining (17). Both sexes were significantly less likely to react with positive emotions (1). Negative reactions, insisting and presenting false facts in return (2, 7, 10) were all more likely to be used.

(k)   The formation of indirect coalitions (11) by one partner increased the probability of the other partner also forming coalitions (11, 12), and also the likelihood of insisting (7) or presenting false facts (10). Reacting with positive emotions (1) was less likely, and there was slightly more probability of offering resources (5) or of reasoned argument (18).

(l)   Direct coalitions (12) produced partially different responses in satisfactory and in unsatisfactory relationships. Satisfied partners reacted particularly sensitively to this tactic: negative emotions (2) were more likely to be employed than usual. The tactic of insisting (7) was even more likely in satisfactory than in unsatisfactory relationships, and integrative bargaining (17) was even less likely to be used. Overall, this tactic also increased the likelihood of forming indirect coalitions (11). There was also a greater probability of withdrawal (8) and of presenting false facts (10). Positive emotions (1) were less likely to be used.

(m)   Trade-offs (16) were most likely to increase the probability of similar trade-offs (16) being offered, but also resulted in increased likelihood of insisting (7) and offering of resources (5). Gender was a significant moderator variable for the reactions of helplessness (3) and presenting false facts (10): Women showed a greater increase than men in using both these tactics in response to trade-offs.

(n)   Regardless of other factors, integrative bargaining (17) led to an increased probability of offering resources (5), open presentation of wishes (9), reciprocal integrative bargaining (17), and reasoned argument (18). The use of integrative bargaining significantly reduced the probability of unfriendly reactions—negative emotions (2), physical force (4), withdrawing resources (6), and the tendency to withdraw from the argument (8).

(o)   The reactions to reasoned argument (18) were similar to those following integrative bargaining (17): friendly reactions (5, 9, 17, 18) were more likely, and unfriendly reactions (2, 4, 6, 8) were less likely. However, the probability of insisting (7) being used as a tactic was increased.

If the study is confined to those action–reaction relationships with a value greater than .10 (within an overall range of reaction probabilities from −1 to +1), and no account is taken of interaction effects between reaction probabilities and gender and relationship characteristics, then a clear picture emerges from the results: "Unfriendly" tactics (2, 4, and 6) led to a signifi-cant increase in unfriendly reactions, with the tactics of negative emotions

(2), physical force (4), withdrawing resources (6), and insisting (7) all having increased probabilities. A common result for these three negative tactics (2, 4, and 6) was also a decreased probability of positive emotions (1) and integrative bargaining (17). The actions of negative emotions (2) and physical force (4) also led to a decreased probability of open presentation of facts (9) and reasoned argument (18). The action of withdrawing resources (6) was associated with an increase in the probability of trade-offs (16). Tactics 2, 4, and 6 were also those where the usual pattern of tactics changed most markedly. The opposite effect—i.e. a reduction in "unfriendly" tactics by the use of friendly tactics—was barely identifiable.

Reciprocity effects were apparent—apart from those already mentioned for tactics 2, 4, and 6—for the tactics of offering resources (5), insisting (7), presenting false facts (10), and trade-offs (16). Use of these tactics resulted in an increased likelihood of the same tactic being employed in the reaction by the other partner.

A hardening of positions, as indicated by an increased probability of a reaction using the tactic of insisting (7), can also be expected if trade-offs (16) are offered or if false facts are presented (10), as well as when the tactics 2, 4, 6, or 7 are used.

Offering resources (5) or open presentation of facts (9) reduced the likelihood of negative emotions (2), particularly for dissatisfied couples who showed a relatively high level of base probability for negative emotions. Presenting false facts (10) resulted in positive emotions (1) being less likely to be used as a reaction.

Comparable results were found in the Vienna Diary Study, where 40 couples recorded the tactics used by each partner in the course of disagreements over financial and non-financial matters. If the number of tactics and reactions are summed together, regardless of the type of conflict involved or the gender of the respondent or the relationship characteristics, then a frequency table can be generated offering information about action and reactions on a broad level. Table 7.9 shows the total frequencies and deviation from the expected values, assuming an even distribution. Figure 7.3 shows the frequency pattern, produced using correspondence analysis, in diagrammatic form. Correspondence analysis produced a multidimensional solution, whereby the first three dimensions explain 34%, 21%, and 14% of the variation. In similar fashion to Hölzl and Kirchler's (1998) study, in the Vienna Diary Study tactics that were emotionally positively charged resulted in positive tactics, and tactics that were emotionally negatively charged produced negative tactics. Insisting (7) often led to withdrawal (8), and the reverse was also often true—withdrawal resulted in insistence by the other partner. The forming of direct and indirect coalitions (11 and 12) was often alternately interlinked as actions and reactions. Integrative bargaining led to similar integrative bargaining on

TABLE 7.9
Frequencies of tactics and reactions to them from the Vienna Diary Study

Tactics Actions	Reactions														
	1	2	3	4	5	6	7	8	9	10	11	12	16	17	18
1. Positive emotions	49 ++	23 +	10	3	4	1	15	13 −	22 −	5	4	5	3	11 −−	26
2. Negative emotions	24	108 ++	15	14 ++	9	9	38	52	44 −−	21	14	2 −	9	11 −−	38 −−
3. Helplessness	5	25 ++	2	4 ++	4 +	1	13	7	12	4	0 −	1	2	8	10
4. Physical force	3	3	5	5 ++	1 ++	2	6	8	4	4	1	1	2	0 −	2 −−
5. Offering resources	6 +	7	3	1	2	5 ++	5	6	3 −−	6	4 +	4 +	2	4	4
6. Withdrawing resources	3	12	5 +	1	3 +	1	12 +	11	6 −	8 ++	0	1	3	2 −	4 −
7. Insisting	14	47	13	4	10 +	6	43	69 ++	37 −−	17	12	9	14 +	41	48 −
8. Withdrawal	14	32	9	2	7	5	59 ++	35	42 −	12	11	6	4	39	43
9. Open presentation of facts	26 −−	79 −	22	5	5 −−	9	70 −−	99	347 ++	41	32	9 −−	13	98 −	108 −−
10. Presenting false facts	0	10	2	0	0	7 ++	9	2 −	13	5 +	1	0	0	1 −−	11
11. Indirect coalition	4	9 −	1	0	3	2	17	22	19 −	8	13 +	12 ++	6	24	36
12. Direct coalition	2	4	1	0	0	1	8	11	12	3	10 ++	10 ++	4	9	8
16. Trade-offs	0	11	1	0	1	1	6	9	5	1 −	7 ++	4 +	2	8	11
17. Integrative bargaining	9 −−	17 −−	7 −	2	3	5	47	49	53 −−	5 −−	15	7	6	198 ++	81
18. Reasoned argument	30	42 −−	20	1	9 −−	6	63	61	103 −	13 −	35 −−	15	16	67 −−	230 ++

Note: Frequencies with a symbol attached to them show significant variation from the expected value, given even distribution. Frequencies with the symbols "+" and "++" attached lie significantly, or highly significantly, above the expected value; frequencies with the symbols "−" or "−−" lie below the expected value.

Source: Kirchler et al. (1999).

the part of the other partner, and reasoned argument similarly led to reasoned argument by the other partner.

The frequency pattern in Table 7.9 and the solution produced by correspondence analysis in Fig. 7.3 suggest some connections of actions and reactions, and permit us to make some speculative remarks about the

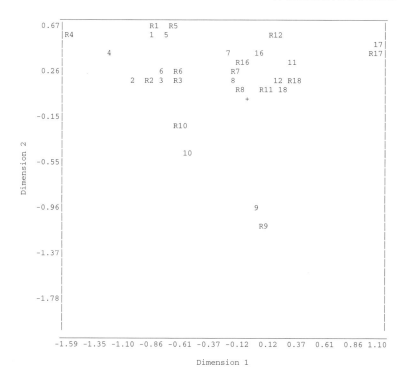

Figure 7.3 Solution produced using correspondence analysis of tactics as actions and reactions from the Vienna Diary Study (Kirchler et al., 1999). The figures from 1 to 18 relate to the tactics as actions; R1 to R18 are used for tactics as reactions (see Table 7.5 for the description of the tactics).

dynamics of conflict situations: It seems that one partner often starts a conversation by expressing his or her wishes and intentions openly, and the other partner will then express their views as a counter-move (tactic R9). As with tactic 9, which is often met by tactic 9 as a reaction, partners often respond to reasoned argument with reasoned argument (18) and respond to integrative bargaining with integrative bargaining (17). Alongside these tactics, which are geared to promoting solutions, there are also emotionally charged tactics: Positive feelings, as expressed through compliments, humour, etc. and through the offer of pleasant things (1, 5), lead to the partner also expressing positive feelings. However, the offer of resources (5) is also associated with withdrawing resources (6) and with presenting false facts (10). A parallel, negative response is associated with negative feelings such as threats, cynicism, compulsion, and aggression, and also with help-lessness (2, 3, and 4). A further link is formed between tactics 7 and 8, insisting and withdrawing from the argument. Finally, a connection is formed between those tactics that are directed towards third parties: Forming direct and indirect coalitions (11, 12) and also trade-offs (16) are frequently linked as actions and reactions. In particular, where attempts are made to convince the other partner using trade-offs, the partners often avoid pursuing the tactic by indicating the advantages of their choice not for themselves, but for the other person.

The main focus of the study by Hölzl and Kirchler (1998) was sequences of actions and reactions, in other words the changes in the probability of tactics being used as a result of the previous action used by the other partner. In summary, it was found that tactics that were emotionally negatively charged, such as the expression of negative emotions (2), the use of physical force (4), and the threat to withdraw resources from the other partner (6), were answered with negative reactions, or by the other partner insisting rigidly on his or her point of view (7), probably annoyed by the actions of the partner. Because negative tactics resulted in negative reactions and insistence, irrespective of the relationship characteristics or the gender of the responding partner, decision-making processes could be obstructed and the search for a jointly agreed solution could be made more difficult by the use of such tactics. In connection with the data about the base probabilities for the use of individual tactics, the conclusion can be drawn that differences of opinion can have a stabilising effect on satisfaction or dissatisfaction with the relationship. People in unhappy relationships indicated a higher level of probability that they would employ "unfriendly" tactics in pursuit of a goal. Unfriendly tactics, however, produced unfriendly reactions—possible compensatory mechanisms could not be identified.

Hardening of negotiating positions, or fixing the attitudes of the partners, also seemed to be probable if one partner presented false facts (10) or formed indirect (11) or direct (12) coalitions. If the other partner was unable to oppose the pressure of these tactics with similar reactions (for example, by attempting to form coalitions for him- or herself), then it was less likely that there would be movement towards the partner's position and agreement over the issue, but more likely that there would be insistence (7) or withdrawal from the argument (8).

Joint agreement over options for a decision seemed to be more easily achieved if tactics that are emotionally positively charged were employed. It is questionable whether tactics that are emotionally positively charged are appropriate methods for changing the attitudes of the partners: Positive emotions (1), the offer of resources (5), but also helplessness (3) and withdrawal from the argument (8), were responded to by the offer of resources (5). It appears that in such interaction situations what is at issue is who is offering the more attractive exchange business as a stimulus to secure concessions in the matter that requires a decision to be made. Whilst annoyance over negative tactics leads to insistence on one's own position, the friendly atmosphere promoted by tactics that are emotionally positively charged is more likely to result in both partners making concessions to the other's point of view. It remains questionable whether this can produce any lasting change in attitudes or is just yielding in the situation.

Tactics that proved to be supportive of the relationship and useful in finding solutions were reasoned argument (18), integrative bargaining (17), and open presentation of an individual's own wishes (9). Where these were given as actions, in none of these three instances did those interviewed indicate that they would be overly likely to respond with any one particular tactic from amongst the range of tactics being investigated. This means that there is scope to respond in a number of different ways, and that there is therefore no fixed interaction sequence determined by a rigid succession of tactics. Apart from the immediate and obvious advantages to the solution-finding process that result from reasoned argument, the integration of different points of view, and clear and open expression of an individual's preferences, it was found that partners who wanted to avoid these tactics most often sought to win over their partners by offering pleasant things (5), a reaction that may possibly not take matters much further in the search for an optimal solution to the question in hand, but preserves the quality of the relationship.

The Vienna Diary Study similarly investigated whether tactics work to preserve the quality of the relationship or to increase influence. In the diaries, participants recorded not only the tactics employed by themselves and their partner in the course of a conflict, but also the relative influence they had and the emotional climate of the discussion. The influence of tactics on the emotional climate of the discussion and ultimately on the relationship, as well as the connection between tactics and influence on the opinions of the partners, was tested using regression analysis. To do this, the tactics a person had used and those which that person perceived as being used by his or her partner were coded as dummy variables and used as predictors of the emotional climate of the discussion or of relative influence. In the regression analyses, the first stage in the analysis measured the effect of relationship characteristics, in a similar way to that carried out in the earlier analyses of decision-making history. After this, calculations were made to determine the degree of variance in the emotional climate of the discussion and in influence that was attributable to the choice of tactics. An individual's own choice of tactics accounted for around 15%, and the perceived tactics of the partner accounted for a further 7% to 8% of the variance in the emotional climate of the discussion (for the sample of women, R^2 values were .17 for their own tactics, and .08 for the perceived tactics of their partner; for the sample of men, the respective R^2 values were .13 and .07). The emotional climate of the discussion was considerably influenced by the choice of persuasion tactics: Negative emotions (2), helplessness (3), and physical force (4) brought about a negative climate, whereas positive emotions (1) improved the climate. In unsatisfactory relationships, the emotional climate of the discussion was also improved by the offer of resources (5) and by open presentation of the facts (9), whereas in happy relationships these tactics barely had any influence on the emotional climate. In happy relationships, the emotional climate of the discussion worsened if one partner insisted on his or her viewpoint (7), whereas this tactic had little influence over the climate in unhappy relationships. The emotional climate of the discussion improved if the partner produced reasoned arguments (18); it worsened if the other partner expressed negative emotions (2), expressed helplessness (3), threatened to withdraw resources (6), insisted on his or her own viewpoint (7), withdrew from the argument (8), presented false facts (10), or reminded the partner of earlier favours (16).

The relative influence of the partners was considerably less dependent on the choice of tactics used. A partner's own choice of tactics accounted for around 3% to 4%, whilst the perceived tactics of the other partner accounted for a further 2% to 3% of the variance in relative influence (for the sample of women, R^2 values were .04 for their own tactics, and .03 for the perceived tactics of their partner; for the sample of men, the respective R^2 values were .03 and .02). A partner's own influence could be increased by the use of negative emotions (2) and physical force (4)—although this worsened the emotional climate of the discussion, as has already been pointed out. Helplessness (3) was shown to be unsuccessful in attempts to convince the other partner, and in addition it had a negative effect on the climate of the discussion. Women gained influence particularly when they used reasoned argument (18) or when they openly expressed their wishes (9). A partner's own influence also tended to be reduced by all the persuasion tactics employed by his or her partner; however, the statistical effects of this were often slight.

In summary, it can be asserted that the choice of tactics by partners has a particularly lasting effect upon the emotional climate of the discussion, and appears to have an effect upon the relative influence of the partners which, although statistically significant, is small in scale. It is persuasion tactics, above all, that determine the emotional climate of the discussion and the relative influence of the partners: tactics that are emotionally negatively charged can appear an appropriate method of asserting one's own opinion, but this happens at the expense of the emotional climate of the discussion, and ultimately of relationship satisfaction. "Harsh" tactics, in particular, can restrict the room for manoeuvre of the other partner and can offer the person employing them influence advantages, as is assumed in the power-act model (Bruins, 1999; Kipnis, 1976). Such influence advantage is often gained at the expense of the emotional climate of the discussion. The choice of tactics also influences the evaluation of the results of conflict situations, such as the fairness of the decision and satisfaction with the outcome of a decision. The next section looks in greater detail at the results of conflict situations.

DECISION OUTCOMES: SENSE, FAIRNESS, AND SATISFACTION

Decisions are about finding acceptable solutions. Particularly where purchasing decisions are involved, this means finding the optimal use of the limited resources available, whilst at the same time intensifying or preserving the quality of the relationship. Even if in practice it is not easy to separate the decision-making process from the results of decisions, it is, however, appropriate to ask, at least at the theoretical level, how good a decision is with respect to the economic management of resources, and what "traces" of the behaviour of the partners have been left behind in the quality of their relationship. Important outcome variables are the perceived fairness of the way in which the conflict is resolved, and a fair distribution of the outcomes. The satisfaction of the partners is bound up not only with procedural and distributive justice, but also with the outcome of the discussions leading to a decision. Fairness and satisfaction should determine the overall quality of the relationship and eventually again be important moderator variables in future conflict situations. Fairness and satisfaction can increase the trust that partners have in one another, or can lead to mistrust. In particular, procedural justice promotes reciprocal trust between partners and distributive justice leads to satisfaction (Greenberg, 1988).

Conflicts about financial matters can also be assessed according to whether they make sensible use of scarce resources, or whether the partners are using their resources in a manner that is sub-optimal, in economic terms. In close relationships, the economically sensible use of resources is not always possible: Particularly if the goal of strengthening the relationship is set alongside economic goals, goal conflicts may arise and the partners may set the goal of strengthening the relationship above economic goals. In happy relationships, money may be spent in order to satisfy the desires of the other partner. People who love their partner, who can "read their partner's wishes in their eyes" and who want to satisfy those wishes, can easily lose sight of economic goals as a result. On the other hand, partners who are in conflict with one another may well seek to spend joint resources on items that satisfy their own individual needs, before their partner claims the money for their own purposes. Happy and unhappy couples spend roughly the same amounts of money, but they spend it in different ways and for different purposes. Schaninger and Buss (1986) demonstrated that, apart from fulfilling individual or altruistic desires, happy couples buy fewer objects for a given level of expenditure than unhappy couples. This suggests that happy couples buy more expensive objects, and (as the authors found) ones that cannot be divided up, whereas unhappy couples prefer to buy goods that can be divided up, as if they were anticipating the break-up of the home and the division of its contents. A German furniture company is even advertising furniture that can be divided up into separate pieces—as if pitching this product at the mind-set of dissatisfied couples!

Although decision-making in close relationships has been described as an incremental, step-by-step process of feeling one's way towards a solution, joint decisions do not necessarily have to be sub-optimal in economic terms. Lindblom (1979) found quite the opposite—that if any kind of decision is to be taken in complex situations, then the decision-makers must deviate from a wholly rational model of behaviour. Partners in close relationships rarely have enough time available to engage in an all-encompassing decision-making process. In order to avoid "steering one's way" into relationship conflicts that are "overly heated", a step-by-step approach is an absolute necessity.

Despite the assertion that incremental decisions are more sensible than economic–rational ones in the given situation, the optimistic view that partners in close relationships would form a good basis for conflict resolution cannot be justified. In Hill's (1972, p. 14) view, close relationships—and particularly the family—are "a poor planning committee, an unwieldy play group and a group of uncertain congeniality. Its leadership is shared by two relatively inexperienced amateurs for most of their incumbency, new to the rules of spouse and parent." The focus of the attention of the partners is not exclusively devoted to any particular problem, because in the private household purchasing decisions and other decisions do not exist as isolated tasks. Purchasing decisions can mutate into power games, and instead of seeking a good solution the partners may be concerned with cancelling out benefit debts that have arisen in completely different situations. Alternatively, partners may be seeking to achieve equality in the distribution of influence and may make moves towards the partner's point of view because this person has in the past made concessions, rather than because the partner is putting forward the better alternative solutions. It is also possible that sub-optimal decisions may be taken in order to improve the quality of the relationship. Where decisions are taken in the private home, the desires of the other person are often agreed to out of a sense of providing a favour to the other person, rather than because one person is convinced that it is sensible to implement what the other desires. Granbois and Summers (1975) demonstrate with reference to purchasing decisions that partners draw up and implement more purchasing decisions than men and women do separately. In their study, whereas men made purchases with a value of US$2417 and women made purchases amounting to US$2960, couples spent US$3354 on purchases per person. If it is sensible to do without goods that are not absolutely necessary and to save the money left over as a result, then purchasing decisions made by individuals were "more cost-favourable" than the decisions made by couples. It is likely that, in this study, people often agreed to the wishes of their partner in order to avoid conflicts and to preserve the existing harmony within the relationship. Uneconomic actions often make good their deficit by their emotional value—which is an obstacle to the economically efficient solution of problems. Alongside a lack of cognitive ability to make a better decision, partners in close relationships often run the risk of making " poor" decisions because too many side-issues and other goals intrude upon the decision-making process.

Weick (1971) also forcefully puts his view that the private household is an unsatisfactory context in which to solve problems. As he puts it, if the partners were exposed to fiercely competitive economic conditions, they would not survive. Aldous (1971, p. 267) shares this pessimistic view:

> The daily routines and the urgency of attention to newly critical situations press the family to dispose of problems and to move on. Families are generally less problem oriented than solution oriented. The emphasis tends to be one of reducing the tension-laden situations to an innocuous level rather than submitting the problem to rigorous analysis and assessing the consequences of possible alternative strategies. One hypothesis reflecting this phenomenon would be that the pressure to work for a quality solution to a problem is generally less among families than among more self-conscious problem solving groups such as committees or task forces.

Rudd and Kohout (1983) compared the capacity of partners in close relationships to process information with that of ad hoc groups, with the hypothesis that people making purchasing decisions could not handle all the possible aspects of product comparison, but would only take something between five and nine elements of information into account. They also hypothesised that ad hoc groups would be more oriented towards problem-solving than partners in close relationships. A total of 64 people decided singly and in couples about four products (toothpaste, a TV, vitamins, and a sofa) with up to 12 attributes per product. Sixteen people worked through the problems presented on their own; 24 people were grouped together to form 12 ad hoc dyads; and 12 married couples took part in the study. In fact, the married couples took less information into account (67% of the information) than the ad hoc groups (80.4%). The amount of information taken into consideration by individuals was noticeably low (63.6%), as a result of the lack of any stimulus to further research which a second person might have provided. The less information being taken into account, the quicker the decision was made: On average, the married couples needed 3.93

minutes, whereas ad hoc groups needed 4.27 minutes and individual participants 3.03 minutes. In comparison with the ad hoc dyads, married couples
made decisions more quickly but took less information into account and
would therefore make sub-optimal decisions more frequently. Whilst ad hoc
groups are oriented towards problem-solving, it appears that partners in
close relationships are more oriented towards solutions (Aldous, 1971).

A single study does not provide enough evidence on which to base the
conclusion that partners in close relationships represent worse "decision-
making forums" than working groups or ad hoc acquaintances; however,
evidence of the problems and interpersonal emotions involved in such
relationships would seem to support this theory. Is it possible that the
consequences for the partnership that arise from a joint decision balance out
the costs of uneconomic decisions?

Although it is possible to represent relationship satisfaction and economic efficiency as two conventional axes at right-angles to each other,
Kourilsky and Murray (1981) found that there was evidence of an extremely
close correlation between the two. The authors hypothesised that satisfaction with a decision was dependent on the quality of the economic–
rational deliberations of the people involved in the decision. They trained 27
parents (of whom 17 were married, and 10 were single parents) and 27
children in how to take rational decisions. Before and after the training, a
parent discussed a budgeting issue with his or her child, and both parties
indicated how satisfied they were with the outcome of the discussion. It was
found that participants in the study were more satisfied with their decision
following their practice in decision-making. Schomaker and Thorpe (1963)
investigated farming families as they solved financial problems, and found
that satisfaction with the decision depended on how many people outside
the family they had discussed the problem with, and on the amount of time
for the decision which allowed the family to take account of "decision-
making traps". Hill and Scanzoni (1982) found that the partners' discussion
style was a decisive factor for satisfaction with the outcome. A competitive
style often causes annoyance or resignation. Compulsion, threats, and
inconsiderate or rigid negotiating tactics result in negative feelings and
threaten the relationship. Emotional tactics and physical force eventually
wear down the other partner, but they do not move the partner away from
their own convictions. If the sum of experiences in past decision-making
processes results in satisfaction with a relationship, then financial decisions
would also bring about high levels of satisfaction unless they were taken in
order "to reach a decision at any cost" and under dogmatic–authoritarian
pressure. Satisfaction depends on whether a decision is taken jointly and
whether both partners influence the decision. For example, if a man informs
his partner about an intended purchase and then acts without any consideration of her views in the matter, then whilst it may be true to say that

the decision has been reached together, the woman has had no right of equal say in the matter and the mood between the partners is bad. Having a say is a decisive factor when it applies to aspects of a particular product that are important to one of the partners. Park (1982) shows that having a say is not a universal guarantee of satisfaction. Where one partner had conceded position over product attributes that seemed important to their partner, the satisfaction of the other partner with the decision was higher even if no concessions had been made in respect of other, relatively unimportant product characteristics.

Klein and Hill (1979) presented a model of problem-solving effectiveness that sought to integrate empirical findings and was based on various theories. Problem-solving effectiveness was defined using the quality of the decision and the degree of acceptance or satisfaction with the decision. Effectiveness depends particularly on the nature of the task and on the interaction process. The interaction process was operationalised using the following, partially interconnected variables: density of verbal communication, which comprises the length of time the partners spend talking to each other; creativity, or the number of alternative solutions taken into consideration; linguistic ability of the partners; support (i.e. the number of positive affects that are communicated); non-verbal communication, such as length of eye contact, intonation, body language, etc.; and the degree of conflict, which is the extent of the difference of opinion, and whether the type of conflict focuses on probabilities or on the persons involved. Moreover, the variables used were: centralisation of power, which comprises the distribution of influence between the partners; coordination, which covers the efforts made by the partners to enable all parties to speak, encouragement to ask further questions, clarification of factual content, etc.; use of expert power—a power that is not fixed normatively, but is based on knowledge and expertise; and rationality, which comprises the time needed to reach a decision, to gather and to evaluate information.

In general terms, tasks are solved effectively if participants in a discussion seek to enable all parties to ask questions and to have their say, if they support one another emotionally and possess high levels of linguistic ability, if the context in which the discussion takes place is relaxed, and if there is adequate time for reflection. Emotional support within a conversation stimulates creative and innovative suggestions for solutions, and guarantees that all parties are involved in the decision. The positive emotions expressed by others encourage people to deviate from routine suggestions and to make unconventional ones instead. Actions that are sensible, in economic terms, will probably result in those cases where the parties make concessions to the partner with the highest level of expert knowledge. Rational decisions, and particularly integrative solutions, are also bound up with creativity. The opposite also holds true: Ineffective decisions can be expected where

TABLE 7.10
The effect of interaction variables on the outcomes of decisions

	Influence on the outcomes of decisions	
	Quality	Acceptance
Elaborate nature of verbal codes	+	
Emotional support	+	
Expert power	+	
Wealth of ideas and linguistic ability	+	+
Degree of conflict	+	–
Concentration of conflict at the start of the decision-making process	+	+
Coordination measures employed by the partners	+	
Creativity of the family members	+	
Legitimation and acceptance of power	+	
Amount of non-verbal communication	+	
Rationality	+	
Verbal communication	+	
Centralisation of power, coordination and legitimate power	+	+
Concentration of creativity		–
Conflict between the members	–	–
Concentration of elaborated "private" codes of speech	–	
Concentration of emotional support	–	
Concentration of non-verbal communication	–	
Concentration of verbal communication	–	
Centralisation of power	–	–

Note: the symbols "+" and "–" represent a positive or negative link between the variable and the quality or the acceptance of the decision.

Source: Based on Klein and Hill (1979, p. 527).

emotional support, verbal communication, and power are concentrated on one person, who alone puts forward possible solutions, and where negative conflicts exist.

On the basis of these considerations, Klein and Hill (1979) formulate a series of hypotheses about the interconnectedness of the interaction variables and problem-solving effectiveness. These are summarised in Table 7.10.

With regard to the nature of the task, Klein and Hill (1979) observe that problem-solving effectiveness reduces when the complexity of the task increases, when there are a multiplicity of possible solutions or when there is no directly apparent correct solution, and as the need for cooperation between the decision-makers increases. The probability of an effective decision increases where events can be controlled and where the partners taking the decision possess the necessary means for a solution.

In summary, the variables that determine relationship satisfaction also prove to be a precondition for decisions to be accepted without negative emotions being left in their wake. In order to take a decision that is sensible in economic terms and minimises the costs to the relationship, the following preconditions are required: a high degree of interdependence between the partners, consideration for the wishes of the other partner, a factual style of communicating to which all parties can contribute and express their ideas without being criticised, egalitarian distribution of influence, clear statements of goals sought, avoidance of indirect strategies to convince the other person, and adequate time in which to make the decision.

The acceptance of decisions was investigated in the Vienna Diary Study in relation to the degree of fairness or unfairness experienced in the process of reaching a decision, and to the fairness of the outcome of a decision. It was also considered in relation to the degree of satisfaction with the outcome of a decision.

Following a conflict situation, partners recorded in the diary on a daily basis how fair the process of resolving the disagreement was, and how fair the outcome was. The scale of possible answers ranged from 1 = unfair to 7 = fair. Partners also used a seven-point scale to indicate their satisfaction with the outcome of the discussion. A number of analyses were carried out to look at fairness and satisfaction. The analyses were limited to the study of distributive fairness, because the assessments of distributive fairness showed a high level of correlation with those for procedural fairness ($r(721) = .79$ for the sample of women, and $r(682) = .68$ for the sample of men).

Fairness and satisfaction were examined firstly as results of the tactics chosen by the partners to resolve disagreements, and secondly as results of the relative influence of the partners, the distribution of benefit between them, the conversation style and the importance of the topic under discussion. Regression analysis was again carried out, taking fairness and satisfaction as dependent variables. In the first stage of the regression models, the importance of the characteristics of the couple were investigated. The couples were included in the regression as dummy variables. At the next stage, the remaining variance in judgements of fairness and satisfaction was examined against the tactics used by one partner and the perceived tactics used by the other partner, and also examined against the pattern of influence, the pattern of benefit, the conversation style and the importance of the subject-matter discussed.

Analysis of the importance of different tactics produced the finding that the choice of tactics made by an individual accounted for around 10% of the variance in judgements of fairness; the tactics perceived as being used by the other partner accounted for a further 9% in the sample of women and 4% in the sample of men. Satisfaction with the outcome of a discussion was equally determined to a considerable extent by the choice of tactics (between 11% to 12% of the variance was determined by the choice of tactics made by an individual, and around 4% was determined by the tactics perceived as being used by the other partner). The outcome of a decision was more likely to be judged as fair and satisfactory if one partner offered resources (5) or used factual and reasoned argument (18); similar results were found where the other partner also used reasoned argument (18), and especially when they put forward integrative solutions (17). Conversely, the outcome was more likely to be judged as unfair if one or the other partner expressed negative emotions (2) or helplessness (3), insisted on their views (7) or withdrew from the argument (8). Similarly, judging the outcome as unfair increased if the other partner presented false facts (10) or used flattery (1) to secure an outcome favourable to him- or herself. Satisfied couples in particular found flattery (1) and insistence by the other partner (7) as unfair methods of gaining influence. Unhappy couples, and particularly women in such relationships, considered threats made by the other partner to withdraw resources (6) to be unfair. Clear expression of an individual's wishes (9) was perceived as a fair tactic when used by the other partner, particularly in unhappy relationships.

In the Vienna Diary Study, fairness was understood as the subjective assessment of a situation on the basis of various principles of justice. These principles of justice were taken as (a) the egoism principle; (b) the equality principle; (c) the needs principle; and (d) the compensation principle:

(a)   According to the egoism principle, a situation in which one's own degree of benefit is high is judged to be fair. On this basis, a positive linear correlation between benefit and the assessment of fairness is to be expected.

(b)   According to the equality principle, fairness results from both partners having an equal amount of benefit. This implies an inverted u-shaped relation between benefit and the assessment of fairness; this formally corresponds to a minus sign in the square of the benefit field in a regression analysis.

(c)   According to the needs principle, the distribution of benefit should be based on the needs of the partners, with the person to whom the topic under discussion is more important having greater benefit from the decision. If this is achieved, the situation is judged to be fair. In formal terms, this corresponds to an interaction between relative importance and the benefit, which is indicated by a plus sign in the regression analysis: the higher the relative importance, the greater the linear correlation between benefit and perceived fairness. Where the level of relative importance is high, it follows that there is increased emphasis on the egoism principle.

(d)   According to the compensation principle, over time a balance of benefit should be achieved. Situations that restore such a balance of benefit are perceived as being fair. In formal terms, this corresponds to an interaction between current and past benefit indicated by a minus sign in the regression analysis: the lower the degree of previous benefit, the greater the linear correlation between benefit and fairness. Where one partner has high benefit debts, it follows that there is increased emphasis on the egoism principle.

A plus sign in the regression parameter for benefit indicates the presence of the egoism principle, whereas a minus sign for the square of benefit indicates the presence of the equality principle. A plus sign in the parameter for the interaction between benefit and relative importance indicates the needs principle, whereas a minus sign in the parameter for the interaction between current and past benefit indicates the compensation principle. These different principles are not mutually exclusive; it is possible that all four principles may operate jointly in bringing about an assessment of fairness. Moreover, in the Vienna Diary Study it was hypothesised that the determinants of the judgement of fairness would have differing levels of influence depending on the relationship structure, as this would affect the importance of the individual principles. Relationship satisfaction and dominance in the relationship were investigated as moderator variables.

Regression analyses were firstly carried out using the remembered degree of benefit, and then using the degree of benefit that was actually recorded at the time. The first figure was obtained from diary records of how high the degree of benefit had been in the last decision, as they remembered it; the second was obtained from the data relating to the last decision as recorded in the diary at that time. The average aggregated benefit for the sample of women was $M = 45.27$, and for the sample of men it was $M = 49.50$. The average aggregated remembered benefit was $M = 46.36$ for the women and $M = 50.57$ for the men. The analyses also distinguished between the last decision and the average of the last three decision-making situations. The analysis was firstly carried out without taking into account the subject-matter of the decision, and was later differentiated by specific type of subject-matter. In total, five regression models were generated (see also Table 7.11): a regression analysis with remembered benefit taken as the independent variable, a last incident model, a moving average model, a specific last incident model, and a specific moving average model. For each model, interactions with relationship satisfaction and dominance in the relationship were investigated. Only the results of the first three models are presented in what follows, as the models that relate to specific subject-matter produced no significantly different results. The findings only differed in respect of subject-matter specific to the relationship, which is not particularly surprising in view of the goals in conflicts about the relationship. Fairness appears to depend on certain conflict variables, regardless of the subject-matter being discussed. We have not included any report about the

TABLE 7.11

Results of regression analyses taking distributive fairness as dependent variable

Model	Women				Men			
	R^2	R^2 adjusted	Difference R^2	Beta	R^2	R^2 adjusted	Difference R^2	Beta
Last incident model (remembered benefit from the last decision):								
1 (Personal parameters)	.27	.24	.27**		.14	.10	.14**	
2 (Benefit variables)	.46	.43	.18**		.23	.18	.08**	
Benefit				.35**				.19**
Benefit²				-.20**				-.10**
Benefit × Importance				.08**				.05
Importance				-.07*				-.09*
3 (History)	.46	.43	.00		.24	.19	.01**	
Benefit ×								
Remembered benefit			.04				-.09**	
Remembered benefit			.03				.01	
Whole model	.46	.43**			.24	.19**		
Last incident model:								
1 (Personal parameters)	.25	.22	.25**		.15	.11	.15**	
2 (Benefit variables)	.41	.38	.16**		.24	.21	.09**	
Benefit				.31**				.21**
Benefit²				-.17**				-.13**
Benefit × Importance				.07**				.01
Importance				-.10**				-.08*

3 (History)	.41	.38	.00		.25	.21	.01
Benefit × Past benefit				-.01			.06
Past benefit				.04			-.03
Whole model	.41	.38**			.25	.21**	

Moving average model:

1 (Personal parameters)	.26	.22	.26**		.17	.13	.17**
2 (Benefit variables)	.42	.39	.16**		.26	.22	.09**
Benefit				.33**			.22**
Benefit²				-.16**			-.11**
Benefit × Importance				.05*			-.04
Importance				-.08*			-.09*
3 (History)	.42	.39	.00		.26	.22	.00
Benefit × Past benefit				-.03			-.01
Past benefit				-.03			-.04
Whole model	.42	.39**			.26	.22**	

Note: 1 (Personal parameters) shows that in the model the couples were considered as dummy variables; 2 (Benefit variables) shows that benefit, the square of the benefit, relative importance and the interaction of benefit and relative importance were considered in the second stage regression; 3 (History) relates to the analysis of influence of the remembered or actually recorded benefit from the last decision and to the interaction between previous benefit and the benefit in the current situation. Statistically significant results are indicated by ** ($p < .01$) and * ($p < .05$).

Source: Kirchler et al. (1999).

different findings for couples in happy and unhappy relationships, and in relationships with different types of dominance structure, because in each category the number of observation statistics was small and therefore the results would be unreliable.

Analyses of the determinants of the experienced degree of fairness in the Vienna Diary Study were related to four different principles for assessing the distribution of benefit as more or less fair. According to the egoism principle, a situation in which a particular individual had a high level of benefit would be judged to be fair. According to the equality principle, a situation is most fair if both partners have equal benefit from it. According to the needs principle, the distribution of benefit should reflect the needs of the partners, whilst the compensation principle states that over time a balance of benefit should be achieved.

In both men and women, the egoism principle proved to have significant influence over the assessment of fairness: The higher the level of benefit obtained, the more likely it was that a decision would be judged to be fair. This finding held true for discussions about financial matters and matters relating to work, children and leisure; however, it was not true of matters that were to do with the relationship.

The equality principle was similarly confirmed: Situations that resulted in a one-sided distribution of benefit were more likely to be assessed as unfair. This effect counteracts the effect of the egoism principle referred to above; in instances where extreme preference is given to an individual's own wishes, the egoism principle does not apply for this reason.

The needs principle was only confirmed in the sample of women. However, regression analyses carried out for specific and separate subject-matters indicated that the needs principle is not applied universally, but particularly when the discussion is about relationship issues.

The compensation principle appeared to have little influence over the assessment of fairness, across all the different areas of subject-matter. The postulated correlation could only be identified in the analysis of remembered benefit for the sample of men.

Satisfaction with the outcome of a decision was also analysed. In the Vienna Diary Study, women recorded 757 instances of decisions and men recorded 743 instances. Despite the relatively high level of aggregated satisfaction ($M = 5.10$ for the sample of women, and $M = 5.30$ for men), the assessments of satisfaction ranged widely (from 1 = completely dissatisfied to 7 = highly satisfied).

Partners in close relationships have two goals in mind during disagreements: On the one hand, there is a need to achieve one's own goal and to assert oneself, but on the other hand there is a need not to jeopardise harmony in the relationship. In this respect, it was hypothesised that satisfaction with the outcome of a decision would contain both goals as evaluation criteria. It is therefore plausible to assert that a positive climate during the conversation and a high degree of distributive fairness will contribute to preserving or restoring harmony in the relationship, resulting ultimately in satisfaction with the relationship. High degrees of benefit and influence in a decision are instrumental in achieving the goal of asserting oneself. However, it is hypothesised that overly high levels of benefit and influence in favour of one partner may disturb the harmony of the relationship—and therefore an inverted u-shaped relation is likely between satisfaction and influence and between satisfaction and benefit. These hypotheses were tested in the Vienna Diary Study.

The first regression analysis, taking satisfaction with the outcome of the decision as the dependent variable, was conducted over several stages: (1) the personal parameters; (2) the climate of the conversation and distributive fairness; (3) relative benefit from the decision and the square of the benefit; and finally (4) relative influence and the square of the influence. Further analyses were carried out using the same variables for the five separate categories of topics: financial matters, and matters relating to work, children, the relationship, and leisure. Table 7.12 summarises the results of the analyses, which were not topic-specific. Overall, the results for the five specific decision-making categories correspond to those of the general analysis. In decisions over financial matters and matters relating to work, children, and leisure, similar variables appear to promote satisfaction; it is only when the topic relates to relationship issues that other variables appear to promote satisfaction.

In investigating the determinants of satisfaction with the outcome of decisions, it was hypothesised that the partners were pursuing two distinct goals: egoistic goals on the one hand, and the goals of stabilising or improving relationship harmony on the other. In all the analyses, the climate of the conversation proved to be an important determinant of satisfaction, whilst distributive fairness was found to be the strongest influencing factor, regardless of the subject-matter of the discussion. The higher the degree of distributive fairness, the higher the satisfaction with the outcome of the discussion, irrespective of the level of satisfaction with the relationship, the dominance relations within it, and the subject-matter of the discussion.

The benefit obtained in a decision, which was a vital aspect in achieving egoistic goals, also proved to be an important determinant of satisfaction. However, excessive benefit resulted in a reduction in satisfaction, probably on account of the feelings of guilt that such an outcome generated.

The influence exerted by an individual was also expected to contribute to achieving egoistic goals. However, this notion was not entirely supported by analysis of the diaries. When the discussion focused on relationship issues, the relative distribution of influence between the partners proved not to be significant in respect of satisfaction with the discussion. In all discussions

TABLE 7.12

Results of regression analysis taking satisfaction with the decision as dependent variable

Model	Women				Men			
	R^2	R^2 adjusted	Difference R^2	Beta	R^2	R^2 adjusted	Difference R^2	Beta
1 (Personal parameters)	.31	.28	.31**		.18	.15	.18**	
2 (Fairness variables)	.66	.64	.35**		.51	.49	.33**	
Conversation climate				.21**				.22**
Fairness				.50**				.47**
3 (Benefit variables)	.68	.66	.02**		.56	.54	.05**	
Benefit				.12**				.19**
Benefit^2				-.03*				-.07**
4 (Influence variables)	.69	.66	.01*		.57	.54	.00	
Influence				.08**				.05*
Influence^2				.00				.03
Whole model	.69	.66**			.57	.54**		

Note: 1 (Personal parameters) shows that in the model the couples were considered as dummy variables; 2 (Fairness variables) shows that the climate of the conversation and assessments of fairness were considered; 3 (Benefit variables) shows that benefit and the square of the benefit were considered in the third stage; 4 (Influence variables) refers to the fourth regression stage, where relative influence and its square were considered. Statistically significant results are indicated by ** ($p < .01$) and * ($p < .05$).

Source: Kirchler et al. (1999).

about other subject-matters, it was found that the level of satisfaction with the decision increased as the level of individual influence over the decision increased. The hypothesis that extremely high levels of individual influence over a decision could lead to feelings of guilt, thereby reducing the level of satisfaction, was not confirmed.

Whilst the reported findings apply equally to happy and unhappy couples, the Vienna Diary Study also reports on differences between egalitarian relationships, those dominated by women and those dominated by men. Particularly in egalitarian partnerships, the degree of fairness that was experienced and the equal distribution of benefit and influence appear significant in determining the level of satisfaction with a decision. This result must be treated with caution, in view of the limited number of couples for each different type of relationship dominance structure in the Vienna Diary Study. However, at the same time it is wholly plausible to argue that, where equality is defined by equal treatment and equal rights for both partners and therefore also applies in the area of benefit, a fair decision will be perceived as one that serves both partners equally well.

CHAPTER EIGHT

Summary

When partners take decisions in the private home, they often start from a position where they have different wishes. Different wishes and opinions about alternative decision options represent conflicts that need to be resolved. It is often possible to discuss differences of opinion in a factual manner and to reach a decision that satisfies all those involved. Sometimes differences of opinion flow into "heated" conflicts, which are broken off or postponed and later resumed until eventually a solution is found or the original wishes become dissipated.

It is not the frequency of conflicts, but the conflict dynamics that have lasting consequences for the quality of close relationships. The tactics partners employ to assert their own wishes and the respect they show towards the wishes of the other partner colour the degree of harmony in the relationship. Moves to realise egoistic desires, consideration for the other partner, and the avoidance of the development of conflicts that might threaten the relationship determine the quality of the relationship and how the partners relate to each other in future conflicts and decision-making situations. Conversely, the relationship quality also determines the type of conflict dynamics.

If decisions, and particularly financial decisions, form the focus of research, then full account needs to be taken of the fact that decisions determine the quality of the relationship, and that conversely the kind of decision-making process is determined by relationship quality, the power relations within the relationship and the level of satisfaction with the relationship. Financial and non-financial decisions taken by women and men, the decision-making dynamics and the outcomes of decisions must be analysed with regard to relationship quality and to power relations between the partners.

If a study is to be made of decisions in the private household, account needs to be taken of the fact that partners do not exclusively devote their attention to the solution of a problem, but discuss different opinions and take decisions alongside their everyday routines. Whilst conflicts are being carried out and decisions are being made, other activities are also being carried out which often demand attention in themselves: In the Vienna Diary Study (Kirchler et al., 1999), the 40 couples who formed the basis of the study reported doing various household tasks in around a third of all cases while a conflict situation was being played out. In around 13% of cases, women discussed issues with their partners while they were doing household tasks, and men were doing household tasks during discussions in around 5% of cases; in a further 12% of cases, both partners were doing household tasks whilst at the same time arguing about differences of opinion and taking decisions.

As a starting-point, it was acknowledged that decisions need to be seen as dependent upon the quality of the relationship between couples and embedded in the complexities of everyday life. Moreover, partners who are acting on current desires, which are driving them to take a decision, and which might sometimes lead to conflict, are also pursuing a goal of reaching a decision that will preserve the relationship. On this basis of disagreements happening when various activities are being performed simultaneously, distracting attention from the conflict at stake, and multiple goals are being pursued, the results of a number of studies were discussed and hypotheses were tested. The following issues were examined in particular: What does the relative influence of the partners depend on? To what extent do past decisions determine current ones? How interconnected are the different matters about which decisions are taken, and to what extent are the dynamics of a decision determined by the outcomes of other past decisions? A study was also made of the tactics that partners use to achieve their own egoistic goals, and those goals that are common to the partnership. In conclusion, the results of decisions, rationality, fairness, and satisfaction were discussed.

This work takes decisions in close relationships as its focus, and these are discussed in the central section of this book. To understand decisions in close relationships better, two chapters of this book address the concepts of decisions themselves and close relationships. A further chapter is devoted to criticism of the methods of empirical research in private households, as this area needs to be given careful consideration if what is actually happening is to be adequately recorded. The opening chapter provides a framework contextualising love, money, and everyday matters and reviewing relevant literature from the social sciences that covers research on decisions in private households.

After years of studying financial and non-financial decisions in the shared home, a diary study was conceived as a means of answering the many questions that had been produced from earlier studies. This book makes detailed and repeated reference to the findings of the Vienna Diary Study

(Kirchler et al., 1999), in which 40 couples took part and recorded information about their relationship and about joint decisions over the course of a year. The Diary Study also provided three case studies, which are set out in the beginning of this book because they provide clear examples of how complex decision-making in the private home can be: The cases, reported on the basis of the recordings made for the Vienna Diary Study, show clearly that partners taking decisions in the private home do not sit down together at a table to reach a decision, freed up from other tasks and weighing up reasoned arguments for or against a particular alternative. Decisions are reached, but only in retrospect does it become clear that wishes have led to discussions and these have resulted in differences of opinion, which finally are ended when a decision is taken. From one case, it is evident that decisions that are ultimately taken autonomously by one partner do not necessarily follow a wholly autonomous decision-making process: The agreement of the partner is repeatedly sought, conflicts are begun and then broken off, and only after no agreement can be reached does the active partner make an autonomous purchasing decision. Another case demonstrates that decision-makers can change their goal over a period of time: whilst at the start of a discussion about a present for their son, both partners are pursuing one goal, in the course of considering the possible alternative presents, the goal the man is pursuing changes, with the result that in the end he is arranging to purchase a present for himself and loses sight of what was the actual (or original) goal. Whilst it may be clear at the outset that the partners are moving in a particular direction in seeking a decision, in the course of taking that decision it is possible to lose sight of the goal as a new goal emerges and is pursued instead. In retrospect it is likely that it will rarely be recalled that the starting-point of the decision-making process was a goal other than the one that has ultimately been realised. Finally, all three case studies also demonstrate impressively that decisions are not isolated events, but are bound up in the complexities of everyday life: Whilst a financial decision is being taken, various other differences of opinion are also being played out, and other everyday tasks repeatedly force their way to the forefront of discussions. All three case-studies also reveal variations in the subjective description of the reality of what went on between the partners. Differences in perception and in recall lead to somewhat different descriptions of shared experiences that lie only a few hours in the past.

In the chapter on "love, money, and everyday matters" (Chapter 2), definitions are offered of what is understood by "being in love" and "love", and theories based on social psychology about love and partnership are presented. Further definitions are offered of what is understood by money, and its significance for close relationships. This section also discusses the grey area that is everyday life, which can at the same time be so thrilling and unusual, as Sherlock Holmes observed. The section about everyday matters in close relationships refers particularly to the complexity of interactions in the private household and proposes a systematic study of the actions of everyday life in preference to other theoretical constructs.

The chapter about "close relationships" (Chapter 3), describes the uniqueness of the male–female dyad, and considers the goals of couples and the structure of relationships. The structure of the relationship is discussed from the perspectives of interaction processes and power relations, asking whether it represents an invariable crystallisation of the experiences of the partners. The chapter closes with a consideration of interaction processes from the viewpoint of exchange and interdependence theory, and critical observations are made about the economic–rational perspective for viewing interpersonal interactions. Romantic partners do not behave according to the desire to optimise egoistic profit in economic terms, but also seek to provide pleasures for their partner. The love model (Kirchler, 1989) differentiates between economic and romantic relationships and describes interaction processes between partners in the private home in a different way to those between partners in ad hoc and economic relationships. Partners in close relationships offer one another a variety of resources; they depend on reciprocal desires and wishes in respect of their behaviour and their decisions; they distribute luxuries and costs not on the basis of the equity principle, but largely in accordance with individual needs; and they offer luxuries to each other without claiming a pay-back, or only seek for the luxury to be repaid "in the longer term". Partners in close relationships also take the wishes of the other person into account when seeking to realise egoistic goals. Those taking decisions may be pursuing multiple goals, but will always be pursuing at least these two goals: the goal of realising an individual's own wishes, and the goal of nurturing their relationship at the same time.

In the chapter on decisions (Chapter 4), a distinction is drawn between decisions and differences of opinion. Similarly, the differences between normative and descriptive decision-making models are examined. Essentially, decision-making situations are categorised as either relating to financial or non-financial decisions, and different types of conflict are discussed. Financial decisions are understood to relate particularly to expenses, money management, savings measures, and the investment of capital. Non-financial decisions cover matters relating to children, work, leisure, and the relationship. Although the current work is mainly concerned with joint decisions by the partners, other areas such as autonomous decisions and spontaneous or habitual decisions are also addressed. With respect to the conflicts that precede joint decisions, a distinction is drawn between probability conflicts, value conflicts, and distributional conflicts. Probability conflicts is the term applied to differences of opinion based on the partners' different factual evaluations of alternatives and possibilities, even though both partners share the same goals. Whereas probability conflicts are rarely perceived as disagreements between the partners, as they tend to lead on to factual discussions, value conflicts can often give rise to "heated" debate: Whilst partners may assess the various alternatives objectively in similar ways, they have different opinions about the value of a particular goal. In distributional conflicts, the debate is about differing interests and the distribution of limited resources. The chapter on "decisions" closes by presenting a model of the course of decision-making in partnerships, developed from the analysis of different models used in market research. The decision-making model does not represent the supposed decision-making processes of the partners, but rather serves as the starting-point for a complex analysis of decisions and as a descriptive framework, although the course of the decision-making structure does not match the temporal course of decision-making by partners. It makes little sense to offer a model of the course of decision-making that is organised along time lines, since decisions in private households are understood to be reached by a process of incremental steps that move from desires to goals—sometimes going back over the steps taken, because goals may change over the course of a decision being taken. Descriptive models of decision-making may serve to draw together the different aspects under investigation.

The chapter on methods for studying decision-making in close relationships (Chapter 5) is quite lengthy. However, the scientific methods involved appear to be of such importance that the length of this chapter is not only justified, but entirely necessary. There is hardly any research field that is as sensitive as everyday life in the private home, and there is hardly any activity that is as easily influenced by the research methods adopted as decision-making processes between partners. Given that everyday life in close relationships unfolds away from public view, that the partners have developed a particular "language" on the basis of long years of intimacy and shared experience which outsiders can only follow with difficulty, that the private world of the couple is protected and some taboo areas are guarded within the relationship, inquisitive questions and insensitive observation can destroy the very thing that is the object of research. As well as considering the shortcomings of observation and the problems inherent in the methodology of questionnaire techniques, diary methods are also discussed. An events diary that is kept by the partners at regular intervals is ultimately preferred to other diary-keeping methods. In the Vienna Diary Study, a diary was kept by 40 couples over the period of a year. The section about research methods concludes with a description of the Vienna Diary Study, those participating in it and how the study was conducted. Finally, the quality of the methods employed is assessed using data from the Vienna Diary Study. All criteria indicate the satisfactory reliability of the diary approach.

The central chapters (6 and 7) focus on influence in decisions and decision dynamics in private households. A wide range of empirical studies into purchasing decisions in the private household conducted since the 1980s are summarised here; detailed data, however, are drawn mainly from the Vienna Diary Study.

The Vienna Diary Study demonstrated that women and men spend a few hours together at home nearly every day, but that they only speak with each other for up to 60 minutes during this time. Consistent with the findings of other studies, it was found that satisfied partners spoke for longer with one another than did dissatisfied partners, although in the Diary Study the happy partners spent less time with one another. During these discussions, financial matters were discussed, together with matters relating to work and housework, children, leisure, and the relationship. Whereas matters relating to children represented the most frequent topic of discussion, financial topics were the most rich in conflicts. Discussions about finances often focused on expenditure, and less often on savings measures or money management in general. The couples mostly held different opinions because they had different value concepts. In financial conflicts, there were also often instances of probability conflicts.

Information from the partners about their conversations often varied. As in other studies, the information provided by the partners agreed about two-thirds of the time; a third of the reports revealed differences. Information was often distorted in a way that conformed to socially desirable stereo-types: The extent of an individual's own influence and benefit tended to be underestimated, while the influence and benefit of their partner tended to be overestimated.

Relative influence in disagreements was distributed fairly evenly between men and women in the Vienna Diary Study. In financial matters, the men were attributed as having somewhat more influence than the women; for all other discussion topics, the relative share of influence of the partners lay close to 50%. In similar studies carried out in the last fifty years, it was found that the distribution of influence between women and men was close to 50% in each case. The results of a number of studies looking at purchasing decisions are summarised in respect of relative influence, which suggest overall that gender-specific distribution of influence obeys the prevailing gender role stereotypes: In questionnaires, women indicate that they have more influence over decisions about kitchen equipment, whereas men decide about technical products and both partners decide jointly about holidays. At least some part of these results may be more attributable to the tendency to provide answers that are socially acceptable and to clichéd views of gender roles than to the decision-making dynamic actually in operation in the private home.

Relative influence in disagreements was attributed on the one hand to gender-specific roles and to the nature of the content being discussed (products, product characteristics, etc.), and on the other hand to social norms which are culturally and historically conditioned. There is further discussion as to the extent to which relative resource contributions define power in decision-making situations. Whereas older studies confirm the validity of the theory of relative resource contribution, current research indicates no significant correlation between the contributions of the partners to the relationship and their relative influence. Finally, the influence of men and women in relationships with different degrees of happiness is discussed, together with the influence of children and young adults and the importance of specialist knowledge and interest in a particular topic. Overall, there is evidence that both specialist knowledge and relative interest in a particular topic about which a decision is to be made are the most important determinants of the partners' influence. Although the significance of relative specialist knowledge speaks in favour of a factually sound solution in taking decisions, subjective awareness of the importance of a decision might suggest that partners may seek to acquiesce with the other's views if a particular decision is of special importance to the other partner. Alongside the goal of taking decisions that are factually sound, the partners also show consideration for the wishes of the other partner.

Together with consideration for the wishes of the other partner, the fact that past decision-making outcomes determine the current decision-making processes also indicates the importance of the relationship in decisions about specific subject-matters. The partners try not to optimise their egoistic desires in isolation from other goals, and therefore it is not only specialist knowledge that counts in taking a decision, but also the urgency of the individual wishes and what has happened in previous disagreements. If one partner has exercised more influence in the past and obtained greater benefit from a decision than the other partner, then it is more likely that in the current disagreements it is the other partner who will assert him- or herself. It appears as if the partners are seeking to distribute relative benefit and relative influence, and therefore power, equally between themselves. Complex analysis of the data recorded in the Vienna Diary Study established that partners seek to equalise influence and benefit over time. It is important to note that the topic areas in which decisions are taken are separate from one another, and that imbalance in influence or benefit in one area of decision-making must be balanced out in exactly the same area. Moreover, it does not appear to be necessary to settle up overdrawn "accounts" immediately in the short term; the distribution of influence and benefit in the last two or three decision-making situations is taken into account. This tendency to seek to equalise the balance was particularly evident in the records provided by men. The records provided by women often revealed "crystallised" influence patterns which favoured either the woman or the man. In addition, attempts to balance the situation were more likely to be found in decisions relating to financial matters, or when it concerned work, leisure or children than in discussions about the relationship. Disagreements and decision-making represent complex tasks with partners keeping record of what is going on, approximately knowing what happened in the past and trying to keep in balance the mutual distribution of resources, influence, and utility, but at the same time not risking the stability of their relationship.

The tactics used to gain influence were then investigated. Alongside tactics of persuasion and negotiation, reasoned argument was also analysed as a tactic. All studies of the use of tactics have shown that reasoned arguments are adduced particularly frequently and partners present their wishes openly. Persuasion tactics follow if reasoned argument fails to enable a goal to be reached. The choice of tactics appears to depend, above all, on the relationship quality. Gender, the subject-matter giving rise to the disagreement and the type of conflict also appear to determine the choice of tactics. The relative dominance of partners was not a determining factor in the choice of tactics. In summary, it was found that tactics often colour the climate of the conversation, but the relative influence of the partners was less dependent on the choice of tactics employed. Some tactics, particularly those involving harsh and negative emotions, can raise the degree of influence, but they have extremely negative effects on the climate of the conversation. Other tactics also worsen the climate of the conversation, for example the tactic of helplessness, but they are also not effective in terms of securing relative influence. Reasoned argument, integrative negotiating measures and the clear expression of one's wishes appear to be tactics that lead to the achievement of goals, both in asserting one's own wishes and in furthering the relationship with their partner.

Economically sensible solutions, the experience of procedural and distributive fairness, and satisfaction with a decision were analysed as aspects of the outcome of decision-making. Although the situations in which decisions are made could make it more difficult to reach optimal solutions, in economic terms, overall it is difficult to judge what is economically optimal and thus research in this area remains speculative. However, the Vienna Diary Study provides some important findings in respect of fairness and satisfaction: Partners appear to perceive decisions to be fair if they obtain some personal benefit from them, and especially if the outcome appears particularly important to them while the benefit which accrues is not excessively great and is not obtained at the expense of the other partner. In addition to this, most couples at least show a tendency to perceive a move to balance out the subjective benefit over time as fair. Satisfaction with a decision increases if the outcome of the decision is perceived as fair, if the climate of the conversation was good, if the degree of benefit obtained by an individual is high, but not excessively so, and if one's own influence over the decision-making process increases.

In summary, a picture of decision-making in partnerships can be drawn that follows closely the models of incremental decisions: Partners move repeatedly from a desire, via discussions and evaluations, postponement and renewed discussion of a topic to arrive at a decision. Sometimes, in the course of reaching a decision, one goal becomes lost in favour of another one. Whereas diaries make it clear that decisions are arrived at via several routes and deviations along the way, people indicate in interviews that they proceed "in a straight line" from desires to decisions. In retrospect, this may appear to be the case; and when asked to replay the process, rationalisation often takes place.

In taking decisions, the partner who knows more about the matter that requires a decision dominates. However, in taking decisions partners are pursuing more goals than simply that of fulfilling their own egoistic desires: It is possible for the partner who is particularly concerned about a particular decision to have their way, even overriding the more knowledgeable partner. It is also possible for the person who has had less influence in the past and less benefit from past decisions to assert their wishes. Partners appear to keep accounts of influence and benefit relating to different topic areas where decisions are taken, and they distribute material and non-material resources equally. Just as the analyses of relative influence reveal egoistic goals and goals that seek to further the relationship, the choice of tactics also indicates different and simultaneously operating goals: various tactics are chosen, depending on relationship quality, and these different tactics may further the individual's influence and the relationship quality, or they may only increase the individual's influence whilst at the same time damaging the quality of the relationship. Finally, the analyses of the outcomes of decisions show how complex and differing goals are pursued at the same time: As influence and benefit increase, a decision is experienced as being fairer and more satisfactory, although too much influence and too great a degree of benefit, at the cost of benefit for the other partner, certainly tend to generate an uncomfortable feeling and dissatisfaction with the decision, even for the partner who has maximised the advantages to him- or herself.

In conclusion, there remains the issue of further questions requiring research in this area, questions that have arisen in the attempt to answer certain other questions. Naturally, some of the findings have not been replicated in other research, and some statements remain speculative even though there are a number of investigations to support them, and these should be tested again in targeted studies. However, from the overview it is clear that what is presented is a complex and consistent picture of decision-making in close relationships. It remains to be seen whether closer observation and even more intensive analysis of decision-making will refine the picture obtained so far still further, or whether the increased closeness to the object of study will result in the loss of the overview or will blur perceptions. However, this question is one that properly relates to the theory of research and social science, and not to the subject of decision-making in close relationships.

References

Adams, J.S. (1965). Inequity in social exchange. In L. Berkowitz (Ed.), *Advances in experimental social psychology* (Vol. 2, pp. 267–299). New York: Academic Press.

Ahuja, R.B.D., & Stinson, K.M. (1993). Female-headed single parent families: An explanatory study of children's influence in family decision making. *Advances in Consumer Research, 20*, 469–474.

Ainsworth, M.D.S., Blehar, M.C., Waters, E., & Wall, S. (1978). *Patterns of attachment: A psychological study of the strange situation*. Hillsdale, NJ: Lawrence Erlbaum Associates Inc.

Aldous, J. (1971). A framework for the analysis of family problem solving. In J. Aldous, T. Condon, R. Hill, M. Straus, & I. Tallman (Eds.), *Family problem solving*. Hinsdale, NH: Dryden Press.

Almeida, D.M., & Kessler, R.C. (1998). Everyday stressors and gender differences in daily distress. *Journal of Personality and Social Psychology, 75*, 670–680.

Almeida, D.M., & Wethington, E. (1996, March). *Daily spillover between marital and parent–child tensions*. Paper presented at the meeting of the Society for Research on Adolescence. Boston, MA.

Almeida, D.M., Wethington, E., & Chandler, A.L. (1999). Daily transmission of tensions between marital dyads and parent–child dyads. *Journal of Marriage and the Family, 61*, 49–61.

Anderson, N.H. (1982). *Methods of information integration theory*. New York: Academic Press.

Argyle, M., & Henderson, M. (1985). *The anatomy of relationships*. London: Heinemann.

Armstrong, M.A., & Anderson, N.H. (Undated). *Influence in marriage studied with information integration theory*. Unpublished manuscript, University of California, San Diego.

Aron, A., Meliant, E., Aron, E.N., Vallone, R.D., & Bator, R.J. (1997). The experimental generation of interpersonal closeness: A procedure and some preliminary findings. *Personality and Social Psychology Bulletin, 23*, 365–377.

Auhagen, A.E. (1987). A new approach for the study of personal relationships: The double diary approach. *The German Journal of Psychology, 11*, 3–7.

Auhagen, A.E. (1991). *Freundschaft im Alltag. Eine Studie mit dem Doppeltagebuch*. Bern: Huber.

Auinger, F. (1987). *Subjektives Wohlbefinden als Klimabarometer in Organisationen. Eine Studie mit dem Zeitstichprobentagebuch*. Unpublished masters thesis, University of Linz, Austria.

Axelrod, R. (1984). *The evolution of cooperation*. New York: Basic Books.

Barry, B., & Oliver, R.R. (1996). Affect in dyadic negotiation: A model and propositions. *Organizational Behavior and Human Decision Processes, 67*, 127–143.

Baxter, L.A., & Wilmot, W.W. (1985). Taboo topics in close relationships. *Journal of Social and Personal Relationships, 2*, 253–269.

Beatty, S.E., & Talpade, S. (1994). Adolescent influence in family decision making: A replication with extension. *Journal of Consumer Research, 21*, 332–341.

Becker, G.S. (1974). A theory of marriage. In T. Schulz (Ed.), *Economics of the family* (pp. 299–244). Chicago: Chicago University Press.

Becker, G.S. (1981). *A treatise on the family*. Cambridge, MA: Harvard University Press.

Becker, G.S. (1982). *Der ökonomische Ansatz zur Erklärung menschlichen Verhaltens*. Tübingen: J.C.B. Mohr.

Belk, R.W. (1988). Possessions and the extended self. *Journal of Consumer Research, 15*, 139–162.

Berg, J.H., & McQuinn, R.D. (1986). Attraction and exchange in continuing and noncontinuing dating relationships. *Journal of Personality and Social Psychology, 50*, 942–952.

Bernard, H.R., Killworth, P.D., Kronenfeld, D., & Sailer, L. (1984). On the validity of retrospective data: The problem of informant accuracy. *Annual Review of Anthropology, 13*, 495–517.

Berscheid, E. (1994). Interpersonal relationships. *Annual Review of Psychology, 45*, 49–129.

Berscheid, E., & Lopes, J. (1997). A temporal model of relationship satisfaction and stability. In R.J. Sternberg, & M. Hojjat (Eds.), *Satisfaction in close relationships*. New York: Guilford.

Bettman, J.R. (1979). *An information processing theory of consumer choice*. Reading, MA: Addison-Wesley.

Bierhoff, H.W. (1991). Liebe. In M. Amelang, H.-J. Ahrens, & H.W. Bierhoff (Eds.), *Attraktion und Liebe. Formen und Grundlagen partnerschaftlicher Beziehungen* (pp. 197–228). Göttingen: Hogrefe.

Bierhoff, H.W., & Grau, I. (1999). *Romantische Beziehungen. Bindung, Liebe, Partnerschaft*. Bern: Huber.

Billig, M. (1987). *Arguing and thinking. A rhetorical approach to social psychology*. Cambridge: Cambridge University Press.

Birchler, G.R., Weiss, R.L., & Vincent, J.P. (1975). Multimethod analysis of social reinforcement exchange between maritally distressed and nondistressed spouses and stranger dyads. *Journal of Personality and Social Psychology, 31*, 349–360.

Blau, P.M. (1964). *Exchange and power in social life*. New York: Wiley.

Bless, H. (1997). *Stimmung und Denken. Ein Modell zum Einfluß von Stimmungen auf Denkprozesse*. Bern: Huber.

Blood, R.O., & Wolfe, D.W. (1960). *Husbands and wives. The dynamics of married living*. Glencoe, IL: Free Press.

Bodenhausen, G.V., & Lichtenstein, M. (1987). Social stereotypes and information-processing strategies: The impact of task complexity. *Journal of Personality and Social Psychology, 52*, 871–880.

Bohner, G., Bless, H., Schwarz, N., & Strack, F. (1988). What triggers causal attributions? The impact of valence and subjective probability. *European Journal of Social Psychology, 18*, 335–345.

Bolger, N., DeLongis, A., Kessler, R.C., & Schilling, E.A. (1989a). Effects of daily stress on negative mood. *Journal of Personality and Social Psychology, 57*, 808–818.

Bolger, N., DeLongis, A., Kessler, R.C., & Wethington, E. (1989b). The contagion of stress across multiple roles. *Journal of Marriage and the Family, 51*, 175–183.

Bolle, F. (1987). The altruistic family: Some remarks on Beckers theory of marriage. In F. Bolle, H. Brandstätter, K. Heinemann, E. Kirchler, H.-G. Krüsselberg, W. Meyer, W. Stroebe, W. Wagner, & U. Witt (Eds.), *Die Familie als Gegenstand sozialwissenschaftlicher Forschung* (pp. 87–98). Berlin: Duncker & Humblot.

Bolle, F. (1992). When and why to love your enemy. *Journal of Economic Psychology, 13*, 509–514.

Bornemann, E. (1976). *Psychology of money*. New York: Urizen.

Bower, G.H. (1981). Mood and memory. *American Psychologist, 36*, 129–148.

Bowlby, J. (1969). *Attachment and loss: Vol. 1. Attachment*. Harmondsworth, UK: Penguin Books.

Bowlby, J. (1973). *Attachment and loss. Vol. 2. Separation*. New York: Basic Books.

Box, G.P., & Jenkins, G.M. (1976). *Time series analysis. Forecasting and control*. San Francisco: Holden-Day.

Bradbury, T.N., & Fincham, F.D. (1990). Dimensions of marital and family interaction. In J. Touligtos, B.F. Perlmutter & M.A. Straus (Eds.), *Handbook of family measurement techniques* (pp. 37–60). Newbury Park, CA: Sage.

Brandstätter, E. (1998). *Ambivalente Zufriedenheit. Der Einfluß sozialer Vergleiche*. Münster, Germany: Waxmann.

Brandstätter, E. & Brandstätter, H. (1996). What's money worth? Determinants of the subjective value of money. *Journal of Economic Psychology, 17*, 443–464.

Brandstätter, H. (1977). Wohlbefinden und Unbehagen. In W.H. Tack (Ed.), *Bericht über den 30. Kongreß der Deutschen Gesellschaft für Psychologie in Regensburg (1976)* (Vol. 2, pp. 60–62). Göttingen, Germany: Hogrefe.

Brandstätter, H. (1981). Time sampling of subjective well-being. In H. Hartmann, W. Molt, & P. Stringer (Eds.), *Advances in Economic Psychology* (pp. 63–76). Heidelberg: Meyn.

Brandstätter, H. (1983). Emotional responses to other persons in everyday life situations. *Journal of Personality and Social Psychology, 45*, 871–883.

Brandstätter, H. (1987). Gruppenleistung und Gruppenentscheidung. In D. Frey, & S. Greif (Eds.), *Sozialpsychologie. Ein Handbuch in Schlüsselbegriffen* (pp. 182–186). Munich: Urban & Schwarzenberg.

Brandstätter, H. (1988). Sechzehn Persönlichkeits-Adjektivskalen (16 PA) als Forschungsinstrument anstelle des 16 PF. *Zeitschrift für experimentelle und angewandte Psychologie, 35*, 370–391.

Brandstätter, H., Kirchler, E., & Wagner, W. (1987). Rücksichtnahme und Betroffenheit von Ehepaaren in Konfliktsituationen. In H. Todt (Ed.), *Die Familie als Gegenstand sozialwissenschaftlicher Forschung* (pp. 147–161). Berlin: Duncker & Humblot.

Brandstätter, H., Stocker-Kreichgauer, G., & Firchau, V. (1980). Wirkung von Freundlichkeit und Argumentgüte auf Leser eines Diskussionsprotokolls. Ein Prozeßmodell. *Zeitschrift für Sozialpsychologie, 11*, 152–167.

Brandstätter, H., & Wagner, W. (1994). Erwerbsarbeit der Frau und Alltagsbefinden von Ehepartnern im Zeitverlauf. *Zeitschrift für Sozialpsychologie, 25*, 126–146.

Brannen, J., & Moss, P. (1987). Dual earner households: Women's financial contributions after the birth of the first child. In J. Brannen & G. Wilson (Eds.), *Give and take in families. Studies in resource distribution* (pp. 75–95). London: Allen & Unwin.

Branscombe, N.R., & Cohen, B.M. (1991). Motivation and complexity levels as determinants of heuristic use in social judgment. In J. P. Forgas (Ed.), *Emotion and social judgments* (pp. 145–160). Oxford: Pergamon Press.

Braybrooke, D., & Lindblom, C.E. (1963). *A strategy of decisions*. Glencoe: Free Press.

Brendl, C.M., Markman, A.B., & Higgins, E.T. (1998). Mentale Kontoführung als Selbstregulierung: Representativität für zielgeleitete Kategorien. *Zeitschrift für Sozialpsychologie, 29*, 89–104.

Brief, A.P., Butcher, A.H., & Roberson, L. (1995). Cookies, disposition, and job attitudes: The effects of positive mood-inducing events and negative affectivity on job satisfaction in a field experiment. *Organizational Behavior and Human Decision Processes, 62*, 55–62.

Bruins, J. (1999). Social power and influence tactics: A theoretical introduction. *Journal of Social Issues, 55*, 7–14.

Bruner, J., & Goodman, C. (1947). Value and need as organizing factors in perception. *Journal of Abnormal and Social Psychology, 42*, 33–44.

Brunswick, E. (1949). *Systematic and representative design of psychological experiments*. Berkeley: University of California Press.

Bui, K.-V.T., Peplau, L.A., & Hill, C.T. (1996). Testing the Rusbult model of relationship commitment and stability in a 15-year study of heterosexual couples. *Personality and Social Psychology Bulletin*, 22, 1244–1257.

Burgess, E.W. (1921). The romantic impulse and family disorganization. *Survey*, 57, 290–294.

Burgess, R.L. (1981). Relationships in marriage and the family. In S. Duck & R. Gilmour (Eds.), *Personal relationships* (Vol. 1, pp. 179–196). London: Academic Press.

Burgess, R.L., & Huston, T.L. (Eds.) (1979). *Social exchange in developing relationships*. New York: Academic Press.

Burghardt, A. (1977). *Soziologie des Geldes und der Inflation*. Vienna: Hermann Böhlau.

Burgoyne, C.B., & Morrison, V. (1997). Money in remarriage: Keeping things simple—and separate. *The Sociological Review*, 45, 363–395.

Burns, A.C. (1976). Spousal involvement and empathy in jointly-resolved and authoritatively-resolved purchase subdecisions. *Advances in Consumer Research*, 3, 199–207.

Burns, A.C., & Gentry, J.W. (1990). Toward improving household consumption behavior research: Avoidance of pitfalls in using alternative household data collection procedures. *Advances in Consumer Research*, 17, 518–520.

Burnstein, E. (1982). Persuasion as argument processing. In H. Brandstätter, J.H. Davis, & G. Stocker-Kreichgauer (Eds.), *Group decision processes*. London: Academic Press.

Buunk, B.P., & Van der Eijneden, R.J.J.M. (1997). Perceived prevalence, perceived superiority, and relationship satisfaction: Most relationships are good, but ours is the best. *Personality and Social Psychology Bulletin*, 23, 219–228.

Byrne, D. (1971). *The attraction paradigm*. New York: Academic Press.

Byrne, D., & Murnen, S.K. (1988). Maintaining loving relationships. In R.J. Sternberg & M.L. Barnes (Eds.), *The psychology of love* (pp. 293–310). New Haven, CT: Yale University Press.

Canary, D.J., & Cupach, W.R. (1988). Relational and episodic characteristics associated with conflict tactics. *Journal of Social and Personal Relationships*, 5, 305–325.

Cantor, J.R., Zillmann, D., & Bryant, J. (1975). Enhancement of experienced sexual arousal in response to erotic stimuli through misattribution of unrelated residual excitation. *Journal of Personality and Social Psychology*, 32, 69–75.

Carli, L.L. (1999). Gender, interpersonal power, and social influence. *Journal of Social Issues*, 55, 81–101.

Caron, A., & Ward, S. (1975). Gift decisions by kids and parents. *Journal of Advertising Research*, 14, 15–20.

Castro-Martin, T., & Bumpass, L. (1989). Recent trends in marital disruption. *Demography*, 26, 37–51.

Chattoe, E., & Gilbert, N. (1997). *Talking about budgets*. Working paper at the Department of Sociology, University of Surrey, Guildford, UK.

Cherlin, A.J. (1992). *Marriage, divorce, remarriage* (2nd ed.). Cambridge, MA: Harvard University Press.

Cialdini, R.B. (1993). *Influence. Science and practice*. New York: Harper Collins.

Clark, M.S. (1984). Record keeping in two types of relationships. *Journal of Personality and Social Psychology*, 47, 549–557.

Clark, M.S., & Chrisman, K. (1994). Resource allocation in intimate relationships: Trying to make sense of a confusing literature. In M.J. Lerner & G. Mikula (Eds.), *Entitlement and the affectional bond* (pp. 65–88). New York: Plenum Press.

Clark, M.S., & Grote, N.K. (1998). Why aren't indices of relationship costs always negatively related to indices of relationship quality? *Personality and Social Psychology Review*, 2, 2–17.

Clark, M.S., & Mills, J. (1979). Interpersonal attraction in exchange and communal relationships. *Journal of Personality and Social Psychology*, 37, 12–24.

Clark, M.S., & Reis, H.T. (1988). Interpersonal processes in close relationships. *Annual Review of Psychology*, 39, 609–672.

Clark, M.S., Mills, J., & Powell, M.C. (1986). Keeping track of needs in communal and exchange relationships. *Journal of Personality and Social Psychology*, *51*, 333–338.

Clark, M.S., Ouelette, R., Powell, M.C., & Milberg, S. (1987). Recipient's mood, relationship type, and helping. *Journal of Personality and Social Psychology*, *53*, 94–103.

Clark, M.S., & Waddell, B. (1985). Perceptions of exploitation in communal and exchange relationships. *Journal of Social and Personal Relationships*, *2*, 403–418.

Clore, G.L., & Byrne, D. (1974). A reinforcement-affect model of attraction. In T.L. Huston (Ed.), *Foundation of interpersonal attraction*. New York: Academic Press.

Clore, G.L., & Itkin, S.M. (1977). Verstärkungsmodelle der zwischenmenschlichen Anziehung. In G. Mikula & W. Stroebe (Eds.), *Sympathie, Freundschaft und Ehe*. Bern: Huber.

Cobb, S., & Jones, J.M. (1984). Social support, support groups and marital relationships. In S. Duck (Ed.), *Personal relationships 5: Repairing personal relationships* (pp. 47–66). London: Academic Press.

Collins, B.E., & Raven, B.H. (1969). Group structure: Attraction, coalitions, communication, and power. In G. Lindzey & E. Aronson (Eds.), *The handbook of social psychology: Vol. 4. Group psychology and phenomena of interaction*. Reading: Addison-Wesley.

Corfman, K.P. (1985). Effects of the cooperative group decision-making context on the test-retest reliability of preference ratings. In R.J. Lutz (Ed.), *Advances in consumer research* (Vol. 13). Provo, UT: Association for Consumer Research.

Corfman, K.P. (1987). Group decision-making and relative influence when preferences differ: A conceptual framework. In J.N. Sheth & E.C. Hirshman (Eds.), *Research in consumer behavior* (Vol. 2, pp. 223–257). Greenwich, CT: JAI.

Corfman, K.P. (1990). Methodological problems in survey and experimental research on family choice processes. *Advances in Consumer Research*, *17*, 520–523.

Corfman, K.P., & Lehmann, D.R. (1987). Models of cooperative group decision-making and relative influence: An experimental investigation of family purchase decisions. *Journal of Consumer Research*, *14*, 1–13.

Coria, C. (1994). *Il denaro nella coppia*. Rome: Editori Riuniti.

Cox, M.J., & Paley, B. (1997). Families as systems. *Annual Review of Psychology*, *48*, 243–267.

Cromwell, R.E., & Olson, D.H. (1975). *Power in families*. New York: Wiley.

Crott, H., Kutschker, M., & Lamm, H. (1977). *Verhandlungen 1 und 2*. Stuttgart: Kohlhammer.

Dahlhoff, H.D. (1980). *Kaufentscheidungsprozesse von Familien*. Frankfurt am Main: Lang.

Davis, H.L. (1970). Dimensions of marital roles in consumer decision-making. *Journal of Marketing Research*, *7*, 168–177.

Davis, H.L. (1972). *Determinants of marital roles in a consumer purchase decision*. Brussels: European Institute for Advanced Studies in Management. Working paper, 72-14.

Davis, H.L. (1976). Decision making within the household. *Journal of Consumer Research*, *2*, 241–260.

Davis, H.L., & Rigaux, B.P. (1974). Perception of marital roles in decision processes. *Journal of Consumer Research*, *1*, 51–62.

De Dreu, C.K.W., Nauta, A., & Van de Vliert, E. (1995). Self-serving evaluations of conflict behavior and escalation of the dispute. *Journal of Applied Social Psychology*, *25*, 2049–2066.

Deutsch, M. (1973). *The resolution of conflict*. New Haven, CT: Yale University Press.

Diener, E., & Larson, R.J. (1984). Temporal stability and cross-situational consistency of affective, behavioral, and cognitive responses. *Journal of Personality and Social Psychology*, *47*, 871–883.

Dijker, A.J., & Koomen, W. (1996). Stereotyping and attitudinal effects under time pressure. *European Journal of Social Psychology*, *26*, 61–74.

Dittmar, H. (1992). *The social psychology of material possessions. To have is to be*. Hemel Hempstead, UK: Harvester Wheatsheaf.

Dörfler-Schweighofer, C. (1996). *Kaufentscheidungen im privaten Haushalt. Analyse von*

Beeinflussungstaktiken der Partner. Unpublished masters thesis, University of Vienna, Austria.

Dörner, D. (1983). Empirische Psychologie und Alltagsrelevanz. In G. Jüttemann (Ed.), *Psychologie in der Veränderung. Perspektiven für eine gegenstandsangemessene Forschungspraxis* (pp. 37–48). Weinheim: Beltz.

Dörner, D. (1989). *Die Logik des Mißlingens. Strategisches Denken in komplexen Situationen.* Reinbeck bei Hamburg: Rowohlt.

Downey, G., Freitas, A., Michaelis, B., & Khouri, H. (1998). The self-fulfilling prophecy in close relationships: Rejection sensitivity and rejection by romantic partners. *Journal of Personality and Social Psychology, 75,* 545–560.

Duck, S.W. (1986). *Human relationships.* London: Sage.

Duck, S.W. (1991). Diaries and logs. In B.M. Montgomery & S.W. Duck (Eds.), *Studying interpersonal interaction.* New York: Guilford.

Duck, S.W. (1994). *Meaningful relationships. Talking, sense, and relating.* Thousand Oaks, CA: Sage.

Duck, S.W., West, L., & Acitelli, L.K. (1996). Sewing the field: The tapestry of relationships in life and research. In S.W. Duck, K. Dindia, B. Ickes, R. Milardo, R. Mills, & B. Sarason (Eds.), *Handbook of personal relationships* (2nd ed., pp. 1–23). Chichester, UK: Wiley.

Duda, A.W. (1994). *Kaufentscheidungen in Familien.* Unpublished masters thesis, Wirtschaftsuniversität Wien. Institut für Werbung & Marktforschung, Vienna.

Dutton, D.G., & Aron, A.P. (1974). Some evidence for heightened sexual attraction under conditions of high anxiety. *Journal of Personality and Social Psychology, 30,* 510–517.

Duval, S., & Wicklund, R.A. (1972). *A theory of objective self-awareness.* New York: Academic Press.

Elias, N. (1978). Zum Begriff des Alltags. In K. Hammerich & M. Klein (Eds.), *Materialien zur Soziologie des Alltags.* Opladen: Westdeutscher Verlag.

Engel, J.F., Blackwell, R.D., & Miniard, P.W. (1993). *Consumer behavior.* Fort Worth, TX: Dryden Press.

Epstein, S. (1986). Does aggregation produce spuriously high estimates of behavior stability? *Journal of Personality and Social Psychology, 50,* 1199–1210.

Falbo, T., & Peplau, L.A. (1980). Power strategies in intimate relationships. *Journal of Personality and Social Psychology, 38,* 618–628.

Faßnacht, G. (1995). *Systematische Verhaltensbeobachtung: Eine Einführung in die Methodologie und Praxis.* Munich: Reinhardt.

Feeney, J.A., Noller, P., & Ward, C. (1997). Marital satisfaction and spousal interaction. In R.J. Sternberg & M. Hojjat (Eds.), *Satisfaction in close relationships* (pp. 160–189). New York: Guilford.

Feger, H., & Auhagen, A.E. (1987). Unterstützende soziale Netzwerke: Sozialpsychologische Perspektiven. *Zeitschrift für Klinische Psychologie, 86,* 353–367.

Fehr, B. (1996). *Friendship processes.* Thousand Oaks, CA: Sage.

Fehr, B., & Russel, J.A. (1991). The concept of love viewed from a prototype perspective. *Journal of Personality and Social Psychology, 60,* 425–438.

Ferber, R. (1973). Family decision making and economic behavior. In E. Sheldon (Ed.), *Family economic behavior* (pp. 29–61). Philadelphia: Lippincott.

Ferber, R., & Lee, L.C. (1974). Husband–wife influence in family purchasing behavior. *Journal of Consumer Research, 1,* 43–50.

Ferreiri, G. (1991). Ma il cuore conta piú della chimica. *Europeo,* 1.11.1991, No. 44, 98–101.

Festinger, L. (1957). *A theory of cognitive dissonance.* Stanford, CA: Stanford University Press.

Fiedler, K. (1991). On the task, the measures and the mood in research on affect and social cognition. In J.P. Forgas (Ed.), *Emotion and social judgments* (pp. 83–104). Oxford: Pergamon Press.

Filiatrault, P., & Ritchie, J.R.B. (1980). Joint purchasing decisions: A comparison of influence structure in family and couple decision-making units. *Journal of Consumer Research*, 7, 131–140.

Fincham, F.D., & Beach, S.R.H. (1999). Conflict in marriage: Implications for working with couples. *Annual Review of Psychology*, 50, 47–77.

Fletcher, G.J.O., Simpson, J.A., & Thomas, G. (2000). The measurement of perceived relationship quality components: A confirmatory factor analytic approach. *Personality and Social Psychology Bulletin*, 26, 340–354.

Fletcher, G.J.O., Simpson, J.A., Thomas, G., & Giles, L. (1999). Ideals in intimate relationships. *Journal of Personality and Social Psychology*, 76, 72–89.

Foa, E.B., & Foa, U.G. (1980). Resource theory: Interpersonal behavior as exchange. In K.J. Gergen, M.S. Greenberg, & R.H. Willis (Eds.), *Social exchange. Advances in theory and research* (pp. 138–147). New York: Plenum.

Foa, U.G., & Foa, E.B. (1974). *Societal structures of the mind*. Springfield, IL: Thomas.

Forgas, J.P. (Ed.) (1991). *Emotion and social judgments*. Oxford: Pergamon Press.

Forman, N. (1987). *Mind over money*. Toronto: Doubleday.

Fraser, C. (1978). Small groups I.: Structure and leadership. In H. Tajfel & C. Fraser (Eds.), *Introducing social psychology*. Harmondsworth, UK: Penguin.

French, J.R.P., & Raven, B.H. (1959). The basis of social power. In D. Cartwright (Ed.), *Studies in social power* (pp. 150–167). Ann Arbor, MI: University of Michigan Press.

Freud, S. (1908). Charakter und Analerotik. In A. Mitscherlich, A. Richards, & J. Strachey, (Eds.), *Sigmund Freud Studienausgabe* (Vol. 7). Stuttgart: Fischer (1969).

Freud, S. (1920). Jenseits des Lustprinzips. In A. Mitscherlich, A. Richards, & J. Strachey (Eds.), *Sigmund Freud Studienausgabe* (Vol. 7). Stuttgart: Fischer (1969).

Fromm, E. (1977). *Die Kunst des Liebens*. Frankfurt am Main: Ullstein.

Furnham, A. (1984). Many sides of the coin: The psychology of money usage. *Personality and Individual Differences*, 5, 95–103.

Furnham, A. (1994). Many sides of the coin: The psychology of money usage. *Journal of Personality and Individual Differences*, 5, 501–509.

Furnham, A. (1996). Attitudinal correlates and demographic predictors of monetary beliefs and behaviours. *Journal of Organizational Behavior*, 17, 375–388.

Gelles, R.J. (1995). *Contemporary families: A sociological view*. Thousand Oaks, CA: Sage.

Gentry, J.W., Stoltman, J.J., & Coulson, K. (1990). A simulation game as a family research paradigm. *Advances in Consumer Research*, 17, 525–528.

Gilly, M.C., & Enis, B.M. (1982). Recycling the family life cycle: A proposal for redefinition. In A. Mitchell (Ed.), *Advances in consumer research* (Vol. 9, pp. 271–276). Ann Arbor, MI: Association for Consumer Research.

Gilmour, R., & Duck, S. (Eds.) (1986). *The emerging field of personal relationships*. Hillsdale, NJ: Lawrence Erlbaum Associates Inc.

Glick, B.R., & Gross, S.J. (1975). Marital interaction and marital conflict: A critical evaluation of current research strategies. *Journal of Marriage and the Family*, 37, 505–512.

Gottman, J.M. (1979). *Marital interactions: Experimental investigations*. New York: Academic Press.

Gottman, J.M. (1994). *What predicts divorce? The relationship between marital processess and marital outcomes*. Hillsdale, NJ: Lawrence Erlbaum Associates Inc.

Gouldner, A.W. (1960). The norm of reciprocity: A preliminary statement. *American Sociological Review*, 25, 161–178.

Granbois, D.H., & Summers, J.O. (1975). Primary and secondary validity of consumer purchase probabilities. *Journal of Consumer Research*, 1, 31–38.

Grau, I., & Bierhoff, H.-W. (1998). Tatsächliche und wahrgenommene Einstellungsähnlichkeit als Prädiktoren für die Beziehungsqualität. *Zeitschrift für Sozialpsychologie*, 29, 38–50.

Greenberg, J. (1988). Equity and workplace status: A field experiment. *Journal of Applied Psychology*, 73, 606–613.

Harvey, J.H., & Omarzu, J. (1997). Minding the close relationship. *Personality and Social Psychology Review, 1*, 224–240.

Harvey, J.H., Wells, G.L., & Alvarez, M.D. (1978). Attribution in the context of conflict and separation in close relationships. In J.H. Harvey, W. Ickes, & R.F. Kidd (Eds.), *New directions in attribution research* (Vol. 2, pp. 235–259). Hillsdale, NJ: Lawrence Erlbaum Associates Inc.

Hassebrauck, M. (1991). ZIP—Ein Instrument zur Erfassung der Zufriedenheit in Paarbeziehungen. *Zeitschrift für Sozialpsychologie, 22*, 256–259.

Hastie, R. (1982). Comment: Consumers' memory for product knowledge. In A. Mitchell (Ed.), *Advances in consumer research* (Vol. 9, pp. 72–73). Ann Arbor, MI: Association for Consumer Research.

Hatfield, E., Utne, M.K., & Traupman, J. (1979). Equity theory and intimate relationships. In R.L. Burgess & T.L. Huston (Eds.), *Social exchange in developing relationships* (pp. 99–133). New York: Academic Press.

Hatfield, E., & Walster, G.W. (1978). *A new look at love.* Lantham, MA: University Press of America.

Hays, R.B. (1985). A longitudinal study of friendship development. *Journal of Personality and Social Psychology, 48*, 909–924.

Heath, C., & Soll, J.B. (1996). Mental budgeting and consumer decisions. *Journal of Consumer Research, 23*, 40–52.

Heider, F. (1958). *The psychology of interpersonal relations.* New York: Wiley.

Heinemann, K. (1987). Innerfamiliäre Folgeerscheinungen der Arbeitslosigkeit von Frauen. In H. Todt (Ed.), *Die Familie als Gegenstand sozialwissenschaftlicher Forschung* (pp. 129–144). Berlin: Duncker & Humblot.

Hempel, D., & Tucker, L. (1980). Issues concerning family decision making and financial services. In J. Olson (Ed.), *Advances in consumer research* (Vol. 7, pp. 216–220). Ann Arbor, MI: Association for Consumer Research.

Hendrick, C., & Hendrick, S.S. (1986). A theory and method of love. *Journal of Personality and Social Psychology, 50*, 392–402.

Hendrick, C., & Hendrick, S.S. (1988). Lovers wear rose colored glasses. *Journal of Social and Personal Relationships, 5*, 161–183.

Hendrick, C., & Hendrick, S.S. (1989). Research on love: Does it measure up? *Journal of Personality and Social Psychology, 56*, 784–794.

Hendrick, C., & Hendrick, S.S. (1990). A relationship-specific version of the Love Attitudes Scale. *Journal of Social Behaviour and Personality, 5*, 239–254.

Hendrick, S.S., & Hendrick, C. (1997). Love and satisfaction. In R.J. Sternberg & M. Hojjat (Eds.), *Satisfaction in close relationships* (pp. 56–78). New York: Guilford.

Henrichsmeyer, W., Gans, O., & Evers, I. (1982). *Einführung in die Volkswirtschaftslehre.* Stuttgart: UTB-Ulmer.

Herkner, W. (1993). *Lehrbuch Sozialpsychologie* (3rd ed.). Bern: Huber.

Hill, R. (1972). Modern systems theory and the family: A confrontation. *Social Science Information, 10*, 7–26.

Hill, W., & Scanzoni, J. (1982). An approach for assessing marital decision-making processes. *Journal of Marriage and the Family, 44*, 927–941.

Hinde, R.A. (1979). *Towards understanding relationships.* New York: Academic Press.

Hinde, R.A. (1997). *Relationships. A dialectial perspective.* Hove, UK: Psychology Press.

Holmberg, D., & Veroff, J. (1996). Rewriting relationship memories: The effect of courtship and wedding scripts. In G.J.O. Fletcher & J. Fitness (Eds.), *Knowledge structures and interaction in close relationships* (pp. 345–368). Hillsdale, NJ: Lawrence Erlbaum Associates Inc.

Holmes, J.G. (1981). The exchange process in close relationships. In M.D. Lerner & S.G. Lerner (Eds.), *The justice motive in social behavior* (pp. 261–284). New York: Plenum.

Holmes, J.G. (1989). Trust and the appraisal process in close relationships. In W.H. Jones & D.

Perlman (Eds.), *Advances in personal relationships* (Vol. 2, pp. 57–104). London: Jessica Kingsley.

Holmes, J.G. (2000). Social relationships: The nature and function of relational schemas. *European Journal of Social Psychology*, *30*, 447–495.

Hölzl, E., & Kirchler, E. (1998). Einflußtaktiken in partnerschaftlichen Kaufentscheidungen. Ein Beitrag zur Analyse von Aktions-Reaktions-Mustern. *Zeitschrift für Sozialpsychologie*, *29*, 105–116.

Homans, G.C. (1961/1974). *Social behavior—its elementary forms.* New York: Harcourt, Brace Jovanovich.

Hormuth, S.E. (1986). The sampling of experiences in situ. *Journal of Personality*, *54*, 262–293.

Hornik, J. (1982). Situational effects on the consumption of time. *Journal of Marketing*, *46*, 44–55.

Howard, J.A., Blumstein, P., & Schwartz, P. (1986). Sex, power and influence tactics in intimate relationships. *Journal of Personality and Social Psychology*, *51*, 102–109.

Hu, M.Y., & Bruning, E.R. (1988). Using prior experience to explain survey versus diary recorded usage data. *Journal of the Market Research Society*, *30*, 59–72.

Huston, T.L., & Burgess, R.L. (1979). Social exchange in developing relationships: An overview. In R.L. Burgess & T.L. Huston (Eds.), *Social exchange in developing relationships.* New York: Academic Press.

Huston, T.L., McHale, S.M., & Crouter, A.C. (1986). When the honeymoon's over: Changes in the marriage relationship over the first year. In R. Gilmour & S. Duck (Eds.), *The emerging field of personal relationships* (pp. 109–132). Hillsdale, NJ: Lawrence Erlbaum Associates Inc.

Hyde, J.S. (1993). *Understanding human sexuality.* New York: McGraw-Hill.

Istvan, J., Griffitt, W., & Weidner, G. (1983). Sexual arousal and the polarization of perceived sexual attractiveness. *Basic and Applied Social Psychology*, *4*, 307–318.

Jasso, G. (1988). Employment, earnings, and martial cohesiveness: An empirical test of theoretical predictions. In M. Webster & M. Foschi (Eds.), *Status generalization. New theory and research* (pp. 123–161). Stanford, CA: Stanford University Press.

Jehn, K.A., & Shah, P.P. (1997). Interpersonal relationships and task performance: An examination of mediating processes in friendship and acquaintance groups. *Journal of Personality and Social Psychology*, *72*, 775–790.

Jenkins, R.L. (1979). The influence of children in family decision-making: Parents' perception. *Advances in Consumer Research*, *6*, 413–418.

Jungermann, H., Pfister, H.-R., & Fischer, K. (1998). *Die Psychologie der Entscheidung.* Heidelberg: Spektrum.

Kahneman, D. (1994). New challenges to the rationality assumption. *Journal of Institutional and Theoretical Economics. Zeitschrift für die gesamte Staatswissenschaft*, *150*, 18–36.

Kahneman, D., & Tversky, A. (1984). Choices, values, and frames. *American Psychologist*, *39*, 341–350.

Karney, B.R., & Bradbury, T.N. (1997). Neuroticism, marital interaction, and the trajectories of marital satisfaction. *Journal of Personality and Social Psychology*, *72*, 1075–1092.

Katona, G. (1951). *Psychological analysis of economic behavior.* New York: Elsevier.

Kellermann, K., & Cole, T. (1994). Classifying compliance gaining messages: Taxonomic disorder and strategic confusion. *Communication Theory*, *4*, 3–60.

Kelley, H.H. (1979). *Personal relationships: Their structures and processes.* Hillsdale, NJ: Lawrence Erlbaum Associates Inc.

Kelley, H.H. (1983). Love and commitment. In H.H. Kelley, E. Berscheid, A. Christensen, J.H. Harvey, T.L. Huston, G. Levinger, E. McClintock, L.A. Peplau, & D.R. Peterson (Eds.), *Close relationships* (pp. 265–314). New York: Freeman.

Kelley, H.H., Berscheid, E., Christensen, A., Harvey, J.H., Huston, T.L., Levinger, G., McClintock, E., Peplau, L.A., & Peterson, D.R. (1983a). *Close relationships.* New York: Freeman.

Kelley, H.H., Berscheid, E., Christensen, A., Harvey, J.H., Huston, T.L., Levinger, G., McClintock, E., Peplau, L.A., & Peterson, D.R. (1983b). Analyzing close relationships. In H.H. Kelley, E. Berscheid, A. Christensen, J.H. Harvey, T.L. Huston, G. Levinger, E. McClintock, L.A. Peplau, & D.R. Peterson (Eds.), *Close relationships* (pp. 20–67). New York: Freeman.

Kelley, H.H., & Schenitzki, D.P. (1972). Bargaining. In C.G. McClintock (Ed.), *Experimental social psychology*. New York: Holt, Rinehart & Winston.

Kelley, H.H., & Thibaut, J.W. (1978). *Interpersonal relations*. New York: Wiley.

Kemp, C.G. (1970). When is a group a group? In C.G. Kemp (Ed.), *Perspectives on the group process. A foundation for counseling with groups* (pp. 29–30). Boston: Houghton Mifflin & Co.

Kenkel, W.F. (1957). Influence differentiation in family decision making. *Sociology and Social Research, 42*, 18–27.

Kim, C., & Lee, H. (1997). Development of family triadic measures for children's purchase influence. *Journal of Marketing Research, 34*, 307–321.

Kipnis, D. (1976). *The powerholders*. Chicago: University of Chicago Press.

Kirchler, E. (1984). Befinden von Wehrpflichtigen in Abhängigkeit von personellen und situativen Gegebenheiten. Psychologie und Praxis. *Zeitschrift für Arbeits- und Organisationspsychologie, 28*, 16–25.

Kirchler, E. (1985). Job loss and mood. *Journal of Economic Psychology, 6*, 9–25.

Kirchler, E. (1988a). Marital happiness and interaction in everyday surroundings. A time-sample diary approach for couples. *Journal of Social and Personal Relationships, 5*, 375–382.

Kirchler, E. (1988b). Household economic decision-making. In F.W. van Raaij, G.M. van Veldhoven, T.M.M. Verhallen & K.-E. Wärneryd (Eds.), *Handbook of economic psychology* (pp. 258–293). Amsterdam: North Holland.

Kirchler, E. (1988c). Diary reports on daily economic decisions of happy versus unhappy couples. *Journal of Economic Psychology, 9*, 327–357.

Kirchler, E. (1988d). *Kaufentscheidungen in der Familie. Eine Replikation der Studie von Davis and Rigaux (1974) unter Berücksichtigung der Kinder*. Unpublished manuscript, University of Linz, Austria.

Kirchler, E. (1989). *Kaufentscheidungen im privaten Haushalt. Eine sozialpsychologische Analyse des Familienalltages*. Göttingen: Hogrefe.

Kirchler, E. (1990). Spouses' influence strategies in purchase decisions as dependent on conflict type and relationship characteristics. *Journal of Economic Psychology, 11*, 101–118.

Kirchler, E. (1993a). Beeinflussungstaktiken von Eheleuten: Entwicklung und Erprobung eines Instrumentes zur Erfassung der Anwendungshäufigkeit verschiedener Beeinflussungstaktiken in familiären Kaufentscheidungen. *Zeitschrift für experimentelle und angewandte Psychologie, 40*, 102–131.

Kirchler, E. (1993b). Spouses' joint purchase decisions: Determinants of influence strategies to muddle through the process. *Journal of Economic Psychology, 14*, 405–438.

Kirchler, E. (1995). Studying economic decisions within private households: A critical review and design for a "couple experiences diary". *Journal of Economic Psychology, 16*, 393–419.

Kirchler, E. (1999). Unbelievable similarity: Accuracy in spouses' reports on their partners' tactics to influence joint economic decisions. *Applied Psychology: An International Review, 48*, 329–348.

Kirchler, E., & Berti, C. (1990). Immagini del dare e ricevere in alcune relazioni sociali. *Giornale Italiano di Psicologia, 17*, 145–157.

Kirchler, E., & Berti, C. (1996). Convincersi a vicenda nelle decisioni di coppia. *Giornale Italiano di Psicologia, 23*, 675–698.

Kirchler, E., Buchleitner, S., & Wagner, J. (1996). Der langsame Wechsel in Führungsetagen. Meinungen über Frauen und Männer als Führungspersonen. *Zeitschrift für Sozialpsychologie, 27*, 148–166.

Kirchler, E., & Hölzl, E. (1996). Vom Austausch zum Altruismus: Profitorientierung versus spontane Angebote in interpersonellen Beziehungen. *Gruppendynamik, 26*, 457–465.

Kirchler, E., & Kirchler, E. (1990). Einflußmuster in familiären Kaufentscheidungen. *Planung und Analyse, 2*, 49–54.

Kirchler, E., & Nowy, C. (1988). Wo bleibt das Glück am Herd? Geschlechtsspezifische Reaktionen auf Arbeitslosigkeit. *Wirtschafts- und sozialpolitische Zeitschrift des ISW, 11*, 69–87.

Kirchler, E., Rodler, C., Hölzl, E., & Meier, K. (1999). *Entscheidungen von 40 Paaren während eines Jahres. Die Wiener-Tagebuchstudie.* Unpublished manuscript, University of Vienna.

Kirchler, E., & Schmidl, D. (2000). Schichtarbeit im Vergleich: Befindensunterschiede und Aufmerksamkeitsvariation während der 8-Stunden- versus 12-Stunden-Schichtarbeit. *Zeitschrift für Arbeits- und Organisationspsychologie, 44*, 2–18.

Kirchler, E., Skilitsi, J., & Radel, S. (1995). *Dynamics of economic decisions within the private household. The couple experiences diary.* IV European Congress of Psychology. Athens, Greece, July 2–7.

Klein, D.M., & Hill, R. (1979). Determinants of family problem-solving effectiveness. In W.R. Burr, R. Hill, F.I. Nye, & I.L. Reiss (Eds.), *Contemporary theories about the family. Research bases theories* (Vol. 1, pp. 493–548). New York: Free Press.

Klein, R., & Milardo, R.M. (1993). Third party influence on the management of personal relationships. In S. Duck (Ed.), *Social context and relationships* (pp. 55–77). Newbury Park, CA: Sage.

König, R. (1974). *Materialien zur Soziologie der Familie.* Cologne: Kiepenheuer & Witsch.

Koski, L.R., & Shaver, P.R. (1997). Attachment and relationship satisfaction across the lifespan. In R.J. Sternberg & M. Hojjat (Eds.), *Satisfaction in close relationships* (pp. 26–55). New York: Guilford.

Kotler, P. (1982). *Marketing-Management. Analyse, Planung und Kontrolle.* Stuttgart: Poeschel.

Kourilsky, M., & Murray, T. (1981). The use of economic reasoning to increase satisfaction with family decision making. *Journal of Consumer Research, 8*, 183–188.

Kövecses, Z. (1991). A linguist's quest for love. *Journal of Social and Personal Relationships, 8*, 77–97.

Krampf, R.F., Burns, D.J., & Rayman, D.M. (1993). Consumer decision making and the nature of the product: A comparison of husband and wife adoption process location. *Psychology & Marketing, 10*, 95–109.

Kurdek, L.A., & Schmitt, S.P. (1986). Relationships quality of partners in heterosexual married, heterosexual cohabiting, and gay and lesbian relationships. *Journal of Personality and Social Psychology, 51*, 711–720.

Lackman, C., & Lanasa, J.M. (1993). Family decision-making theory: An overview and assessment. *Psychology & Marketing, 10*, 81–93.

Laermann, K. (1975). Alltags-Zeit. Bemerkungen über die unauffölligste Form sozialen Zwangs. *Kursbuch, 41*, 87–105.

Laireiter, A.-R., Baumann, U., Reisenzein, E., & Untner, A. (1997). A diary method for the assessment of interactive social networks: The interval-contingent diary SONET-T. *Swiss Journal of Psychology, 56*, 217–238.

Larson, R.W., & Csikszentmihalyi, M. (1983). The experience sampling method. In H. Reis (Ed.), *New directions for naturalistic methods in the behavioral sciences* (pp. 41–56). San Francisco: Jossey-Bass.

Larson, R.W., & Almeida, D.M. (1999). Emotional transmission in the daily lives of families: A new paradigm for studying family process. *Journal of Marriage and the Family, 61*, 5–20.

Larson, R.W., & Bradney, N. (1988). Precious moments with family members and friends. In R.M. Milardo (Ed.), *Families and social networks* (pp. 106–126). Beverly Hills, CA: Sage.

Lea, S.E.G., Webley, P., & Levine, R.M. (1993). The economic psychology of consumer debt. *Journal of Economic Psychology, 14*, 85–119.

Lederer, W.J., & Jackson, D.D. (1972). *Ehe als Lernprozeß*. Munich: Pfeiffer.

Lee, J.A. (1973). *The colors of love*. Englewood Cliffs, NJ: Prentice Hall.

Lersch, P. (1970). *Aufbau der Person*. Munich: Barth.

Levinger, G. (1979). A social exchange view on the dissolution of pair relationships. In R.L. Burgess & T.L. Huston (Eds.), *Social exchange in developing relationships*. New York: Academic Press.

Levy, M.B., & Davis, K.E. (1988). Lovestyles and attachment styles compared: Their relations to each other and to various relationship characteristics. *Journal of Social and Personal Relationships, 5*, 439–471.

Lewin, K. (1953). Der Hintergrund von Ehekonflikten. In G.W. Lewin (Ed.), *Die Lösung sozialer Konflikte*. Bad Nauheim, Germany: Christian.

Lewis, R.A., & Spanier, G.B. (1979). Theorizing about the quality and stability of marriage. In W.R. Burr, R. Hill, F.I. Nye, & I.C. Reiss (Eds.), *Contemporary theories about the family* (Vol. 1, pp. 268–294). London: Free Press.

Liebowitz, M.R. (1983). *The chemistry of love*. Boston: Little, Brown.

Lindblom, C.E. (1959). The science of "muddling through". *Public Administration Review, 19*, 79–88.

Lindblom, C.E. (1979). Still muddling, not yet through. *Public Administration Review, 39*, 517–526.

Livingstone, S.M., & Lunt, P.K. (1992). Predicting personal debt and debt repayment: psychological, social and economic determinants. *Journal of Economic Psychology, 13*, 111–134.

Losh-Hesselbart, S. (1987). Development of gender roles. In M.B. Sussman & S.K. Steinmetz (Eds.), *Handbook of marriage and the family* (pp. 535–563). New York: Plenum.

Lott, B.E., & Lott, A.J. (1960). The formation of positive attitudes toward group members. *Journal of Abnormal and Social Psychology, 44*, 964–976.

Luhmann, N. (1984). *Soziale Systeme. Grundriß einer allgemeinen Theorie*. Frankfurt: Suhrkamp.

Lujansky, H., & Mikula, G. (1983). Can equity theory explain the quality and the stability of romantic relationships. *British Journal of Social Psychology, 22*, 101–112.

Lydon, J., Pierce, T., & O'Regan, S. (1997). Coping with moral commitment to long-distance dating relationships. *Journal of Personal and Social Relationships, 73*, 104–113.

Lynch, J. (1977). *The broken heart: The medical consequences of loneliness*. New York: Basic Books.

Maccoby, E.E. (1986). *The parent child relationship: An analysis of influence process*. Paper presented at the 3rd International Conference on Personal Relationships, Herzlia, Israel.

Madden, C.S. (1982). *The effect of conflict awareness on interspousal decision making in highly involving purchases*. Unpublished philosophical dissertation, University of Nebraska (Lincoln), Nebraska.

March, J.D., & Shapira, Z. (1992). Behavioral decision theory and organizational decision theory. In M. Zey (Ed.), *Decision making. Alternatives to rational choice models*. Newbury Park, CA: Sage.

March, J.G., & Simon, H.A. (1958). *Organizations*. New York: Wiley.

Maslow, A.H. (1954). *Motivation and personality*. New York: Harper & Row.

Mauri, C. (1996). L'influenza dei bambini sugli acquisti della famiglia. *Micro & Macro Marketing, 1*, 39–57.

Mayer, H., & Boor, W. (1988). Familie und Konsumverhalten. *Jahrbuch der Absatz- und Verbrauchsforschung, 34*, 120–153.

Mayerhofer, W. (1994). Kaufentscheidungsprozeß in Familien. *Werbeforschung & Praxis, 19*, 126–127.

Mayers, S.A., & Berscheid, A. (1997). The language of love: The difference a preposition makes. *Personality and Social Psychology Bulletin, 23*, 347–362.

McClelland, D.C. (1986). Some reflections on the two psychologies of love. *Journal of Personality, 54*, 334–353.

McDonald, G.W. (1980). Family power: The assessment of a decade of theory and research, 1970–1979. *Journal of Marriage and the Family, 42*, 841–854.

McGonagle, K.A., Kessler, R.C., & Schilling, E.A. (1992). The frequency and determinants of marital disagreements in a community sample. *Journal of Social and Personal Relationships, 9*, 507–524.

McGrath, J.E. (1984). *Groups: Interaction and performance.* Englewood Cliffs, NJ: Prentice Hall.

Meeks, B.S., Hendrick, S.S., & Hendrick, C. (1998). Communication, love and relationship satisfaction. *Journal of Social and Personal Relationships, 15*, 755–773.

Meffert, H., & Dahlhoff, H.-D. (1980). *Kollektive Kaufentscheidungen und Kaufwahrscheinlich-keiten.* Hamburg: Gruner & Jahr AG & Co.

Mehrotra, S., & Torges, S. (1977). Determinants of children's influence on mother's buying behavior. *Advances in Consumer Research, 4*, 56–60.

Meier, K., Kirchler, E., & Hubert, A.-C. (1999). Savings and investment decisions within private households: Spouses' dominance on various forms of investment. *Journal of Economic Psychology, 20*, 499–519.

Meyers Großes Taschenlexikon (1987). Mannheim, Germany: B.I. Taschenbuchverlag.

Michaels, J.W., Acock, A.C., & Edwards, J.N. (1986). Social exchange and equity determinants of relationship commitment. *Journal of Social and Personal Relationships, 3*, 161–175.

Michaels, J.W., Edwards, J.N., & Acock, A.C. (1984). Satisfaction in intimate relationships as a function of inequality, inequity, and outcomes. *Social Psychology Quarterly, 47*, 347–357.

Mikulincer, M. (1998). Attachment working models and the sense of trust: An exploration of interaction goals and affect regulation. *Journal of Personality and Social Psychology, 74*, 1209–1224.

Mikula, G., & Leitner, A. (1998). Partnerschaftsbezogene Bindungsstile und Verhaltenserwar-tungen an Liebespartner, Freunde und Kollegen. *Zeitschrift für Sozialpsychologie, 29*, 213–223.

Miller, G.R., & Boster, F. (1988). Persuasion in personal relationships. In S.W. Duck (Ed.), *Handbook of personal relationships* (pp. 275–288). New York: Wiley.

Mills, J., & Clark, M.S. (1986). Communications that should lead to perceived exploitation in communal and exchange relationships. *Journal of Social and Clinical Psychology, 4*, 225–234.

Montada, L., Dabert, C., & Schmitt, M. (1988). Ist prosoziales Handeln im Kontext Familie abhängig von situativen, personalen oder systematsichen Faktoren? In: H.W. Bierhoff (Ed.), *Altruismus. Bedingungen der Hilfsbereitschaft.* Göttingen, Germany: Hogrefe.

Moschis, G.P. (1987). *Consumer socialization: A life-cycle prospective.* Lexington, MA: D.C. Heath.

Murphy, P., & Staples, W. (1979). A modernized family life cycle. *Journal of Consumer Research, 6*, 12–22.

Murray, S.L., & Holmes, J.G. (1997). A leap of faith? Positive illusions in romantic relationships. *Personality and Social Psychology Bulletin, 23*, 586–604.

Nedelmann, B. (1983). Georg Simmel—Emotion und Wechselwirkung in intimen Gruppen. In F. Neidhardt (Ed.), *Gruppensoziologie. Sonderheft Nr. 25 der Kölner Zeitschrift für Soziologie* (pp. 19–30). Opladen: Westdeutscher Verlag.

Nelson, M.C. (1988). The resolution of conflict in joint purchase decisions by husbands and wives: A review and empirical test. *Advances in Consumer Research, 15*, 436–441.

Newcomb, T.M. (1971). Dyadic balance as a source of clues about interpersonal attraction. In B.I. Murstein (Ed.), *Theories of attraction and love.* New York: Springer.

Nisbett, R., & Ross, L. (1980). *Human inference: Strategies and shortcomings of social judgment.* New York: Prentice Hall.

Nisbett, R., & Wilson, T.D. (1977). Telling more than we know: Verbal reports on mental processes. *Psychological Review, 84*, 231–259.

Noller, P. (1984). *Nonverbal communication and marital interaction*. New York: Pergamon.

Nye, F.I. (1979). Choice, exchange, and the family. In W.R. Burr, R. Hill, F.I. Nye, & I.L. Reiss (Eds.), *Contemporary theories about the family* (Vol. 2, pp. 1–43). New York: Free Press.

Olson, D.H., & Cromwell, R.E. (1975). Power in families. In R.E. Cromwell & D.H. Olson (Eds.), *Power in families* (pp. 3–14). New York: Sage.

Pahl, J. (1989). *Money and marriage*. London: Macmillan.

Pahl, J. (1995). His money, her money: Recent research on financial organisation in marriage. *Journal of Economic Psychology, 16*, 361–376.

Park, C.W. (1982). Joint decisions in home purchasing: A muddling-through process. *Journal of Consumer Research, 9*, 151–162.

Park, J.-H., Tansuhaj, P.S., & Kolbe, R.H. (1991). The role of love, affection, and intimacy in family decision research. *Advances in Consumer Research, 18*, 651–656.

Park, J.-H., Tansuhaj, P., Spangenberg, E.P., & McCullough, J. (1995). An emotion-based perspective of family purchase decisions. *Advances in Consumer Research, 22*, 723–728.

Parsons, T., & Bales, R.F. (1955). *Family, socialisation and interaction process*. New York: Free Press.

Pauleikhoff, B. (1965). Die Rolle des Tageslaufs in der Persönlichkeits- und Ganzheitspsychologie. *Archiv für die gesamte Psychologie, 117*, 67–77.

Pawlik, K., & Buse, L. (1982). Rechnergestützte Verhaltensregistrierung im Feld: Beschreibung und erste psychometrische Überprüfung einer neuen Erhebungsmethode. *Zeitschrift für Differentielle und Diagnostische Psychologie, 3*, 101–118.

Pennebaker, J.W., Dyer, M.A., Caulkins, R.S., Litowitz, D.L., Ackreman, P.L., Anderson, D.B., & McGraw, K.M. (1979). Don't the girls get prettier at closing time: A country and western application to psychology. *Personality and Social Psychology Bulletin, 5*, 122–125.

Perlman, D., & Duck, S. (1987). *Intimate relationships. Development, dynamics, and deterioration*. Beverly Hills, CA: Sage.

Pervin, L.A. (1976). A free-response description approach to the analysis of person-situation interaction. *Journal of Personality and Social Psychology, 34*, 465–474.

Piel, E. (1983). Die Flucht ins Private. In E. Noelle-Neumann & E. Piel (Eds.), *Allensbacher Jahrbuch der Demoskopie. 1978–1983* (pp. 19–30). Munich: Saur.

Pollay, R.W. (1968). A model of family decision making. *British Journal of Marketing, 2*, 206–216.

Prince, M. (1993). Women, men, and money styles. *Journal of Economic Psychology, 14*, 175–182.

Pross, H. (1979). *Die Wirklichkeit der Hausfrau*. Reinbeck bei Hamburg: Rowohlt.

Pruitt, D.G. (1986). Achieving integrative agreements in negotiation. In R.K. White (Ed.), *Psychology and the prevention of nuclear war* (pp. 463–478). New York: New York University Press.

Pruitt, D.G., & Lewis, S.A. (1977). The psychology of integrative bargaining. In D. Druckman (Ed.), *Negotiations: A social-psychological perspective* (pp. 161–192). London: Sage.

Pulver, U. (1991). *Die Bausteine des Alltags. Zur Psychologie des menschlichen Arbeitens und Handelns*. Heidelberg: Asanger.

Qualls, W.J. (1987). Household decision behavior: The impact of husbands' and wives' sex roles orientation. *Journal of Consumer Research, 14*, 264–279.

Qualls, W.J., & Jaffe, F. (1992). Measuring conflict in household decision behavior: Read my lips and read my mind. *Advances in Consumer Research, 19*, 522–531.

Raschke, H.J. (1987). Divorce. In M.B. Sussman & S.K. Steinmetz (Eds.), *Handbook of marriage and the family* (pp. 597–624). New York: Plenum Press.

Raven, B.H. (1999). Kurt Lewin Address: Influence, power, religion, and the mechanisms of social control. *Journal of Social Issues, 55*, 161–186.

Raven, B.H. (1993). The bases of power: Origins and recent developments. *Journal of Social Issues, 49*, 227–251.

Raven, B.H., & Kruglanski, A.W. (1970). Conflict and power. In P. Swingle (Ed.), *The structure of conflict*. New York: Academic Press.

Regan, P.C. (1998). What if you can't get what you want? Willingness to compromise ideal mate selection standards as a function of sex, mate value, and relationship context. *Personality and Social Psychology Bulletin, 24*, 1294–1303.

Regan, P.C., Kocan, E.R., & Whitlock, T. (1998). Ain't love grand! A prototype analysis of the concept of romantic love. *Journal of Social and Personal Relationships, 15*, 411–420.

Rehn, M.L. (1981). *Die Theorie der objektiven Selbstaufmerksamkeit und ihre Anwendung auf eine neue Methode der Befindensmessung: Das Tagebuch*. Unpublished masters thesis, University of Erlangen-Nürnberg.

Reis, H.T., & Patrick, B.C. (1996). Attachment and intimacy: Component processes. In E.T. Higgings & A.W. Kruglanski (Eds.), *Social psychology. Handbook of basic principles* (pp. 523–563). New York: Guilford Press.

Robertson, A.M. (1990). Spousal decision processes for financial/professional services. *Journal of Professional Services Marketing, 6*, 119–135.

Robinson, J.P., Yerby, P., Fieweger, J., & Somerick, N. (1977). Sex-role differences in time use. *Sex Roles, 3*, 443–458.

Rodler, C., & Kirchler, E. (2000). Everyday life of commuters' wives. In H. Brandstätter & A. Eliasz (Eds), *Persons, situations and emotions: An ecological approach* (pp. 163–183). New York: Oxford University Press.

Rodman, H. (1967). Marital power in France, Greece, Yugoslavia, and the United States: A cross-national discussion. *Journal of Marriage and the Family, 29*, 320–324.

Rogen, S., & Amato, P.R. (1997). Is marital quality declining? The evidence from two generations, *Social Forces, 75*, 1089–1100.

Roland-Lévy, C., & Viaud, J. (1994). *Social representations of consumption: An understanding of people's behaviour concerning debts and credit*. Paper presented at the 6th SASE conference, Paris, France.

Rosen, D.L., & Granbois, D.H. (1983). Determinants of role structure in family financial management. *Journal of Consumer Research, 10*, 253–258.

Ross, L. (1977). The intuitive psychologist and his shortcomings: Distortion in the attribution process. In L. Berkowitz (Ed.), *Advances in experimental social psychology* (Vol. 10, pp. 174–221). New York: Academic Press.

Ross, L., & Nisbett, R. (1991). *The person and the situation*. New York: McGraw-Hill.

Ross, M.A. (1989). The relation of implicit theories in the construction of personal histories. *Psychological Review, 96*, 341–357.

Rosso, D. (1991). L'amore fa bene ma . . . *Europeo*, 1.11.1991, Nr. 44, 78–83.

Rubin, J.Z. (1983). Negotiation. An introduction to some issues and themes. *American Behavioral Scientist, 27*, 135–147.

Rubin, Z. (1970). Measurement of romantic love. *Journal of Personality and Social Psychology, 16*, 265–273.

Rubin, Z. (1973). *Liking and loving. An invitation to social psychology*. New York: Holt, Rinehart & Winston.

Rubin, J.Z., & Brown, B.R. (1975). *The social psychology of bargaining and negotiation*. New York: Academic Press.

Rudd, J., & Kohout, F.J. (1983). Individual and group consumer information requisition brand choice situations. *Journal of Consumer Research, 10*, 303–309.

Ruhfus, R. (1976). *Kaufentscheidungen von Familien*. Wiesbaden, Germany: Gabler.

Rumiati, R., & Lotto, L. (1996). Varieties of money. Experts' and non-experts' typicality judgments. *Journal of Economic Psychology, 17*, 403–413.

Rusbult, C.E. (1980). Commitment and satisfaction in romantic associations: A test of the investment model. *Journal of Experimental Social Psychology, 16*, 172–186.

Rusbult, C.E. (1991). Commentary on Johnson's commitment to personal relationships: What's interesting, and what's new? *Advances in Personal Relationships*, *3*, 151–169.

Rusbult, C.E., & Buunk, B.P. (1993). Commitment processes in close relationships: An interdependence analysis. *Journal of Social and Personal Relationships*, *10*, 175–204.

Safilios-Rothschild, C. (1970). The study of family power structure: A review 1960–1969. *Journal of Marriage and the Family*, *32*, 539–553.

Saltfort, N.C., & Roy, L.A. (1981). Family clothing consumption: Comparison of two methods for collecting data. *Home Economic Research Journal*, *2*, 203–211.

Scanzoni, J. (1979a). Social processes and power in families. In W.R. Burr, R. Hill, F.I. Nye, & I.L. Reiss (Eds.), *Contemporary theories about the family. Research based theories* (Vol. 1, pp. 295–316). New York: Free Press.

Scanzoni, J. (1979b). Social exchange and behavioral interdependence. In R.L. Burgess & T.L. Huston (Eds.), *Social exchange in developing relationships* (pp. 61–98). New York: Academic Press.

Scanzoni, J., & Polonko, K. (1980). A conceptual approach to explicit marital negotiation. *Journal of Marriage and the Family*, *42*, 31–44.

Scanzoni, J., & Szinovacz, M. (1980). *Family decision making.* Beverly Hills, CA: Sage.

Schachter, S., & Singer, J.E. (1962). Cognitive, social and physiological determinants of emotional state. *Psychological Review*, *69*, 379–399.

Schaninger, C.M., & Buss, W.C. (1986). A longitudinal comparison of consumption and finance handling between happily married and divorced couples. *Journal of Marriage and the Family*, *48*, 129–136.

Schneewind, K.A. (1993). Familienpsychologie. In A. Schorr (Ed.), *Handwörterbuch der Angewandten Psychologie* (pp. 222–226). Bonn: Deutscher Psychologen Verlag.

Schomaker, P.K., & Thorpe, A.C. (1963). Financial decision-making as reported by farm families in Michigan. *Michigan Quarterly Bulletin*, *46*, 334–353.

Schultz, A. (1973). *A theory of consciousness.* New York: Philosophical Library.

Schütz, A. (1999). It was your fault! Self-serving biases in autobiographical accounts of conflicts in married couples. *Journal of Social and Personal Relationships*, *16*, 193–208.

Schwarz, N. (1987). *Stimmung als Information. Untersuchungen zum Einfluß von Stimmungen auf die Bewertung des eigenen Lebens.* Heidelberg: Springer.

Schwarz, N. (1996). *Cognition & communication. Judgment biases, research methods, and the logic of conversation.* Mahwah, NJ: Lawrence Erlbaum Associates Inc.

Schwarz, N. (1998). Warmer and more social: Recent developments in cognitive social psychology. *Annual Review of Sociology*, *24*, 239–264.

Schwarz, N. (1999). Self-reports: How the questions shape the answers. *American Psychologist*, *54*, 93–105.

Schwarz, N., & Clore, G.L. (1983). Mood, misattribution, and judgments of well-being: Informative and directive functions of affective state. *Journal of Personality and Social Psychology*, *45*, 513–523.

Schwarz, N., & Hippler, H.J. (1987). What response scales may tell your respondents. In H.J. Hippler, N. Schwarz, & S. Sudman (Eds.), *Social information processing and survey methodology* (pp. 163–178). New York: Springer.

Schwarz, N., & Scheuring, B. (1988). Judgments of relationship satisfaction: Inter- and intraindividual comparisons as a function of questionnaire structure. *European Journal of Social Psychology*, *18*, 485–496.

Schwarz, N., Strack, F., Kommer, D., & Wagner, D. (1987). Soccer, rooms, and the quality of your life: Mood effects on judgments of satisfaction with life in general and with specific domains. *European Journal of Social Psychology*, *17*, 69–79.

Schwarzwald, J., & Koslowsky, M. (1999). Gender, self-esteem, and focus of interest in the use of power strategies by adolescents in conflict situations. *Journal of Social Issues*, *55*, 15–32.

Scott, F.G. (1962). Family group structure and patterns of social interaction. *American Journal of Sociology*, *68*, 214–228.

Seymour, D., & Lessne, G. (1984). Spousal conflict arousal: Scale development. *Journal of Consumer Research*, *11*, 810–821.

Shackelford, T.K., & Buss, D.M. (1997). Marital satisfaction in evolutionary psychological perspective. In R.J. Sternberg & M. Hojjat (Eds.), *Satisfaction in close relationships* (pp. 7–25). New York: Guilford.

Shanteau, J., & Troutman, C.M. (1990). Information integration theory approach to husband-wife decision making. *Advances in Consumer Research*, *17*, 528–529.

Shaver, P.R., & Hazan, C. (1988). A biased overview of the study of love. *Journal of Social and Personal Relationships*, *5*, 473–501.

Shaver, P.R., & Hazan, C. (1993). Adult romantic attachment: Theory and evidence. In D. Perlman & W. Jones (Eds.), *Advances in personal relationships* (Vol. 4, pp. 29–70). London: Jessica Kingsley.

Sheth, J.N. (1974). A theory of family buying decisions. In J.N. Sheth (Ed.), *Models of buyer behavior: Conceptual, quantitative, and empirical* (pp. 17–33). New York: Harper & Row.

Sheth, J.N., & Cosmas, S. (1975). *Tactics of conflict resolution in family buying behavior.* Paper presented at the American Psychological Association Meeting, Chicago, IL.

Shim, S., Snyder, L., & Gehrt, K.C. (1995). Parents' perception regarding children's use of clothing evaluative criteria: An exploratory study from the consumer socialization process perspective. *Advances in Consumer Research*, *22*, 628–632.

Siegel, B.S. (1986). *Love, medicine & miracles.* New York: Harper & Row.

Sillars, A.L., & Kalbflesch, P.J. (1989). Implicit and explicit decision-making styles in couples. In D. Brinberg & J. Jaccard (Eds.), *Dyadic decision making* (pp. 179–215). New York: Springer.

Sillars, A.L., & Wilmont, W.W. (1994). Communication strategies in conflict and mediation. In J.A. Daly & J.M. Wiemann (Eds.), *Strategic interpersonal communication* (pp. 163–190). Hillsdale, NJ: Lawrence Erlbaum Associates Inc.

Simmel, G. (1921). Fragmente über die Liebe. *Logos*, *10*, 1–54.

Sixtl, F. (1967). *Meßmethoden der Psychologie.* Weinheim: Beltz.

Smith, R.E., Leffingwell, T.R., & Ptacek, J.T. (1999). Can people remember how they coped? Factors associated with discordance between same-day and retrospective reports. *Journal of Personality and Social Psychology*, *76*, 1050–1061.

Smith, W.P. (1987). Conflict and negotiation: Trends and emerging issues. *Journal of Applied Social Psychology*, *17*, 641–677.

Snelders, H.M.J., Hussein, G., Lea, S.E.G., & Webley, P. (1992). The polymorphous concept of money. *Journal of Economic Psychology*, *13*, 71–92.

Snyder, J., & Serafin, R. (1985). Auto makers set new ad strategy to reach women. *Advertising Age*, *56*, 3.

Sorensen, A. (1998). Life course and family dynamics under social science perspecives. In L.A. Vaskovics & H.A. Schattovits (Eds.), *Living arrangements and family structures—facts and norms* (pp. 23–30). Vienna: Austrian Institute for Family Studies.

Sorrels, J.P., & Myers, B. (1983). Comparison of group and family dynamics. *Human Relations*, *36*, 477–492.

Spiro, R.L. (1983). Persuasion in family decision-making. *Journal of Consumer Research*, *9*, 393–402.

Sprecher, S. (1986). The relations between inequity and emotions in close relationships. *Social Psychology Quarterly*, *49*, 309–321.

Sprey, J. (1972). Family power structure: A critical comment. *Journal of Marriage and the Family*, *34*, 235–238.

Sternberg, R.J. (1987). Liking versus loving: A comparative evaluation of theories. *Psychological Bulletin*, *102*, 331–345.

Sternberg, R.J. (1996). Construct validation of a triangular love scale. *European Journal of Social Psychology, 27*, 313–335.

Sternberg, R.J., & Barnes. M.L. (Eds.) (1988). *The psychology of love.* New Haven, CT: Yale University Press.

Sternberg, R.J., & Dobson, D.M. (1987). Resolving interpersonal conflicts: An analysis of stylistic consistency. *Journal of Personality and Social Psychology, 52*, 794–812.

Sternberg, R.J., & Grajek, S. (1984). The nature of love. *Journal of Personality and Social Psychology, 47*, 312–329.

Sternberg, R.J., & Hojjat, M. (Eds.) (1997). *Satisfaction in close relationships.* New York: Guilford.

Stinnett, N., & DeFrain, J. (1985). *Secrets of strong families.* Boston: Little, Brown & Co.

Stone, A.A., Kessler, R.C., & Haythornthwaite, J.A. (1991). Measuring daily events and experiences: Decisions for the researcher. *Journal of Personality, 59*, 575–607.

Strack, F., Martin, L.L., & Schwarz, N. (1988). Priming and communication: Social determinants of information use in judgments of life satisfaction. *European Journal of Social Psychology, 18*, 429–442.

Straus, M.A. (1979). Measuring intrafamily conflict and violence: The conflict tactics (CT) scales. *Journal of Marriage and the Family, 41*, 75–87.

Straus, M.A., & Sweet, S. (1992). Verbal/symbolic aggression in couples: Incidence rates and relationships to personal characteristics. *Journal of Marriage and the Family, 54*, 346–357.

Strauss, A. (1978). *Negotiations: Varieties, contexts, processes and social order.* San Francisco: Jossey Bass.

Stroebe, W., & Stroebe, M. (1983). Who suffers more? Sex differences in health risk of the widowed. *Psychological Bulletin, 93*, 279–301.

Stroebe, W., & Stroebe, M.S. (1987). *Bereavement and health. The psychological and physical consequences of partner loss.* New York: Cambridge University Press.

Surra, C.A., & Longstreth, M. (1990). Similarity of outcomes, interdependence, and conflict in dating relationships. *Journal of Personality and Social Psychology, 59*, 501–516.

Swensen, C.H. Jr (1972). The behavior of love. In H.A. Otto (Ed.), *Love today: A new exploration* (pp. 86–101). New York: Association Press.

Szinovacz, M.E. (1987). Family power. In M.B. Sussman & S.K. Steinmetz (Eds.), *Handbook of marriage and the family* (pp. 651–693). New York: Plenum.

Tansuhaj, P.S., & Foxman, E.R. (1990). The use of triad data to study family purchase decisions. *Advances in Consumer Research, 17*, 523–525.

Tedeschi, J.T., & Lindskold, S. (1976). *Social psychology.* New York: Wiley.

Thaler, R.H. (1980). Toward a positive theory of consumer choice. *Journal of Economic Behavior and Organization, 1*, 30–60.

Thaler, R.H. (1985). Mental accounting and consumer choice. *Marketing Science, 4*, 199–214.

Thaler, R.H. (1992). *The winner's curse. Paradoxes and anomalies of economic life.* New York: Free Press.

Thaler, R.H. (Ed.) (1994). *Quasi rational economics.* New York: Sage.

Thibaut, J.W., & Kelley, H.H. (1959). *The social psychology of groups.* New York: Wiley.

Thomas, G., Fletcher, G.J.O., & Lange, C. (1997). On-line empathic accuracy in marital interaction. *Journal of Personality and Social Psychology, 72*, 839–850.

Trivers, R.L. (1972). Parental investment and sexual selection. In C. Campbell (Ed.), *Sexual selection and the descent of man* (pp. 136–179). Chicago: Aldine.

Tschammer-Osten, B. (1979). *Haushaltswissenschaft.* Stuttgart: Fischer.

Tversky, A., & Kahneman, D. (1974). Judgment under uncertainty: Heuristics and biases. *Science, 185*, 1124–1131.

Van Lange, P.A.M., Rusbult, C.E., Drigotas, S.M., Arriaga, X.B., & Witcher, B.S. (1997). Willingness to sacrifice in close relationships. *Journal of Personality and Social Psychology, 72*, 1373–1395.

Van Ypern, N.W., & Buunk, B.P. (1994). Social comparison and social exchange in marital relationships. In M.J. Lerner & G. Mikula (Eds.), *Entitlement and the affectional bond* (pp. 89–115). New York: Plenum Press.

Vanek, J. (1974). Time spent in housework. *Scientific American, 231*, 116–120.

Vankatesh, A. (1990). Longitudinal methods for family consumer research. *Advances in Consumer Research, 17*, 529–530.

Verbrugge, L.M. (1979). Marital status and health. *Journal of Marriage and the Family, 41*, 267–285.

Vertone, S. (1991). Ma è l'illusione erotica la causa della sofferenza. *Europeo*, 1.11.1991, Nr. 44, 85–86.

Vetere, A., & Gale, A. (1987). *Ecological studies of family life.* New York: Wiley.

Vetter, A. (1966). *Anthropologie der Person.* Freiburg, Germany: Alber.

Vogler, C., & Pahl, J. (1994). Money, power and inequality within marriage. *Sociological Review, 42*, 263–288.

Von Rosenstiel, L. (1992). *Grundlagen der Organisationspsychologie.* Stuttgart: Schäffer-Poeschel.

Wagner, W. (1994). *Alltagsdiskurs. Die Theorie sozialer Repräsentationen.* Göttingen, Germany: Hogrefe.

Wagner, W., Kirchler, E., & Brandstätter, H. (1984). Marital relationships and purchase decisions—to buy or not to buy, that is the question. *Journal of Economic Psychology, 5*, 139–157.

Walker, C.M. (1994). *Economic man's missing teenage years: Adolescents' views about money, credit and debt.* Paper presented at the IAREP/SABE conference. Rotterdam, The Netherlands.

Walster, E., & Berscheid, E. (1974). A little bit about love: A minor essay on a major topic. In T.L. Huston (Ed.), *Foundations of interpersonal attraction* (pp. 355–381). New York: Academic Press.

Walster, E., Walster, G.W., & Berscheid, E. (1978). *Equity: Theory and research.* Boston: Allyn & Bacon.

Walster, E., Walster, G.W., & Traupmann, J. (1978). Equity and premarital sex. *Journal of Personality and Social Psychology, 36*, 82–92.

Walters, L.H. (1982). Are families different from other groups? *Journal of Marriage and the Family, 44*, 841–850.

Ward, S., & Wackman, D.B. (1973). Children's purchase influence attempts and parental yielding. In H.H. Kassajian & T.S. Robertson (Eds.), *Perspectives in consumer behavior* (pp. 369–374). Glenview, IL: Scott, Foresman & Co.

Wärneryd, K.-E. (1995). *A study of saving behavior towards the end of the life cycle.* Tilburg University: Center for Economic Research. VSB-CentER Savings Project. Report 28.

Wärneryd, K.-E. (1999). *The psychology of saving. A study on economic psychology.* Cheltenham, UK: Edgar Elgar.

Waxler, N.E., & Mishler, E.G. (1970). Experimental studies of families. In L. Berkowitz (Ed.), *Advances in experimental social psychology* (Vol. 5, pp. 249–304). New York: Academic Press.

Webb, P.H. (1978). A new method for studying family decision making. *Journal of Marketing, 42*, 12 and 126.

Webley, P. (1994). *The role of economic and psychological factors in consumer debt.* Tilburg University: Center for Economic Research. VSB-CentER Savings Project. Report 21.

Webster, C. (1994). Effects of hispanic ethnic identification on marital roles in the purchase decision process. *Journal of Consumer Research, 21*, 319–331.

Webster, C. (1995). Determinants of marital power in decision making. *Advances in Consumer Research, 22*, 717–722.

Weick, K. (1971). Group processes, family processes, and problem solving. In J. Aldous, T.

Condon, R. Hill, M. Straus, & I. Tallman (Eds.), *Family problem solving: A symposium on theoretical, methodological and substantive concerns* (pp. 3–33). Hillsdale, NJ: Dryden Press.

Weigel, D.J., & Ballard-Reisch, D.S. (1999). Using paired data to test models of relational maintenance and marital quality. *Journal of Social and Personal Relationships, 16*, 175–191.

Wilkes, R.E. (1995). Household life-cycle stages, transitions, and product expenditures. *Journal of Consumer Research, 22*, 27–42.

Willer, D. (1985). Property and social exchange. In E.F. Lawler (Ed.), *Advances in group processes* (Vol. 2, pp. 123–142). Greenwich, CT: JAI.

Williams, R., & Thomson, E. (1995). Can spouses be trusted? A look at husband/wife. *Proxy Reports, 22*, 115–123.

Wilson, G. (1987). Money: Patterns of responsibility and irresponsibility in marriage. In J. Brannen & G. Wilson (Eds.), *Give and take in families. Studies in resource distribution* (pp. 136–154). London: Allen & Unwin.

Winch, R.F., & Gordon, M.T. (1974). *Family structure and function as influence.* Lexington, MA: Lexington Books.

Winter, M., & Mayerhofer, W. (1983a). Kind-Familie-Fernsehen-Werbung (Part I). *WWG Information*, Issue 92, 38–44.

Winter, M., & Mayerhofer, W. (1983b.) Kind-Familie-Fernsehen-Werbung (Part II)—Empirische Studie. Die Effekte der Fernsehwerbung auf die Position des Kindes beim Kaufentscheidungsprozeß in der Familie. *WWG Information*, Issue 93, 79–84.

Winter, W.D., Ferreira, A.J., & Bowers, G. (1973). Decision making in married and unrelated couples. *Family Process, 12*, 81–94.

Wish, M., Deutsch, M., & Kaplan, S.J. (1976). Perceived dimensions of interpersonal relations. *Journal of Personality and Social Psychology, 33*, 409–420.

Wiswede, G. (1995). *Einführung in die Wirtschaftspsychologie* (2nd edn.). Munich: UTB.

Witte, E.H. (1986). *Sozialpsychologie. Ein Lehrbuch.* Munich: Psychologie Verlags Union.

Wolfe, D.M. (1959). Power and authority in the family. In D. Cartwright (Ed.), *Studies in social power.* Ann Arbor, MI: University of Michigan Press.

Wolfe, J.B. (1936). The effectiveness of token rewards for chimpanzees. *Comparative Psychological Monographs*, 12, No. 60.

Wright, P., & Rip, P. (1980). Retrospective reports on consumer decision processes: I can remember if I want to, but why should I bother trying? In J.C. Olson (Ed.), *Advances in consumer research* (Vol. 7, pp. 146–147). Ann Arbor, MI: Association for Consumer Research.

Zani, B., & Kirchler, E. (1993). Come influenzare il partner: processi decisionali nelle relazioni di coppia. *Giornale Italiano di Psicologia, 20*, 247–281.

Zelditch, M.J. (1971). Experimental family sociology. In J. Aldous, T. Condon, R. Hill, M. Straus, & J. Tallman (Eds.), *Family problem solving: A symposium on theoretical, methodological and substantive concerns* (pp. 55–89). Hinsdale, NH: Dryden Press.

Author Index

Subject Index